Routledge Questions & Answers Series

European Union Law

2013–2014

Mike Cuthbert

Routledge
Taylor & Francis Group

LONDON AND NEW YORK

Ninth edition published 2013
by Routledge
2 Park Square, Milton Park, Abingdon, Oxon OX14 4RN

Simultaneously published in the USA and Canada
by Routledge
711 Third Avenue, New York, NY 10017

Routledge is an imprint of the Taylor & Francis Group, an informa business

© 2013 Mike Cuthbert

The right of Mike Cuthbert to be identified as the author of this work has been asserted by him in accordance with sections 77 and 78 of the Copyright, Designs and Patents Act 1988.

First edition published by Cavendish Publishing 1993
Eighth edition published by Routledge 2011

British Library Cataloguing in Publication Data
A catalogue record for this book is available from the British Library

Library of Congress Cataloging in Publication Data
Cuthbert, Mike, LL. M.
   European Union law : 2013-2014 / Mike Cuthbert.—Ninth edition.
      pages cm.—(Q&A, Routledge–Cavendish questions & answers series)
   Includes bibliographical references and index.
   ISBN 978–0–415–50797–4 (pbk)
   1. Law—European Union countries.   2. Law—European Union countries—Examinations, questions, etc.
   3. European Union.   I. Title.
   KJE949.C884 2013
   341.242'2076—dc23

                                                                                    2012017481

ISBN: 978–0–415–50797–4 (pbk)
ISBN: 978–0–203–08385–7 (ebk)

Typeset in TheSans
by RefineCatch Limited, Bungay, Suffolk

Printed and bound in Great Britain by the MPG Books Group

Contents

Table of Cases

OPINIONS

Table of Legislation

REGULATIONS

TREATIES AND CONVENTIONS

UK LEGISLATION

Statutes

Statutory Instruments

International Legislation

Table of Equivalences

Treaty Establishing the European Community (EC Treaty) (Pre Amsterdam Treaty)	Treaty Establishing the European Community (EC Treaty) (Post Amsterdam Treaty)	Treaty on the Functioning of the European Union (Post Lisbon Treaty)
		Art 1(3) (new)
		Art 2 (new)
		Art 3 (new)
		Art 7 (new)
Art 3	Art 3 (repealed)	
		Art 10 (new)
		Art 13 (new)
Art 4	Art 7 (repealed)	
Art 5	Art 10 (repealed)	
Art 6	Art 12	Art 18
Art 6(a)	Art 13	Art 19
Art 8	Art 17	Art 20
Art 8a	Art 18	Art 21
Art 8b	Art 19	Art 22
Art 8c	Art 20	Art 23
Art 8d	Art 21	Art 24
Art 7	Art 14	Art 26
Art 9	Art 23	Art 28
Art 10	Art 24	Art 29
Art 12	Art 25	Art 30
Art 19 (repealed)		
Art 25 (repealed)		
Art 30	Art 28	Art 34
Art 31 (repealed)		
Art 34	Art 29	Art 35
Art 36	Art 30	Art 36
Art 37	Art 31	Art 43
Art 48	Art 39	Art 45
Art 52	Art 43	Art 49
Art 54	Art 44	Art 50
Art 55	Art 45	Art 51

Treaty Establishing the European Community (EC Treaty) (Pre Amsterdam Treaty)	Treaty Establishing the European Community (EC Treaty) (Post Amsterdam Treaty)	Treaty on the Functioning of the European Union (Post Lisbon Treaty)
Art 56	Art 46	Art 52
Art 57	Art 47	Art 53
Art 58	Art 48	Art 54
Art 221	Art 294	Art 55
Art 59	Art 49	Art 56
Art 60	Art 50	Art 57
Art 66	Art 55	Art 62
	Art 30 (TEU)	Art 88
Art 75	Art 71	Art 91
Art 85	Art 81	Art 101
Art 86	Art 82	Art 102
Art 89	Art 85	Art 105
Art 90	Art 86	Art 106
Art 92	Art 87	Art 107
Art 93	Art 88	Art 108
Art 95	Art 90	Art 110
Art 114 (repealed)		
Art 3a	Art 4	Art 119
Art 117	Art 136	Art 151
Art 119	Art 141	Art 157
		Art 205 (new)
Art 110	Art 131	Art 206
Art 113	Art 133	Art 207
Art 128	Art 180	Art 210
Art 228	Art 300 (replaced)	Art 218
Arts 229–231	Arts 302–304	Art 220
Art 138	Art 190	Art 223
Art 138a	Art 191	Art 224
Art 138b	Art 192 (2nd para)	Art 225
Art 138c	Art 193	Art 226
Art 138d	Art 194	Art 227
Art 138e	Art 195	Art 228
Art 139	Art 196	Art 229
Art 140	Art 197 (2nd, 3rd, 4th paras)	Art 230
Art 141	Art 198	Art 231
Art 142	Art 199	Art 232
Art 143	Art 200	Art 233

Treaty Establishing the European Community (EC Treaty) (Pre Amsterdam Treaty)	Treaty Establishing the European Community (EC Treaty) (Post Amsterdam Treaty)	Treaty on the Functioning of the European Union (Post Lisbon Treaty)
Art 144	Art 201	Art 234
		Art 236 (new)
Art 148	Art 204	Art 237
Art 150	Art 205 (paras 1 & 3)	Art 238
Art 151	Art 206	Art 239
Art 152	Art 207	Art 240
Art 153	Art 208	Art 241
Art 154	Art 209	Art 242
Art 154	Art 210	Art 243
		Art 244 (new)
Art 157	Art 213	Art 245
Art 159	Art 215	Art 246
Art 160	Art 216	Art 247
Art 161	Art 217 (para 2)	Art 248
Art 162	Art 218 (para 2)	Art 249
Art 163	Art 219	Art 250
Art 165	Art 221	Art 251
Art 166	Art 222	Art 252
Art 167	Art 223	Art 253
Art 168	Art 224	Art 254
		Art 255 (new)
Art 168a	Art 225	Art 256
Art 168a	Art 225(a)	Art 257
Art 169	Art 226	Art 258
Art 170	Art 227	Art 259
Art 171	Art 228	Art 260
Art 172	Art 229	Art 261
Art 172	Art 229(a)	Art 262
Art 173	Art 230	Art 263
Art 174	Art 231	Art 264
Art 175	Art 232	Art 265
Art 176	Art 233	Art 266
Art 177	Art 234	Art 267
Art 178	Art 235	Art 268
		Art 269 (new)
Art 179	Art 236	Art 270
Art 180	Art 237	Art 271

Treaty Establishing the European Community (EC Treaty) (Pre Amsterdam Treaty)	Treaty Establishing the European Community (EC Treaty) (Post Amsterdam Treaty)	Treaty on the Functioning of the European Union (Post Lisbon Treaty)
Art 181	Art 238	Art 272
Art 182	Art 239	Art 273
Art 183	Art 240	Art 274
		Art 275 (new)
		Art 276 (new)
Art 184	Art 241	Art 277
Art 185	Art 242	Art 278
Art 186	Art 243	Art 279
Art 187	Art 244	Art 280
Art 188	Art 245	Art 281
Art 189	Art 249	Art 288
		Art 289 (new)
Art 189a	Art 250	Art 293
Art 189b	Art 251	Art 294
Art 190	Art 253	Art 296
Art 191	Art 254	Art 297
		Art 300 (new)
Art 194	Art 258 (1st, 2nd, 4th paras)	Art 301
Art 199	Art 267	Art 309
Art 199	Art 268	Art 310
Art 203	Art 272 (paras 2–10)	Art 314
Art 205	Art 274	Art 317
Art 210	Art 181 (repealed)	
Art 215	Art 288	Art 340
Art 222	Art 295	Art 345
Art 235	Art 308	Art 352

Guide to the Companion Website

http://cw.routledge.com/textbooks/revision

Visit the Routledge Q&A website to discover even more study tips and advice on getting those top marks.

On the Routledge revision website you will find the following resources designed to enhance your revision on all areas of undergraduate law.

The Good, The Fair, & The Ugly

Good essays are the gateway to top marks. This interactive tutorial provides sample essays together with voice-over commentary and tips for successful exam essays, written by our Q&A authors themselves.

Multiple Choice Questions

Knowledge is the foundation of every good essay. Focusing on key examination themes, these MCQs have been written to test your knowledge and understanding of each subject in the book.

Bonus Q&As

Having studied our exam advice, put your revision into practice and test your essay writing skills with our additional online questions and answers.

Don't forget to check out even more revision guides and exam tools from Routledge!

Lawcards

Lawcards are your complete, pocket-sized guides to key examinable areas of the undergraduate law.

Routledge Student Statutes

Comprehensive selections; clear, easy-to-use layout; alphabetical, chronological, and thematic indexes; and a competitive price make *Routledge Student Statutes* the statute book of choice for the serious law student.

Introduction

This book is intended to be of help to students studying EU law who feel that they have acquired a body of knowledge, but do not feel confident about using it effectively in exams. This book sets out to demonstrate how to apply the knowledge to the question and how to structure the answer. Students, especially first-year students, are faced with acquiring knowledge and understanding of English common law and then along comes EU law with seemingly different language, different approaches and traditions. If they have the knowledge then they often find the technique of answering problem questions particularly hard to grasp, so this book contains a large number of answers to such questions. This technique is rarely taught in law schools and the student who comes from studying science or maths A levels may find it particularly tricky. Equally, a student who has studied English literature may find it difficult to adapt to the impersonal, logical, concise style that problem answers demand. It is hoped that this book will be particularly useful at exam time, but may also prove useful throughout the year. The book provides examples of the kind of questions that are usually asked in end-of-year examinations, along with suggested solutions. Each chapter deals with one of the main topics covered in EU law courses and contain typical questions on that area. The aim is not to include questions covering every aspect of a course, but to pick out the areas that tend to be examined because they are particularly contentious or topical. Many courses contain a certain amount of material that is not examined, although it is important as providing background knowledge. You should look at past examination papers or assignments to get a feel for the topics favoured by your examiner. Seminar topics are usually a good guide to what your tutor has identified as being key topics and possible question.

PROBLEM AND ESSAY QUESTIONS

Some areas tend to be examined only by essays, some mainly – although not invariably – by problems, and some by either. The questions chosen reflect this mix, and the introductions at the beginning of each chapter discuss the type of question usually asked. It is important not to choose a topic and then assume that it will appear on the exam paper in a particular form unless it is in an area where, for example, a problem question is never set. If it might appear as an essay or a problem, revision should be geared to either possibility: a very thorough knowledge of the area should be acquired, but also an awareness of critical opinion in relation to it. As a rule of thumb think that the essay question will ask you to discuss an area of law, perhaps looking at how it has developed, criticisms and possible ways forward, whereas the problem question wants you to state the law and apply it to a given factual situation.

LENGTH OF ANSWERS

The answers in this book are about the length of an essay that a good student would expect to write in an exam. Some are somewhat longer and these will also provide useful guidance for students writing assessed essays, which typically are between 2,000 and 3,000 words. In relation to exam questions, there are a number of reasons for including lengthy answers as the examination in some universities are by tradition three hours with you having to answer four questions and in others it is the luxurious two hours to answer two questions. Some students can write long answers – about 1,800 words – under exam conditions; other students cannot, but nevertheless can write two very good and lengthy essays and two reasonable but shorter ones. Such students tend to do very well, although it must be emphasised that it is always better to aim to spread the time evenly between all four, three or two essays. Therefore, some answers indicate what might be done if very thorough coverage of a topic were to be undertaken.

EXPRESSING A POINT OF VIEW

Students sometimes ask, especially in an area such as EU law, which can be quite topical and politically controversial, whether they should argue for any particular point of view in an essay. It will be noticed that the essays in this book tend to do this. In general, the good student does argue for one side but he or she always uses sound arguments to support his or her view. Further, a good student does not ignore the opposing arguments; they are considered and, if possible, their weaknesses are exposed. Of course, it would not be appropriate to do this in a problem question or in some essay questions, but where an invitation to do so is held out, it is a good idea to accept it rather than sit on the fence. You have the knowledge flaunt it!

EXAM PAPERS

EU law exam papers reflect the assessment strategy for that module. Some university courses have an emphasis towards what is called the constitutional aspects of EU law such as the institutions, supremacy, direct effect and the various direct and indirect actions before the ECJ or General Court. Other courses concentrate on the substantive areas of EU law such as the freedom of movement of goods, people, companies or professionals and competition law. Whatever the emphasis of your course the examination paper you will receive will reflect the main topics identified in your course guide but probably more importantly by the length of time the tutor spent on 'making sure that you understand this important point'! The questions in this book seek to give examples of the various types of questions that are asked on the topics found within undergraduate EU law courses.

SUGGESTIONS FOR EXAM TECHNIQUE

Below are some suggestions that might improve exam technique; some failings are pointed out that are very commonly found on exam scripts.

(1) When tackling a problem question, do not write out the facts in the answer. Quite a number of students write out chunks of the facts as they answer the question – perhaps to help themselves to pick out the important issues. It is better to avoid this and merely to refer to the significant facts. Remember the marker wrote the question so she does not need to be told what was in it!

(2) Use an impersonal style in both problem and essay answers. In an essay, you should rarely need to use the word 'I' and it should not be used at all in a problem answer. (Of course, examiners may differ in their views on this point.) Instead, you could say 'it is therefore submitted that' or 'it is arguable that'; avoid saying 'I believe that' or 'I feel that'.

(3) In answers to problem questions, try to explain at the beginning of each section of your answer what point you are trying to establish. You might say, for example: 'In order to show that an article of the Treaties has direct effect three tests must be satisfied.' You should then consider all three, come to a conclusion on each, and then come to a final conclusion as to whether or not direct effect will apply. If you are really unsure whether or not it will arise (which will often be the case – there is not much point in asking a question to which there is one very clear and obvious answer), then consider what you have written in relation to the three tests and what alternative remedies would be available to assist the individual in enforcing their right under EU law.

(4) As you will see, there are some basic cases that are the authority for a number of principles of Union law. They appear in answers to many questions. You should ensure that you are familiar with these, and gradually build up your confidence with the topics. Start with the definitions and basic principles, looking for an authority either through a case or an Article of the Treaty, for example. This approach will help you when you come to the examination hall and read the questions for the first time.

(5) Read the question paper carefully. Underline or highlight what appear to you to be the key points. This is especially important for problem questions, which may be quite long.

Write, on the question paper or one of the pages of the answer book, any ideas you have when you first read the question. This might include definitions, cases, Treaty Articles, quotations or other references. This is good practice because it may help you decide the best questions to tackle but, more importantly, when you return to answer that particular question these notes will help you to concentrate on the new topic. As you are writing other answers, ideas and cases may suddenly come to mind. Write them down before you forget them! You can always put a line through these notes at the end of the examination, so that the examiner will not regard them as part of your answer.

(6) When you start to answer a particular question, plan your answer carefully. This will help you to adjust to the topic, but it will also help you recover from those moments when your concentration lapses through some distraction. It may also help you find your next point in your answer when you ask yourself 'what shall I write next?'

Remember that you will get little credit for rambling, so planning and following your plan are very important.

(7)   Make sure that you deal with all the parts of the question. This applies to all questions and not just those that have separate (a) and (b) parts. If you do not answer the question fully, you are limiting the range of marks you can obtain for your answer. When you are dealing with problem questions remember that the examiner is not just looking for an answer that shows knowledge of principles. Your answer should show understanding of the principles and the ability to apply them to the facts in the question.

Common Pitfalls ✘

The most common mistake made when using Questions & Answers books for revision is to memorise the model answers provided and try to reproduce them in exams. This approach is a sure-fire pitfall, likely to result in a poor overall mark because your answer will not be specific enough to the particular question on your exam paper, and there is also a danger that reproducing an answer in this way would be treated as plagiarism. You must instead be sure to read the question carefully, to identify the issues and problems it is asking you to address and to answer it directly in your exam. If you take our examiners' advice and use your Q&A to focus on your question-answering skills and understanding of the law applied, you will be ready for whatever your exam paper has to offer!

the absence of what some observers see as the fundamental involvement of
representatives in the governance of the EU. This arises where individuals
e the EU with the governance of an individual Member State, when any analysis
nion shows that such a comparison is limited due to its international
ation structure. Attempts have been made since the Single European Act 1987 to
the democratic element and the Treaty of Lisbon is the latest treaty amendment
. The Treaty of Lisbon did not have an easy birth as it followed the aborted
utional Treaty and was challenged in the German Courts and concessions had to
n to Ireland before it was ratified in a second referendum of the Irish people. The
of Lisbon finally came into force on 1 December 2009 and made changes in an
t to lessen the democratic deficit within the EU due to the interrelationship
n the main institutions of the European Parliament, European Council, Council of
rs and the European Commission.

racy has always been identified as an important principle to the EU and is seen as
cteristic of all member States. The Copenhagen criteria for membership of the
listed three requirements including 'candidate country to have achieved stability of
tions guaranteeing democracy, the rule of law, human rights and respect for and
tion of minorities'. How democratic are the EU institutions? Since 1989 the only
y elected institution has been the European Parliament (EP), with MEPs being
d every five years. The original EEC Treaty in 1957 provided for the 'European
bly' to be consulted but that body was made up of Member State nominees who
bly' mandate or constituency. Every amendment to the Treaties since 1987 has
ed more authority to the EP in relation to European legislation; first with the
ration procedure and then the co-decision procedure established in the Maastricht
of 1992. The co-decision procedure gave equal authority to the EP on specific areas
cy which were gradually increased but the political power still remained with the
il of Ministers who are the representatives of the Member States. The EP gained
involvement in the setting of the EU budget in 1975 but this was restricted to
ompulsory' expenditure, which included all expenditure that was committed under
eaties, such as the common agricultural policy. The 'non-compulsory' expenditure is
significant at about 42% of the total budget and included Union social policy,
al and industrial policies. However, at the start of the twenty-first century the EP
t have the authority that was recognisable in a national parliament.

stitutions of the EU are not a mirror of those found in the Member States, as it is an
ational organisation. The legislative procedure of the EU has to be instigated by the
ean Commission making a proposal (Art 294 TFEU) which then goes to the EP and
ouncil of Ministers. The EP has gradually obtained more authority in the
ntment of the Commission to add to its long standing power to dismiss the whole
iate body (now Art 234 TFEU). The EP has to approve the appointment of the
nission President, who is nominated by the European Council after taking into
nt the results of the EP elections (Art 17(7) TEU). The EP then has to approve the

Community Institutions

1

INTRODUCTION

It is very important to develop a good understanding of the functions, powers and
relationships between the main institutions of the European Union. This requires
knowledge of four key institutions, which have their origin in the first Community,
the European Coal and Steel Community, established in 1952 with a fixed life of fifty
years. Although there have been some changes since then, the basic principles have
remained the same. The Treaty of Lisbon came into force on 1 December 2009 and
this is the latest example of changes made to the institutions and the numbering of the
articles relating to the institutions. With regard to the Treaty of Lisbon you should
remember that there are in fact two Treaties under that one umbrella: Treaty
on European Union (TEU) and the Treaty on the Functioning of the European
Union (TFEU).

You should try to get a feel for the need for such institutions. It is sometimes forgotten
that the European Community was an innovative idea, in the sense that a supranational
body was being created by the transfer of sovereignty from Member States to a
Community which was to act on behalf of all its members. Therefore, it was important to
ensure that the institutions established would provide a forum for an input by the
Member States, a body to implement and police policies decided by the Community, a
court to settle disputes and provide authoritative judgments and, finally, a body which
would allow an input from a wider base of views from the Member States. Hence, the
Treaty of Rome established the Council of Ministers, the European Commission, the
European Court of Justice (ECJ) and the European Assembly, later to be called the
European Parliament in the Single European Act.

The starting point for an understanding of the EU institutions is their origin, that is, the
Treaty Articles. Although these need not be learned by heart, there are key points which
must be grasped as you build up an understanding of their functions and relationships.
Do not be confused by the fact that the numbering of the Articles has been affected by
the Treaty of Lisbon, where the opportunity was taken to reorder them. As some
textbooks and old judgments still refer to the 'traditional' numbering, a Table of
Equivalences is included on pp. xxi–xxiv to help you. This details old and new Treaty
numbers.

One of the best ways to get an overview of the variety of institutions is to read material that is intended for the non-specialist reader. Some of the publications produced by the European Commission are very good and have the added advantage of being free. There is also a very good website (www.europa.eu). Once you have an overview, you should begin to build up a more detailed picture, which shows the more complex functions and relationships between the institutions. However, you should always be alert to practical examples of the friction or otherwise generated by these institutions and reported in the media. Such examples are invaluable in impressing the examiner but, more importantly, they should convince you that you are not dealing with a theoretical group of institutions, but 'a living community'.

Checklist ✔

You need to have a good understanding of the functions, procedures and membership of the main Community institutions, plus an awareness of the less significant ones. You should also look at Chapter 12, where some of the proposed changes to the institutions are discussed. In particular, you should concentrate on:

- the European Parliament – **Arts 223–234 TFEU**;
- the Council of Ministers – **Arts 237–243 TFEU**;
- the European Commission – **Arts 244–250 TFEU**;
- the Court of Justice (ECJ) – **Arts 251–281 TFEU**; and
- the European Council, the General Court, the European Economic and Social Committee (EESC), the Committee of Permanent Representatives (COREPER), the Committee of the Regions and the Court of Auditors.

QUESTION 1

What has been the impact, if any, of the Lisbon Treaty on the democratic deficit within the EU?

How to Answer this Question

This type of question has become very popular in recent years. This is largely due to developments that have affected the Parliament and the emphasis given to democracy in the European Union. The main points to cover in your answer are:

- ❖ powers and composition of the European Parliament;
- ❖ procedures of the Parliament;
- ❖ role of the Parliament in the legislative process;
- ❖ the Lisbon Treaty.

Answer Structure

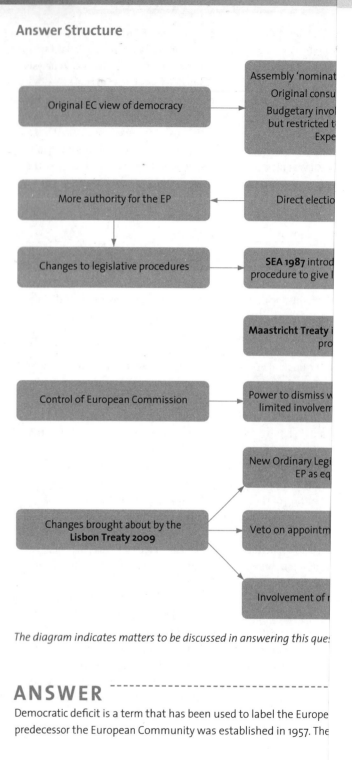

The diagram indicates matters to be discussed in answering this que:

ANSWER

Democratic deficit is a term that has been used to label the Europe
predecessor the European Community was established in 1957. The

appointment of the remaining members of the Commission before they can be formally appointed by the European Council. The European Commission is therefore not democratically elected in the sense of involving the citizens of the EU exercising their universal suffrage! It could be said that the 'democratic element' in the EU is of two types: representative democracy and participatory democracy. Representative democracy is where the EU citizens directly elect their MEP once every five years and this is in addition to the members of the European Council and Council of Ministers who are members of their national governments and accountable to their national electorate via their national parliaments or assemblies. It maybe that in the 'representative democracy' sense the Commission has been appointed 'democratically'. Participatory democracy, on the other hand, does not involve an election or electorate but is a process by which EU citizens and their representative associations have an opportunity to influence Union policy. How has the Lisbon Treaty impacted on these types of democratic participation and the democratic deficit?

Title II of the Treaty on European Union (TEU) now provides for 'provisions on democratic principles' and a number of articles are to be found here demonstrating how Art 2 TEU which lists the values that the Union is founded upon, including democracy. Article 10(1) TEU then states that the 'functioning of the Union shall be founded on representative democracy'. This provides the clue that the EP has gained the most from the Lisbon Treaty as it is the only 'directly elected institution'. The EP has been given more authority by being put onto an equal footing with the Council of Ministers as far as the legislative procedure is concerned. The co-decision procedure has gone to be replaced by the 'ordinary legislative procedure' under Art 289 TFEU and specified under Art 294 TFEU. If the EP does not agree with a proposal put forward by the Commission or the amendments of the Council the measure falls. This puts the EP on the same footing as the Council of Ministers on all the areas of EU policy where 'qualified majority voting (QMV)' is required in the Council. This means that the EP has had its rights increased from approximately 45 to 85 areas of policy, including the most important ones. The Lisbon Treaty also abolished the distinction between 'compulsory and non-compulsory expenditure' that limited the EP's powers of amendment. Article 314 TFEU gives the EP equal power of budgetary approval along with the Council.

In an attempt to boost the representative democracy of the Union Protocol 1 of the Lisbon Treaty gives more involvement to the national parliaments with the introduction of what have been referred to as 'yellow card' and 'orange card' provisions. All national parliaments have their own systems and procedures when dealing with EU proposals. The UK Westminster Parliament has a system of scrutiny committees that report to the House. The purpose of these 'cards' is so that national parliaments can report to the EP, Council and Commission if they consider that the principle of subsidiarity, stated in Art 5 TEU, has been complied with. If at least one-third of the national parliaments are of the view that the principle has not been followed the Commission can be required to review the proposal (the yellow card). If the Commission decide to proceed they have to provide a reasoned opinion and refer the matter to the EP and Council for a final decision. If more than a simple majority of the national parliaments raise concerns then the orange card is used and this allows the EP and Council to reject the proposal before the first reading under Art 294 TFEU. The Treaty also requires more information to be provided to national parliaments on EU proposals and for them to have early notice in order to have more time for discussion in their national deliberations.

The Maastricht Treaty in 1992 attempted to provide a response to the electorates of the Member States' view that the EU was something abstract and solely for business by creating the notion of EU citizens, so the Lisbon Treaty has sought to appeal to the individual in the Member States. The voter turnout for EP elections has been in decline, although new Member States' have bolstered the figures. In the 2009 EP elections there was an overall voter turnout of 43% of the 375 million Europeans entitled to vote, with only 34.7% in the UK. In an attempt to increase the feeling of involvement of EU citizens the Lisbon Treaty has introduced European Citizens Initiatives (ECI) (Art 11(4) TEU) and Regulation 211/2011 outlines the procedure. This ECI can invite the Commission to submit a legislative proposal which has the support of more than one million citizens from a 'significant' number of Member States.

Has the Lisbon Treaty had any impact on the democratic deficit within the EU? The measures discussed above were intended to achieve this result but like all amendments to the EU Treaties much depends upon how the changes are implemented and the interaction of the various institutions involved. Article 16(1) TEU states that the Council and the EP shall jointly exercise legislative and budgetary functions that is 'as laid down in the Treaties'. However, although the EP has more authority there are still many policy areas where the Council can exercise authority without sharing it with the Parliament. If the EP is assertive then the powers that the institution now has could provide a more democratic involvement of the only directly elected institution within the EU. The fact that now the Commission appointments will take place after the EP elections should mean that there will be more empathy between the two institutions and the proposals put forward by the Commission. The measures to give greater involvement of the national parliaments may also have an impact on the decisions taken in the Council. In the judgement in the case of *Matthews v UK* (Case 24833/94) the European Court of Human Rights said at paragraph 52: 'The Court considers that whatever its limitations, the European Parliament, which derives democratic legitimation from the direct elections by universal suffrage, must be seen as that part of the European Community structure which best reflects concerns as to 'effective political democracy'. However, to put the changes of the Lisbon Treaty in context the German Constitutional Court, when considering whether that Treaty was compatible with the German Basic Law in June 2009, said that the actual democratic legitimacy of the EU is obtained from the national parliaments whereas the appointment and decision-making of the EU remain those of an international organisation. As the Lisbon Treaty is fully implemented the impact on the democratic deficit may become clearer.

QUESTION 2

'The Court of Justice is unlike any English court.'

▶ Discuss.

How to Answer this Question

This illustrates a common type of essay question on the ECJ. The task is to discuss the special features of the Court. This has a special impact for the UK because it is very different from the national courts, including the House of Lords.

The main points of the question are:

- ❖ function of the ECJ as defined by Art 19 of the TEU;
- ❖ personnel, term of office, function – judges and Advocates General;
- ❖ procedures and languages;
- ❖ form of judgments; and
- ❖ comparison with the English courts.

Answer Structure

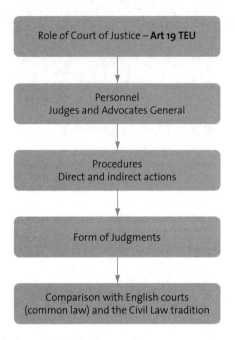

This diagram shows the key points to be discussed.

ANSWER

The European Court of Justice (ECJ) is one of the main institutions of the European Union. It provides the independent judicial function necessary to ensure, as Art 19 of the TEU states, 'that in the interpretation and application of this Treaty the law is observed'. The main influence on the characteristics of the ECJ was the French legal system, notably the highest administrative court in France, the Conseil d'Etat. However, this is not the only reason why the Court is different from any English court. Another important factor is that the Court was established to work not within a State, but within a community which brought together a number of States in a new relationship, which had implications for their own legal systems.

There are 27 judges on the ECJ, with each Member State providing one judge. Appointed for a term of six years, the judges elect their own President of the Court, who serves in that post for three years. Like all posts within the Court, it is possible for the period in office to be renewed. Although this fixed but renewable term of office is not found in English courts, the attributes the judges should have are the same. Article 253 TFEU specifies that they should be independent and qualified for the highest judicial office within their respective countries. However, an important difference is that, whereas

English judges are selected from barristers and, to a lesser extent, solicitors, judges in some Member States are chosen from a much wider field, including academic lawyers. Thus, when the judges in the European Court deliberate, they are bringing together a variety of legal backgrounds which would not be found in an English court.

Perhaps a striking difference about the ECJ is the role given to Advocates General, a post derived from the French legal system and unknown in English law. There are eight Advocates General appointed to the Court. They have the same backgrounds as judges, the same term of office and, perhaps most importantly, the same status. Therefore, Advocates General should not be seen as inferior to judges, as the precedence within the Court for both depends upon the date of appointment, and not the designated office. Advocates General are given a specific role under **Art 252 TFEU**, which states that 'it should be the duty of the Advocate General, acting with complete impartiality and independence, to make, in open court, reasoned submissions on cases brought before the ECJ, in order to assist the Court in the performance of its tasks'. Unlike in senior English courts, where a full judgment is given, including dissenting views, only one judgment is given by the ECJ. All the judges must agree to the one judgment, which is why they appear so terse and lacking in any real discussion of the law. They do not contain the *obiter dicta* or the *ratio decidendi* found in the common law tradition.

The importance of the Advocate General is that he hears and reads all the evidence as a judge would do, but he gives his opinion to the Court as to what the judgment should be before the judges themselves reach their decision. In his opinion, the Advocate General can range over the case law of the Court or, if appropriate, the jurisprudence of the Member States. In this way, some insight is given as to the direction European Community law may take in the future. Obviously, the judges do not have to follow the Advocate General's opinion, but if they do not it can be just as illuminating as when they do! In order to speed up the judicial process in the last few years the Advocate General, with the agreement of the judges, may not give an opinion.

The workload of the ECJ has increased tremendously since the Court was established in 1957. To help the Court deal with cases, the 27 judges sit in chambers of up to five judges, but always with an odd number, so that there can be a clear decision in a case. In 1989, the Court of First Instance (now called the General Court under the Treaty on the Functioning of the EU) was set up to assist the ECJ by taking a specific jurisdiction with the safeguard of appeal to the ECJ itself. This is not unusual, as all Member States have a hierarchy or structure for their courts. The ECJ itself has a general jurisdiction with regard to Union law, only fettered by the types of action specified in the Treaty. There are a number of direct actions available which include judicial review (**Art 263 TFEU**), actions against a Member State for failure to fulfil an obligation (**Arts 258** and **259 TFEU**) and illegality (Art 277). It is also possible to obtain interim measures under Art 279, such as interlocutory injunctions.

In addition, there is the special procedure for preliminary references under Art 267. Under this procedure, courts in the Member States can ask the ECJ questions regarding the interpretation of the Treaty or validity and interpretation of Community Acts. This does not amount to an appeal relationship, but is the recognition of a 'co-operation' between the national courts and the ECJ. The nearest procedure to this in English law is appeal by case stated in criminal cases, but this is insignificant compared to the preliminary reference procedure. With regard to the doctrine of precedent so familiar to common law systems, such as in the UK, there is no such rigid adherence in the ECJ. There is, however, the Community law general principle of certainty and therefore it is unlikely that the ECJ would depart from its previous decisions without good reason.

As indicated above, the greatest influence on the ECJ has been the French judicial system. Perhaps it is to be expected, therefore, that although cases may be brought in any of the 23 official languages recognised by the Court, the working language of the Court is French. Whenever a case is brought to the ECJ, whether as a direct action which is heard in its entirety only by the Court or a request for a preliminary reference from a Member State under Art 267, it is processed by the Court Registry to ensure that the progress of the case can be recorded. This is especially important with preliminary references, where the whole procedure is dominated by the 'file' of written documentation sent by the national court. The procedure is that on receipt by the Registrar, the President of the Court will assign the case to one of the six chambers and nominate one of the judges to act as *rapporteur*. The First Advocate General will, at the same time, designate the Advocate General for the case.

The role of the judge *rapporteur* is that, although all the papers will go to every judge hearing the case, only he will have studied them closely in order to produce a preliminary report. This report, together with any views expressed by the Advocate General, will help the Court decide what the relevant issues are. It may be decided that the case should be heard by the full Court, as normally happens with cases between the Member States or Community institutions. These early stages, covering the written proceedings and the preparatory inquiry, are held in private. Where oral proceedings follow as with direct actions, these are held in open court in Luxembourg, although some of the recently appointed judges do not value oral hearings that are the cornerstone of English judicial tradition. The next stage is for the Advocate General to deliver his opinion to the Court or for the judges to agree for an opinion not to be given if no new point of law is raised in the case. Sometime after this, the Court will deliver its judgment. If it is a preliminary reference, the answers given by the Court to the questions raised by the national court will be sent back to that court so that it can complete its hearing. If it is a direct action the Court will deliver its judgment, which may take the form of a declaration, as with Art 260. However, if the judgment needs to be enforced, for example against a company, the Court itself has no mechanism for enforcing its judgments. Any enforcement has to be left to the appropriate judicial machinery of the Member State.

NOTE

See Chapter 4 on Direct Actions and Chapter 5 on Indirect Action before the ECJ and the Court of First Instance.

QUESTION 3

Briefly describe the role of at least two of the following:

❖ the Committee of Permanent Representatives;
❖ the Court of First Instance;
❖ the Economic and Social Committee.

How to Answer this Question

This question follows the tradition, mentioned above, of essay questions on the institutions. However, instead of asking a narrower question on only one institution, this question gives you the opportunity to exercise some choice. It must be remembered that this type of question is not as easy as it looks with regard to obtaining marks!

Answer Structure

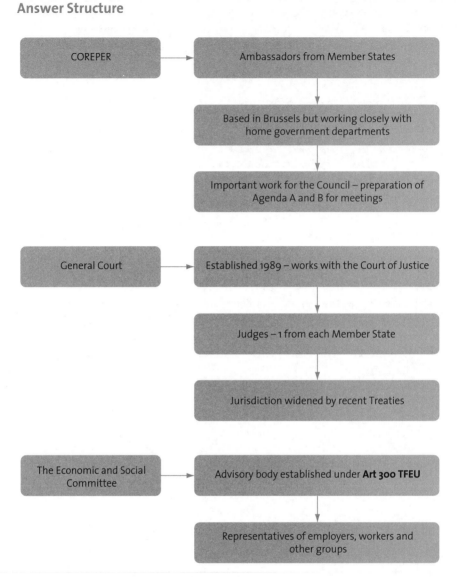

COREPER → Ambassadors from Member States

Based in Brussels but working closely with home government departments

Important work for the Council – preparation of Agenda A and B for meetings

General Court → Established 1989 – works with the Court of Justice

Judges – 1 from each Member State

Jurisdiction widened by recent Treaties

The Economic and Social Committee → Advisory body established under **Art 300 TFEU**

Representatives of employers, workers and other groups

This diagram shows the key points to be discussed.

ANSWER

(A) THE COMMITTEE OF PERMANENT REPRESENTATIVES (COREPER)

The Council of Ministers is the main political power within the Community, bringing together the government ministers of the 27 Member States. However, such ministers are busy individuals with many demands upon their time. They are members of their national parliaments and governments. They do not have the time to spend in long debate on routine Community matters. To assist them, COREPER, an acronym from the name of the Committee in French, was established first under the Council's Rules of Procedure but then formally under the **Merger Treaty 1965**. The Committee of Permanent Representatives is composed of individuals of ambassador rank who are accredited to the European Community. Their main task is to carry out work preparatory to Council meetings and other work delegated to them by the Council. This is listed in **Art 240 TFEU**.

The Committee works very closely with the Commission, as it seeks to represent the views of its governments in the discussion of Commission proposals. In order to carry out this task effectively, it is very important that there is very good liaison between members of COREPER and the appropriate national government departments. Thus, in discussing draft Community legislation, national viewpoints can be aired. This is not just a one-way transmission of information, in that the views of the representatives of other governments can be channelled back. In this way, disagreements can usually be ironed out before the proposal comes before the Council to make its decision.

When the Council of Ministers meets to discuss Commission proposals, there are two agendas, A and B. Items on the A agenda are those upon which provisional agreement has been reached in the course of the preparatory COREPER meetings. This allows the Council to concentrate on the items on the B agenda, where there is still disagreement and where political compromise is needed.

As the activity of the Community has increased, so the workload on COREPER has led to it being divided into two. COREPER I is composed of deputy Permanent Representatives, who generally discuss matters of a more technical nature, and COREPER II is composed of the Ambassadors, who discuss politically important matters.

(B) THE GENERAL COURT

This Court was established under the **Single European Act (SEA) 1986** and came into operation in 1989 when it was called the Court of First Instance (CFI). The ECJ, which had been established by the **Treaty of Rome**, had experienced increasing difficulties in coping with the workload, as the number of Member States had increased and the policy area had expanded. The solution finally accepted by the Council of Ministers was to 'attach' the CFI to the ECJ and to give it a limited jurisdiction with a possible appeal to the ECJ itself. As the CFI has been very successful in its operations, the scope of its jurisdiction has been widened. This is listed in Art 256 of TFEU.

Although it is quite common for judicial structures in the Member States to form a hierarchy of courts, the SEA uses the word 'attach' quite deliberately. The General Court is not a separate institution. It shares not only the building in Luxembourg with the ECJ, but also other facilities, such as the library. It appoints its own Registrar, but other administrative services are shared.

The General Court is based on Art 256 TFEU. There are 27 judges appointed to the Court, one from each Member State. Although there are no Advocates General specifically appointed to the CFI, the need for such a role to be fulfilled is recognised. Where an Advocate General is required in a particular case, one of the judges will be requested to carry out this role. This will not happen in every case before the General Court. The Court may sit in chambers of three or five judges in order to hear cases brought before it and provide a more efficient use of its resources.

Like the judges appointed to the ECJ, those appointed to the General Court have a six-year term of office, which is renewable. Unlike their colleagues, the criteria for selection as a judge in the General Court are not as high as in the ECJ. In the ECJ, prospective judges must possess the ability for appointment to high judicial office. Article 254 states that for the General Court, judges are to be chosen 'from persons whose independence is beyond doubt and who possess the ability required for appointment to judicial office'.

As already indicated, the ECJ's workload increased dramatically in the 1980s, and concern was expressed about the effect this was having on the time it was taking it to deal with cases. The resultant jurisdiction of the General Court indicates that one of the problems encountered by the ECJ was those cases which required a long examination of questions of fact. These are very time-consuming and involve sifting through a great deal of evidence. Originally, there were three categories of case which came before the General Court. These were: staff cases, where employees of the Community have a dispute with regard to their employment; cases brought under the European Coal and Steel Community Treaty (now repealed), concerned with production and prices; and, most importantly, competition cases. In 1994, this jurisdiction was extended to include any action brought by any natural or legal persons against an act of a Community institution. If these cases also contain a claim for damages, the General Court can hear that claim as part of the action. However, the General Court itself now has a 30-month wait for cases to be heard. This is unsatisfactory for the individual concerned. Therefore, the Treaty of Nice reduced some aspects of the General Court's workload, for example by setting up specialist chambers to deal with staff cases. In November 2004 the Council adopted a decision to establish the EU Civil Service Tribunal, with an appeal to the General Court on points of law only. However, it also added others to relieve the pressure on the ECJ, such as giving the General Court some requests for preliminary rulings. The Court has become more efficient but there has also been more pressure on it as the Union has grown in the number of Memeber States. The 2011 statistics for the General Court showed a record number of cases being decided (+35%) but there was also a 10% growth in new cases so the Court cannot be complacent.

Appeals from the General Court are to the ECJ and have to be brought within two months. The appeal will only be heard on points of law and not of fact. Some writers believe that large companies involved in competition cases will always seek to appeal to the ECJ and therefore the reduction on the ECJ's workload envisaged by establishing the General Court will not materialise. It is an issue where only experience will tell, but the time-consuming factual aspects of the case will not be something that can be raised on appeal and will not therefore take up the time of the ECJ. The three grounds of appeal mirror the grounds of annulment under Art 263, namely, lack of competence, breach of procedure or infringement of Union law by the General Court.

(C) THE ECONOMIC AND SOCIAL COMMITTEE (ECOSOC)

The Committee is established under the EC Treaty, but it is not an institution of the Union. It is in fact an advisory committee appointed under Art 300 TFEU. It consists of representatives of the various sections of economic and social life of the community. It provides a sounding board for informed and general opinion of matters relating to the policies of the Union and this helps the Council and Commission as they develop European legislation. Although the opinions of the Committee are not binding, they do appear to have influence. The Commission has a very good working relationship with the Economic and Social Committee. This is perhaps reflected by the fact that generally, the Committee supports the proposals put forward by the Commission. The relationship with the Council has not been so well developed, although attempts have been made in recent years to improve this. Since 1987, it has become a regular practice for the person holding the office of President of the Council to address the Committee on matters discussed at the European Council. This has spread to ministers from the Member State holding the presidency to address meetings of the Committee.

Although advisory, the Commission or Council consults the Committee when it considers it appropriate, in addition to those instances where it is obligatory to do so under some Articles of the Treaty. An example of this is Art 91 TFEU, which deals with international transport within the Community and the common rules established to implement the policy.

There are a total of 350 members of the Economic and Social Committee. These are allocated to the different Member States to reflect their size, with the large countries such as France, Italy, Germany and the UK having 24 each, down to five for Malta. The Committee reflects three particular groups of people: the Employers' Group, which is made up of representatives of employers' organisations and chambers of commerce; the Workers' Group, which represents trade unions, and a group of 'Other Interests', which includes small businesses, family, environmental and similar representatives. Within these groups can be found the representatives of the various categories of economic and social activity specified in **Art 300**. It is impossible, given the limited number of members from each country, for all the interest groups within that country to be represented. This is recognised by the obligation placed on the Council to ensure that the total Committee at Community level reflects the requirement of **Art 300** as stated in the case of *Confederazione Italiana Dirigenta di Azienda v EC Council* (1988). In order to achieve this, each Member State submits a list of potential members amounting to twice its actual allotted members. The Council appoints the members on the basis of unanimity. Once appointed, the members of the Economic and Social Committee act in their personal capacity, and not as representatives following instruction from their Member State or interest group. In preparation for enlargement of the EU, the **Treaty of Nice** had set a ceiling of 350 members to the Committee and this is now stated in **Art 301 TFEU**.

QUESTION 4

What has been the impact of the Treaty of Lisbon on the Council? Have there been any changes in how it operates?

How to Answer this Question

This type of essay question is very common for EU courses. It allows you to draw upon other parts of the syllabus to demonstrate your knowledge and to look critically at the work of the Council of Ministers. The main points to cover are:

- ❖ **Art 16 TEU** and **Arts 237–243 TFEU** which are the Articles providing the Treaty sources for the Council;
- ❖ membership and procedures of the Council;
- ❖ the relationship between the Council of Ministers and the European Council;
- ❖ the support given by COREPER;
- ❖ the voting procedures in the Council and the impact of enlargement; and
- ❖ the future voting weightings after 2014.

Answer Structure

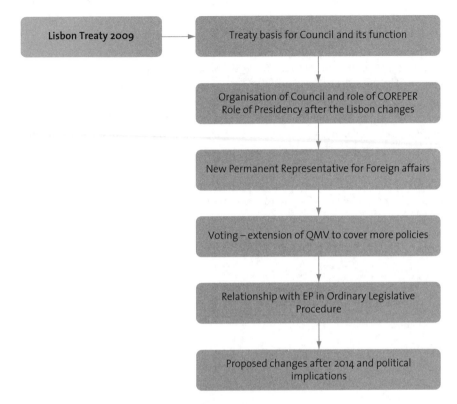

This diagram shows the key points to be discussed.

ANSWER

The Council of Ministers is a very important part of the EU institutional framework as it brings together the political representatives of the governments of the 27 Member States who are authorised to bind the Member State they represent. The Treaties refer to this body as 'the Council', but this does not reflect the composition of that body so in this essay they shall be referred to as the Council of Ministers to avoid any confusion with the European Council which brings together the Heads of Government. The Treaty of Lisbon came into force on 1 December 2009 and immediately made some changes to the composition of the Council of Ministers with changes in the voting procedures to come into force in 2014 and 2017. The important Articles of the Treaties concerning the composition and work of the Council of Ministers are Art 16 TEU and Arts 237–243 TFEU.

The composition of the Council of Ministers has always been one minister for each Member State so the numbers attending such meetings have grown as enlargement has taken place. The current 27 ministers are now joined by the by the High Representative of the Union for Foreign Affairs, Baroness Catherine Ashton, who chairs the Foreign Affairs Council established by **Art 16(6) TEU**. The Presidency of the Council has, since the start of the European Union, been based upon a six-monthly rotation, but this was heavily criticised as not being fit for purpose for an enlarged Union, so a vision of a 'team presidencies' was introduced by the **Treaty of Lisbon**. **Article 16(9) TEU** and **Art 236 TFEU** indicate that this will happen but the old system of six-monthly rotation is still being used. Spain held the Presidency of the Council for the first six months followed by Belgium. The importance of the Presidency used to be that the government holding that position would often make statements on behalf of the Member States or represent the EU at important international gatherings. This has been superseded by the fact that the EU now has a President of the European Council, a full-time post which **Art 15(5) TEU** states is for a term of two-and-a-half years, renewable once. The President is currently Mr Herman Van Rompuy. However, the Presidency of the Council of Ministers is still important because the minister from that Member State chairs the meeting of the Council and its various configurations apart from the Foreign Affairs Council. The setting of agendas and 'moving the Union's business through to a decision' is a powerful influence. The Presidency's basic duty is simply to get results. Each Presidency usually begins with the holder making a statement to the European Parliament with regard to what he or she hopes to achieve during his or her six months in office.

The main preparatory work for the Council of Ministers has always been by the national civil servants of ambassadorial rank who resolve technical issues and political questions as far as they can. This body is known as the Committee of the Permanent Representatives (COREPER), and is identified in **Art 16(7) TEU** and **Art 240 TFEU**. The Committee operates on two levels with senior rank ambassadors sitting on COREPER I with their deputies being on COREPER II. Given that government ministers of all Member States have other duties as members of a national government and elected politician the work in COREPER is crucial for the progress of EU legislation especially as the ordinary legislative procedure is used with its tight timescales. Under the ordinary legislative procedure the Council of Ministers shares the legislative decision making with the European Parliament and as the number of Union competences that fall under this procedure increase the burden on the Council and COREPER increases as well.

The voting within the Council of Ministers has often given rise to political confrontations between the Member States. In the original Treaties it was envisaged that the Council would move, after the transitional period, to majority voting, except for those specific matters identified by the Treaty as requiring unanimity. This was not to be a simple majority, but generally a qualified one on the basis of **Art 205** (now **Art 238(1) TFEU**). This Article gave each Member State a number of votes depending roughly upon the size of its population. On any issue before the Council, it requires a combination of the larger and smaller Member States to accumulate the necessary votes to adopt the measure. This seeks to ensure that no interest group in the Council can dominate the voting and encourages a compromise in the sense that the measure must be acceptable to a range of Member States. The necessary voting majority was 62 votes in favour of the measure. The intention of the Treaty was hindered by the events of 1966 that led to the Luxembourg Accord or Compromise, which was instituted to obtain the co-operation of the French Government in the working of the EU. This recognition of a 'veto', in the sense that unanimity was required on particular issues not specified as requiring unanimity under the Treaty, slowed down the actions of the Council, in that it could not proceed faster than its slowest participating government. Although academic debate still continues on whether the veto still exists, it is important to recognise the political nature of the Council. If the President of the Council is aware of the political implications of calling for a vote where a minority of the Council have strong objections, it is likely that such a vote will be postponed for further discussion.

The Inter-Governmental Conference (IGC) at the end of 2000 in Nice was dominated by the implications for voting in the Council of Ministers of the planned enlargement of the EU to 27 members. As Protocol 36 to the Treaty of Lisbon illustrates, the weighted votes for qualified majority voting now vary from 29 for Germany as the largest Member State down to three for Malta. There is a need for 255 votes in favour of an act for it to be adopted and a member of the Council or the European Council may request that this number represents at least 62% of the total population of the Union. If this is not the case the act will not be adopted. After 1 November 2014 the configuration of this voting will change so that the qualified majority will be defined as at least 72% of the members of the Council, representing Member States comprising at least 65% of the population of the Union (Art 238 TFEU). The Council of Ministers after the Treaty of Lisbon is still the most important political institution within the EU, but since the Single European Act 1986 it has had to increasingly share authority with the European Parliament. The original co-decision procedure has been replaced by the ordinary legislative procedure in the Treaty of Lisbon as the Union seeks to demonstrate a more democratic framework for its legislative process.

Aim Higher ★

Look out for news media coverage of the practical implications of the changes brought about by the **Treaty of Lisbon**. Are there any difficulties brought about by having important full-time posts in Foreign Affairs and the Presidency of the Council outside the normal Council membership?

QUESTION 5

What is the role of the Commission? Is it sufficiently accountable?

How to Answer this Question

This question allows you to draw upon the other areas of a European Law syllabus to illustrate the powers and functions of the European Commission. The main points to cover are:

❖ Art 17 of the TEU and Arts 244–250 TFEU for the general duties of the Commission;

❖ the appointment and organisation of the European Commission;

❖ the role of the Commission and Community legislation;

❖ the Commission's role in external relations;

❖ the enforcement powers of the Commission under Art 258 TFEU;

❖ the powers of the Commission with regard to competition policy; and

❖ elements of the Constitutional Treaty 2004 dealing with the relationship between the Commission and the European Parliament and the final Treaty of Lisbon changes.

Answer Structure

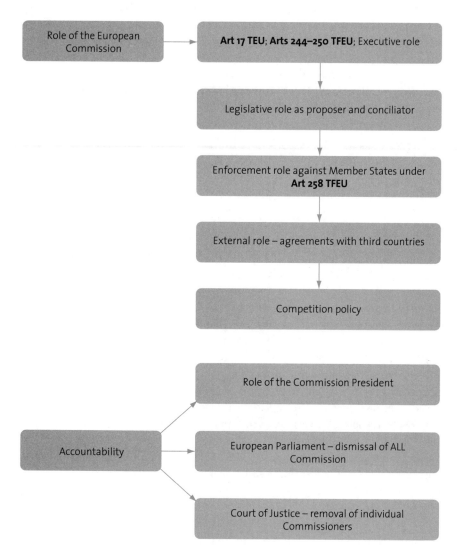

This diagram shows the key points to be discussed.

ANSWER

The main roles of the European Commission are given in Art 17 TEU, and indicate the key functions envisaged for it by the Treaty of Lisbon. Perhaps the most important role given to the Commission is its power to initiate European laws in the form of draft regulations and directives, and as the executive arm of the Union once those laws are passed. Although the main political power of the Union rests with the Council of

Ministers, the Council is dependent upon receiving a proposal from the Commission before it can act. These proposals cover the full range of EU policy specified in the Treaty and the general power under Art 352 TFEU. In exceptional cases the Council, and more latterly the European Parliament, can request proposals under Art 241 TFEU, but even here a proposal must come from the Commission. The introduction in 1993 of the co-decision procedure whereby the European Parliament's legislative role in certain policy areas was greatly increased and now the ordinary legislative procedure of the Treaty of Lisbon requires the involvement of the Commission. If the European Parliament wishes to amend the Council's common position, such amendments are first considered by the European Commission which can either adopt them or give reasons for their refusal to the Council. It can also put forward new drafts in an attempt to get a compromise agreement between the parties. The role of the Commission in directing and stimulating the development of the EU cannot be underestimated.

Following the passing of Community Acts, such as those mentioned in Art 288 TFEU, it is for the Commission to ensure that they are applied. Some observers refer to this as the policing role of the Commission, but it goes further than this. The Commission is acting in an executive role, implementing the agreed policy of the Community. In order to ensure that Member States implement the Community Act and generally fulfil their obligations under the Treaty, the Commission is granted a power under Art 258 TFEU. This power can lead to an 'enforcement action' before the ECJ but first the Commission has to deliver a reasoned opinion to any Member States which it feels is failing to fulfil an obligation. If the Member State is unable to satisfy the Commission that it is not failing to do so, the Commission can bring the matter before the European Court of Justice. If the Court agrees with the Commission's view it can make a declaration under Art 260 TFEU requiring the Member State to comply with its judgment and, if appropriate, imposing a fine. This is a very powerful weapon given to the Commission, which has led to it being called 'the guardian of the Treaties'. The Commission has complete discretion as to whether to bring an action under Art 258 TFEU, but this has to be seen within the context of its overall duty under Art 17 TEU to ensure that the Treaty and the associated measures taken are applied. Therefore there is a mixture of legal and political pressure on the Member State to comply.

There is no 'EU government' in the sense that one would associate with a sovereign national state, but the Commission does play some of the roles of a government. The Commission is seen as the body representing the Community interest as a whole and therefore it is understandable that the original treaties gave a special role to the Commission with regard to the Community's external relations. The Community is a large economic trading area and as such belongs to a number of international organisations, such as GATT. International trade is an area of policy that was transferred to the Community when the EEC Treaty was signed in 1957 and so there is a division of 'sovereignty' between the Member States and the Community. In addition the Community is party to bilateral and multilateral agreements with countries or trading blocs. Under Art 251 TFEU such international agreements are to be negotiated by the Commission, although they are concluded by the Council of Ministers after receiving the approval of the European Parliament.

Given that the free market is seen as a fundamental principle of the EU, the important area of competition policy provides an example of the wide powers of the Commission. The competition policy of the Community is founded upon Arts 101, 102 and 105 TFEU covering both the private sector and the activities of governments of Member States. The authority of the Commission with regard to the private sector is not restricted to those undertakings based in the European Community, but includes all those who are involved in an economic activity within the Community. This was a lesson learnt by ICI, before the UK became a member of the Community, in the *Dyestuffs* case in 1972. As indicated above, the Commission is involved in the Community Acts specified in Art 88 TFEU. In the specific area of competition policy this results in decisions being taken that are binding upon those to whom they are addressed. Thus the Commission, exercising its powers under Regulation 1/2003, can investigate restrictive practices or abuses of a dominant position affecting the Community and if the competition policy has been breached, it can impose very large fines. Many of the undertakings involved in such cases complain that the Commission's powers are excessive in that they are 'prosecutor, judge and jury'. However, there is the possibility of appeal to the Court of First Instance. The Commission's role with regard to mergers was also increased by the Merger Regulation 4064/89 and now Regulation 139/2004. Under Regulation 4064/89 the Commission must approve such mergers between undertakings with a worldwide turnover of more than €5,000 million, where at least two of the firms have a combined turnover of more than €250 million in the European Community. Actions by governments of Member States which may affect undertakings by providing subsidies or other unfair treatment are also subject to the powers of enforcement of the Commission, much to the annoyance of the Member States concerned.

It can be seen that the roles and powers of the European Commission are very wide. Without the European Commission, the European Community could never have been constructed and developed to the extent it has. Although it should operate on a collegiate basis, the increased number of Commissioners and the policies of the Community make this difficult. With enlargement in May 2004 and January 2007 there are now 27 Member States, each with one Commissioner. The Constitutional Treaty 2004 proposed that the number of Commissioners should be reduced in size from 2014 and then consists of Commissioners corresponding to two-thirds of the number of Member States, based on a system of rotation. Such a system was designed to meet the problems of an ever-larger number of Commissioners but it was always a sensitive issue and was considered to be a factor in the Irish vote against the Lisbon Treaty in June 2008. As the Constitutional Treaty was not ratified at all and in response to the failure in the first Irish referendum on the Lisbon Treaty there is still one Commissioner for each Member State. So although Art 17 TEU sets a date of 1 November 2014 for a reduction in the size of the Commission the concession given to Ireland in order for the referendum to have a positive outcome is to be incorporated into a legally binding protocol to be attached to the next accession treaty. This is likely to be when Croatia joins.

The Commissioners are not 'elected' but nominated by the Member States. Even though they have to be approved or confirmed in office by the European Parliament since the Treaty of Amsterdam, the question arises as to how accountable they are. They are not to be 'mandated' by their Member State or to be seen favouring one Member State or organisation, so once in office there is no control by the Member State, which is in line with the functions of the Commissioner envisaged by the treaties. The term of office of the Commission is synchronised with the European Parliament elections so that the political profile of the Commissioners is matched to that of the EP. They can only be removed as a group by the European Parliament and the ECJ, under Arts 245 and 247 TFEU, only deals with individual Commissioners who breach their obligations under the Treaty. Neither of these possible actions has ever been taken. The problems in 1999 of the Santer Commission led to informal arrangements so that the President of the Commission gained in authority and there was an arrangement whereby Commissioners would agree to resign from office if requested to do so by the President. There was also the possibility of the President of the Commission changing the portfolio or area of responsibility for a Commissioner, a form of 'reshuffle'. This was all formalised in the Treaty of Lisbon where Art 17(6) and (7) TEU provide a legal base for the relationship between the President of the Commission and the other Commissioners. But again, this gives more authority to the President of the Commission, and how accountable is she? Also the nomination of Commissioners by Member States after the 2009 EP elections did have some regard to the outcome of the elections but many still reflected the party allegiances of the governments of the member States. The President of the Commission was 'elected' by the European Parliament to emphasise the responsibility of the President to the Commission but it is unlikely to increase accountability. It raises the question 'who will guard the guardians'?

NOTE

You should look at Chapter 4 on Direct Actions, where Art 258 TFEU actions are dealt with in more detail, and Chapter 7 on Competition Policy.

Sources of Law

2

INTRODUCTION

As you are no doubt aware, the European Union is based upon treaties which have a special significance under international law. They form the basis not only of the institutions, but also of the powers that can be exercised by those institutions and the procedures under which they must operate. Therefore, it is no wonder that the starting point for any discussion of the legal basis of the European Union is the treaties upon which it is founded. The treaties are considered to be the primary source of Community law. The basis of any legal action must be founded on a treaty provision.

Although it is perhaps an over-simplification to use this analogy, if you think of the treaty as an enabling Act, then what is required is the equivalent of delegated legislation to provide the structure and detail necessary to produce an effective measure upon which individuals can base their actions and which the legal system can enforce. Hence we come to what are generally called secondary sources of Community law. These are listed in Art 288 TFEU as regulations, directives and decisions. Although recommendations and opinions are mentioned, these are not legally binding. This Article provides the key definitions of these Community administrative acts which are so important to the study of European law.

As every student of a common law system is aware, the judiciary, in their deliberation and judgments on the law, create rules or principles which are followed in subsequent cases. Although the European legal system does not have such a rigid adherence to precedent as found in the common law, the judges in the European Court of Justice (ECJ) have provided an additional secondary source of law to add to the administrative acts found in Art 288. Examples of this will be found in specific questions throughout the later chapters of this book, but a few points can be made now to show the impact of this source of law. As will be discussed in Chapter 3, there is a clear acceptance within the EU that the ECJ provides definitive and authoritative judgments on points of European Union law which are followed by the courts of the Member States.

Checklist ✔

You need to have a good understanding of the role of the **EU Treaty** as an authority for Community Acts or judgments of the Court of Justice (ECJ). When you are tracing the authority of a particular EU Act, you will generally go back to a Treaty Article. In addition, you should cover the following points:

- primary and secondary sources of Community law;
- administrative acts defined in **Art 288 TFEU**;
- general principles of Community law; and
- methods of interpretation used in Community law.

QUESTION 6

Critically review the development of general principles of law as part of the law of the European Union.

How to Answer this Question

Generally, questions covering only general principles of Community law are essay questions, similar to this one. However, you must be prepared to deal with this topic within problem questions, where a particular general principle may be the ground which will allow a remedy to be granted to one of the parties. The most common question where these occur asks you to deal with an action for judicial review under Art 263 TFEU. You should look at Chapter 4 to see how the topic of general principles can be integrated into a problem question drawing upon a number of topics in the syllabus.

With regard to this question, the main points for discussion are:

- ❖ the role of general principles within a legal system;
- ❖ authority for the development of general principles within the EC legal system; and
- ❖ specific examples of Community general principles, including the most important ones.

Answer Structure

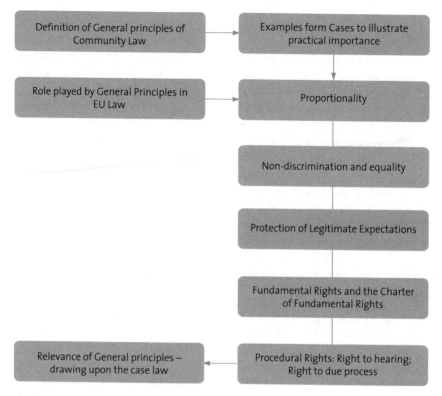

This diagram shows the key points to be discussed.

ANSWER -

General principles of law are found in all legal systems, including the common law system. Within the common law system of England, they are seen as a device to hide judge-made law, whereby a judge seeks to show that his ruling was derived from a principle of sufficient generality so as to command common assent. In this way, a firm legal base could be provided for the judgment. Within the legal systems of the Member States, the development of general principles has taken place over a number of years and has been cloaked in historical respectability or authority. However, the European Union was facing the possible development of general principles in a modern era and therefore had to be more conscious of what it was undertaking. The ECJ has developed a doctrine that rules of EU law may be derived from general principles of law in addition to treaties and EU legislation. There has also been the important development of the Charter of Fundamental Rights which has built upon the European Convention of Human Rights to include many economic and social rights.

The ECJ has pointed to three Articles of the EU Treaty to provide some justification for general principles as a source of law. These are:

(a) **Article 19 TEU**, which states that 'The Court of Justice shall ensure that in the interpretation of the Treaty the law is observed'. In view of the word 'law' being used, it is considered that it must refer to something over and above the Treaty itself, and it is not unreasonable for this Article to oblige the judges of the Court to take general principles into account.

(b) **Article 263 TFEU** deals with judicial review and specifies the grounds upon which an annulment can be based. The first paragraph of the Article includes the words 'infringement of this Treaty, or of any rule of law relating to its application . . .'. The phrase 'any rule of law' must refer to something other than the Treaty itself. This has been used by the ECJ as a basis for the principle that a Community Act may be quashed for the infringement of a general principle of law.

(c) **Article 340 TFEU** is concerned with non-contractual liability (tort), and expressly provides that the liability of the Community is based on the 'general principles common to the laws of the Member States'.

Given this authority from the Treaty, three points should be noted before going on to specific general principles:

(a) the Court is prepared to apply principles of law, even if they are not found in the legal system of every Member State;

(b) whatever the factual origin of the principle, it is applied by the ECJ as a principle of EU law and not of national law. This is very important, as can be noted by the development of the general principle of protection of fundamental rights given below and now encapsulated in the Charter;

(c) there is little doubt that the ECJ would have applied general principles of law even if none of these Treaty provisions existed, because of the function of such general principles.

PROPORTIONALITY

This principle is derived from German law, where it underlies certain provisions of the German Constitution. 'A public authority may not impose obligations on a citizen except to the extent to which they are strictly necessary in the public interest to attain the purpose of the measure' (*Internationale Handelsgesellschaft* (1970)).

Thus, if the burdens imposed are clearly out of proportion to the object in view, the measure will be annulled. Proportionality is important in economic law and therefore has a wide application within the EU. It frequently involves imposing taxes, levies, duties, etc, in the hope of achieving economic advantages. The ECJ will not interfere unless there is a very clear and obvious infringement of the principle. The principle has also been widely used by the English courts in domestic disputes.

An example is the *Skimmed Milk Powder* case (*Bela-Muhle Josef Bergman v Grows Farm* (1977)), where the Council had sought to reduce a surplus of skimmed milk powder in the Community by forcing animal feed producers to incorporate it in their product in place of soya, which was the normal protein element used. The drawback to the producers was that the skimmed milk was three times more expensive than the soya. The ECJ held that the regulation embodying the scheme was invalid, partly because it was discriminatory and partly because it offended against the principle of proportionality. The effect of making animal feed producers use skimmed milk was to increase the price of animal feed and thus harm all livestock breeders. The imposition of the obligation to purchase skimmed milk powder was not necessary in order to diminish the surplus. On the other hand, the benefits of the policy were felt only by dairy farmers. Therefore, the policy worked in a discriminatory fashion between different categories of farmers.

NON-DISCRIMINATION OR EQUALITY

Specific reference to this principle can be found in the Treaty, notably in the original Art 7 (now Art 3 TEU), which dealt with discrimination on the grounds of nationality, and Art 57 TFEU which deals with equal pay. However, the ECJ has gone beyond these provisions in holding that there is a general principle of non-discrimination in Union law. This does not mean that Community institutions must treat everybody alike, but that there must be no arbitrary distinctions between different groups within the Community. For an example concerning a business, see the *Skimmed Milk Powder* case, above. The case of *Sabbatini v European Parliament* (1972) illustrates how the principle applies to discrimination between the sexes. The Court went further in the case of *Prais v Council* (1976), where it held that the principle also covered discrimination on the basis of religion.

PROTECTION OF LEGITIMATE EXPECTATIONS

According to this principle, derived from German law, Community measures must not, in the absence of an overriding matter of public interest, violate the legitimate expectations of those concerned. Thus, a business, holding a reasonable expectation which it has acted upon in the normal cause of business and having suffered a loss, may seek to have the Community measure annulled. The ECJ sometimes seeks to avoid annulment by adopting a strained interpretation of the measure concerned.

In *Deuka v EVGF* (1975), the German intervention agency (EVGF) was the national authority concerned with the payment of premiums to processors who made wheat unfit for human consumption and only suitable for animal feed. In order to qualify for a premium, Deuka had to obtain the prior agreement of EVGF and to carry out the process under their supervision. A European Commission regulation increased the premium payable as from 1 June 1970, that is, during a crop year. Deuka processed a quantity of wheat which had been purchased before 1 June, and thus claimed they were entitled to the increased premium. This was refused. Following legal proceedings in the German courts, a reference was made to the ECJ. The regulation was not declared invalid, but the

Court stated that, in view of the principle of legal certainty, it should be interpreted so that the increase was payable, even if processing took place after 1 June, provided that the wheat was purchased and the relevant authority approved before 1 June. Therefore, this interpretation gave full protection to the legitimate expectations of the processors (see also *Commission v Council* (1973), which is concerned with salary payments to Community staff).

FUNDAMENTAL RIGHTS

It was not until the case of *Stauder v City of Ulm* (1969) that the ECJ recognised this general principle. The refusal to do so earlier had created pressure between the Court and some of the Member States, notably Germany and Italy, where such rights had been enshrined into the respective constitutions. The matter was resolved when an administrative judge in Stuttgart asked the ECJ whether a particular requirement was compatible with the general principles of Community law. The result was that the ECJ expressly included the protection of 'fundamental human rights enshrined in the general principles of Community law and protected by the Court'. In the later case of *Internationale Handelsgesellschaft* (1970), the Court stated that 'fundamental rights form an integral part of the general principles of the law, the observance of which it ensures; [and] in safeguarding those rights, the Court is bound to draw inspiration from constitutional traditions common to the Member States . . .'. The European Convention on Human Rights was recognised in the Preamble to the Single European Act 1986 and the ECJ has accorded a special significance to the Convention (*ERT* (1989)). At the IGC held in December 2000 in Nice, it was decided not to include the Charter of Fundamental Rights in the Treaty. Although a joint proclamation by the Council, Parliament and the Commission was made in support of the Charter, there is legal uncertainty as to its status. It was included in the Constitution Treaty 2004, but this treaty has not yet been ratified. However, following the Treaty of Lisbon, Art 6(1) TEU recognises the Charter as an integral part of EU law.

PROCEDURAL RIGHTS

These rights have been developed to fill the gaps where EC legislation does not provide specific safeguards for a person's rights. Examples include:

(a) *the right to a hearing* – this is drawn from the tradition of English law and was first used in *Transocean Marine Paint Association v Commission* (1974), where Advocate General Warner submitted that there was a general rule that a person whose interests are perceptibly affected by a decision taken by a public authority must be given the opportunity to make his views known. As the Commission had failed to do so in this competition case, its decision was annulled;

(b) *the right to due process* – in the case of *Johnston v Chief Constable of the Royal Ulster Constabulary* (1986), Mrs Johnston claimed that she had been subject to sex discrimination by her employer, contrary to Directive 76/207 (now Directive

2002/73). A certificate issued by the Secretary of State sought to provide conclusive evidence that the derogation from Community obligations was on the grounds of national security. The Court held that such a provision was contrary to the 'requirement of judicial control stipulated by [Art 6 which] reflects a general principle of law which underlies the constitutional traditions common to the Member States'.

The advantages of general principles are the same for the Community legal system as for Member States. They help to fill the gaps which always arise when it is not possible to have a written text to cover every legal eventuality. They constitute the unwritten law of the Community. Also within the Community, the characteristic role of general principles as limiting the power of the administration to take measures affecting the citizen has been continued.

General principles of law are relevant in the context of EU law in a number of ways:

(a)   they may be invoked as an aid to interpretation in the sense that 'the measure should not conflict with general principles';
(b)   general principles may be invoked by both Member States and individuals in order to challenge Union Acts;
(c)   general principles may also be invoked as a means of challenging action by a Member State, where the action is performed in the context of a right or obligation arising from Community law; and
(d)   general principles may be invoked to support claims for damages against the Community (Art 340 TFEU).

Aim Higher ★

If you extend your coverage of general principles of law beyond those mentioned here you will increase your potential mark. It will demonstrate your wider reading.

QUESTION 7

Explain the nature and legal effect of regulations, directives and decisions made by the Council of Ministers, the European Parliament and the Commission of the European Community.

How to Answer this Question

Most questions on sources of law are essay questions like this one. However, you must remember that a good understanding of these topics can be invaluable when answering problem questions, which come up in later chapters. The best example is that of cases brought under Art 263 TFEU, where the ability to discuss what is meant by a regulation is very important.

This question is looking for a clear understanding of the definitions in Art 288 TFEU and the legal effect of a regulation, a directive and a decision!

Answer Structure

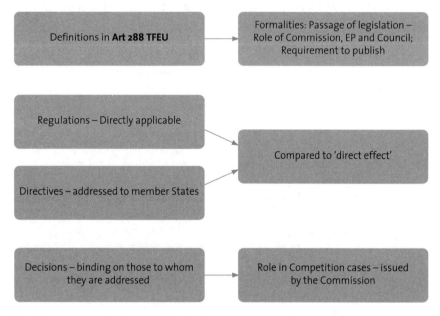

This diagram shows the key points to be discussed.

ANSWER

The forms of EU legislation or administrative acts are listed in Art 288. This provides the basic definitions for a regulation, directive and decision. Article 288 does not give the authority to issue such legislative measures, as they have to be authorised by specific Articles of the Treaty. However, where the Council and the EP or the Commission, in order to carry out their tasks, do need to issue a legally binding act, it is to Art 288 TFEU that attention must be given.

Under Art 288 TFEU, the definition of a regulation is that it shall have general application and be binding in its entirety and directly applicable in all Member States. It does not mean that a regulation necessarily has to apply to all Member States. It could be applicable in only one Member State. However, as long as it retains its character of being applicable to an abstract group of persons it will still be a regulation. This is important if an individual is seeking to challenge the validity of a regulation by using the **Art 263** procedure, as was discussed in *Zuckerfabrik Watenstedt* (1968).

Under **Art 296 TFEU**, it is a requirement that certain formalities be completed in order for a valid regulation to be made. The reasons upon which the regulation is based must be given and any proposals or opinions which were required by the Treaty to be obtained must be referred to. The next Article, **Art 297 TFEU**, requires that regulations are published in the Official Journal of the Community. The Council's Rules of Procedure for regulations require them to be numbered, dated and signed. Regulations also carry a formula describing their legal effects, that is, 'this Regulation is binding in its entirety and directly applicable in all Member States'.

This formula raises two points about the effects of regulations. The first is whether national legislation is required by the Member State to implement the regulation. The view of the ECJ is that regulations have a mandatory effect and have the force of law in the Member States without the need for transformation or confirmation by their legislatures. The Court went further in the 1972 case of *EC Commission v Italy*, when it stated that 'all methods of implementation are contrary to the Treaty which would have the result of creating an obstacle to the direct effect of Community regulations and jeopardising their simultaneous and uniform application in the whole of the Community'. Although there are exceptional cases where such national legislation is required, in such cases, the national law must not disguise its Community character by altering the wording of the regulation or its date for coming into force.

The second point concerns the meaning of 'directly applicable in all Member States'. 'Directly applicable' means that the regulation does not require a national measure to become binding upon the citizens and also that national authorities and national measures cannot prevent its application. There is often confusion between 'direct applicability' and the term 'direct effect', especially as the ECJ itself seems to use the terms interchangeably. The Treaty and other sources of Community law can have direct effect, but only regulations are directly applicable. In *Politi v Italian Ministry of Finance* (1971), the ECJ held that, under **Art 288 TFEU**, 'Regulations shall have general application and shall be directly applicable in Member States . . . Therefore by reason of their nature and their function in the system of the sources of EU law, regulations have direct effect and are as such capable of creating individual rights which national courts must protect'. Therefore, not only may individuals rely on specific provisions as against other individuals and Member States, they may invoke the general objective and purpose of regulations as against national legal provisions. Thus, in *Amsterdam Bulb BV v Producktschap voor Siergewassen* (1977), it was stated that 'the moment that the Community adopts regulations under **Art 20 TEU** establishing a common organisation of the market in a specific sector, the Member States are under a duty not to take any measure which might create exemptions from them or affect them adversely'.

Aim Higher ★

Try to use current examples to show the nature and legal effect of
regulations and directives. There is always something in the media if you
research the *Daily Telegraph* or the *Daily Mail*!

QUESTION 8

Critically review the methods of interpretation used by the European Court of Justice
(ECJ).

How to Answer this Question

This question is seeking an answer which shows knowledge and understanding of how
the ECJ goes about the process of interpreting Community law.

The main points raised by this question are:

* ❖ purpose of methods of interpretation;
* ❖ influences on the ECJ; and
* ❖ methods used by the ECJ – teleological, contextual, literal, historical.

Answer Structure

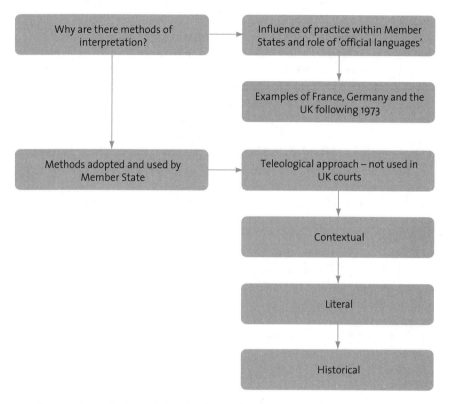

This diagram shows the key points to be discussed.

ANSWER

With regard to EC law, the ECJ is the final arbiter. There are no appeals against judgments it gives. Under the preliminary ruling procedure of Art 267 TFEU, the ECJ can be requested to provide a definitive interpretation of the Treaty or of a Union Act. This can be extended under other Articles of the Treaty to include other sources of law that are legally binding in the European Union. In order to carry out its tasks, the ECJ has developed a number of tools of interpretation. The European Court 'tool box' is not unlike the English methods of literal, golden, mischief, etc, but with the very important difference that it has been developed in the context of influence of domestic law (mainly France and Germany) and international law. However, like English judges, the judges of the ECJ very rarely use one method of interpretation in a particular case. They use a variety of rules of interpretation and then decide, as part of the judicial art, which is the most appropriate in the circumstances. Given the authority of the ECJ, this gives the judges a great deal of influence over the character and effectiveness of EU law.

Whatever method or approach to interpretation the Court may utilise, it must be remembered that they are operating in a legal system that has a strong linguistic dimension. There are 23 official languages, so all the Community texts written in the languages of the Member States are recognised as having equal validity. The main approaches to interpretation are characterised by the teleological approach, which is increasingly favoured by the ECJ. The teleological approach requires the judge to look to the purpose or object of the text before him. As Lord Denning observed in *Bulmer v Bollinger* (1974): '. . . the **[EC] Treaty** is quite unlike any of the enactments to which we have become accustomed . . . It lays down general principles. It expresses its aims and purposes . . . But it lacks precision.' Faced with a body of law couched in such terms, the ECJ uses the teleological approach. In the **Art 102 TFEU** competition case of *Continental Can*, the ECJ referred to the 'spirit, general scheme and wording of **Art 106**, as well as to the system and objectives of the Treaty'. In the *Colditz* (1967) case, certain social security regulations were before the Court, which declared that 'the solution to this question . . . can only emerge from the interpretation of those regulations in the light of the objectives of the Treaty'.

The contextual approach involves the Court placing the provision, whether from a treaty or an EU Act, within its context and interpreting it in relation to other provisions of Union law. Given the lack of precision in many Community provisions, it is no wonder that frequent reference is made to the 'framework of Community law', as in *Costa v ENEL*, or 'one must have regard to the whole scheme of the Treaty no less than to its specific provisions', in the *ERTA* case. Contextual interpretation is also used for Community legislation.

In the important case of *Defrenne* (1976) , the ECJ was considering whether the **Equal Pay Article**, now **Art 157 TFEU**, had direct effect. It brought together a teleological approach when looking at the socio-economic purpose of the Article, but within a particular context (or contextual approach), in that **Art 157** has a close relationship with **Art 151** (**Art 117** at the time of the case), which concerned the need to promote improved working conditions and an improved standard of living for workers.

Although not stated in the judgments of the Court, writings of retired members of the ECJ indicate that they favour the teleological and context approaches to interpretation because they reflect the way that the Community is changing as it seeks to fulfil its aims and objectives in the future.

The literal interpretation is an approach which every court takes when faced with the question 'What does this mean?' The ECJ is no exception, but whereas the national judge may feel that his task is then at an end, the ECJ may decide that the plain meaning of the words should not be followed, but preference should be given to allow for the aims and objectives of the treaties to be achieved. In other words, the teleological or contextual approaches are given priority. In the *ERTA* case, the Commission sought to have the

Council decision to co-ordinate the Member States' negotiations under the European Road Transport Agreement annulled. The Council argued that the action under Art 263 (then Art 173) was not valid, in that the Community Acts mentioned were those found in Art 288 (then Art 189), namely, regulations, directives or decisions. Despite the clear wording of Art 288, the ECJ held that the purpose of Art 263 was to subject to judicial review all those measures which had legal effect. They declared: 'It would be inconsistent with this objective to interpret the conditions under which the action is admissible so restrictively as to limit the availability of this procedure merely to the categories of measures referred to by Art 189 [now Art 288].' In *Stauder v City of Ulm*, the ECJ had to consider the different wording of a Commission decision permitting the sale of cheap butter to those in receipt of welfare benefits. Stauder was a German national who, under German law implementing the decision, was required to give his name when purchasing the butter, something which he claimed was contrary to his fundamental rights. The Dutch text followed the German text, but the Court referred to the French and Italian texts, which only stipulated that a coupon referring to the person concerned needed to be presented. The Court adopted this more liberal version of the decision, which would enable its objectives to be achieved without any breach of fundamental rights.

Historical interpretation is associated with the attempt to ascertain the subjective intention of the author of the text before the Court. It is not used very often, because of the lack of documentation available to help the Court. The negotiations surrounding the original treaties are shrouded by secrecy and thus the *travaux preparatoires* are not available. However, the Official Journal publishes all legislative proposals by the Commission as well as formal opinions of the European Parliament. In addition, the legislative Acts of the Community are required, under Art 253 (Art 296 TFEU), to state in their Preamble the reasons on which they are based and to refer to any proposals or opinions which were required by the Act. These Preambles give some assistance to the Court, as they did in *Markus v Hauptzollamt Hamburg-Jonas* (1969) a case involving agricultural tariffs.

EC Law and National Law

3

INTRODUCTION

One of the central principles established by the Court of Justice (ECJ) is that of the supremacy of European Union law over national law. Having gained acceptance for this, the Court went on to establish the principle or doctrine of direct effect, which gives rights to individuals which can be enforced in the courts of the Member States. Both of these developments were signalled in the early cases of *Van Gend en Loos* (1963) and *Costa v ENEL*. (1964)

However, it is also important to note that the Court has built upon these principles in other topics, such as preliminary references, which are dealt with in Chapter 5. Generally, the specific questions on this topic are essay types, but aspects of the principles associated with the relationship of EU law and national law also arise in questions on other topics which can be in both essay and problem format.

Checklist ✔

You should understand the principle of supremacy of EU law and direct effect developed in the following cases: *Van Gend en Loos, Costa, Simmenthal SpA (No 2)* **(1978)** and *Internationale* **(1970)**. In addition, the following specific points should be covered:

- the principle of direct effect in relation to direct applicability;
- the direct effect of treaty provisions, regulations, directives and decisions;
- the test for direct effect; and
- vertical and horizontal direct effect.

QUESTION 9

Critically discuss the development of the principle of supremacy of EU law.

How to Answer this Question

This essay question requires a discussion of the supremacy of Community law over national law and how it has come about. The main points for this question are:

- ❖ the Treaty basis used to justify supremacy of EU law, notably Art 10;
- ❖ the foundations of the Community referred to in *Van Gend en Loos, Costa, Internationale* and *Simmenthal*;
- ❖ how Community, now EU, law is incorporated into national law;
- ❖ the reaction of the Member States to this development.

Answer Structure

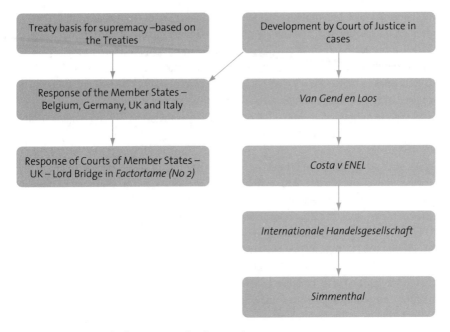

This diagram shows the key points to be discussed.

ANSWER

When the European Community was established in 1957, it required a transfer of sovereignty for certain specific areas of policy from the Member State to the Community. This meant that some legal matters that had been the sole prerogative of a Member State were no longer within its control. This inevitably led to a situation of conflict between national and EU law. Yet if the Community was to fulfil its aims, it was necessary that such conflicts were speedily resolved, with a minimum of uncertainty. However, this question raised constitutional problems of varying magnitude for all Member States.

The primary source of EU law, the Treaties, contains no specific mention of any priorities in the relationship between national and EU law. However, in the view of the ECJ, the legal basis on which the Community rests necessarily presupposes the supremacy or primacy of Community law. Under international law, the question is resolved by the constitutional rules of the Member State concerned. Principally, it will depend on the means by which international law is incorporated into the domestic law of that Member State. There are two approaches to this incorporation, in that the legal systems of States are generally either monist or dualist in their approach to international law. In monist States, such as France, all law is treated equally, in the sense that national courts can apply international treaties, as long as the appropriate constitutional procedures have been followed. In cases of conflict with national law, monist countries usually recognise the supremacy of Treaty provisions. However, in dualist States, such as the UK, international law and national law are considered to be fundamentally different. As such, international treaties can never be applied by national courts, and only domestic legislation can be brought about by the international treaties. Thus, the EC Treaty has to be specifically incorporated into domestic law. In the UK, this was achieved by the European Communities Act 1972, specifically ss 2 and 3. However, whatever the method of incorporation used by the Member State, this does not in itself settle the question of priorities.

The ECJ has placed great importance upon the uniformity of application of EU law in the Member States, and the desire to see that the Community was not weakened by diversity in interpretation or application. Therefore, it is understandable that the Court would develop its own constitutional rules to ensure that where there was a conflict between EU and national law, it would be EU law which prevailed. It was in the case of *Van Gend en Loos* that the ECJ took its first tentative steps in this process. The case was an Art 263TFEU (then Art 177) preliminary reference from the Dutch courts on whether Art 30 (then Art 12) of the Treaty had direct effect. The Court took the opportunity of declaring that 'the Community constitutes a new legal order in international law, for whose benefit the States have limited their sovereign rights, albeit within limited fields'. In *Costa v ENEL* (1964), the Court went further when asked a specific question by the Italian court on the priority of EU law and national law. With the transfer of sovereignty mentioned in *Van Gend* 'comes . . . a clear limitation of their sovereign rights upon which a subsequent unilateral law, incompatible with the aims of the Community, cannot prevail'. Thus, by establishing a European Community, now the EU, with real powers, the Member States created a body of law which applies to their nationals as well as to themselves.

In the important case of *Internationale Handelsgesellschaft mbH* (1970), the Court was concerned with a conflict between an EC regulation and provisions of the German Constitution protecting fundamental rights. Under German law, the Constitution was superior to a statute. As a country with a mitigated dualist legal system, it was necessary for the EC Treaty to be incorporated into the national legal system and the vehicle used to do this was a statute. Thus, given that there was no provision in the Constitution to allow it to be overridden by EC law, the plaintiff claimed that the regulation should be nullified. Which should prevail: the regulation or the Constitution? The ECJ took a very strong view and insisted that the legality of a Community Act cannot be nullified by national law. The German Constitutional Court was concerned about the lack of protection for fundamental rights within the Community and stated that until this changed, the fundamental rights provision of the German Constitution would take priority. This would not mean that they would rule on the validity of a Community Act, but rather they would conclude that such a measure could not be applied in Germany. This did not happen in the *Internationale* case or in any subsequent German case, but it does indicate a possible conflict in particular circumstances. A similar conclusion occurred in the *Frontini* (1974) case, only here it was the Italian Constitution's protection of fundamental rights which was involved. The Constitutional Courts in both Germany and Italy were not happy with the hard line taken by the ECJ. The important difference is that the Italian Constitutional Court has repeated the possibility of declaring that a Community measure may not apply in Italy. This was in the *Fragd* case in 1990.

Thus, as far as the ECJ is concerned, all EU law, regardless of whether it is a Treaty provision, a EU Act or an agreement with a third country, must take priority over all conflicting domestic law. This applies whether the national law is enacted prior or subsequent to Community law. In the absence of any specific Treaty provision, how can this be justified? It in fact reflects the approach of the Court, which is pragmatic and pro-Community based on the purpose, the general aims and the spirit of the Treaty. In its view, Member States apply to join the Community and must therefore take the necessary measures to comply with EU law. The Community was established with its own institutions which have powers under **Art 288 TFEU**, with no qualification or reservation, to make laws binding upon all Member States. Regulations are specifically said in **Art 288** to have 'binding force' and to be directly applicable in all Member States. To the Court, this shows a clear indication of the supremacy of the legislative provisions conferred on the Community. If a State could unilaterally nullify its effects by means of domestic legislation overruling EU law, Union legislation would be quite meaningless.

The ECJ has repeatedly used **Art 20 TEU** to emphasise the fundamental obligation upon Member States to implement Community legislation, so that it receives uniform application throughout the Community. Under **Art 20 TEU**, Member States are required to abstain from any measure that could jeopardise the attainment of the objectives of the Treaty. Where Member States fail to fulfil their obligations, **Art 258 TFEU** gives authority to the Commission to instigate enforcement procedures. The Community would not survive if States were free to act unilaterally in breach of such obligation. If the aims of the Community are to be achieved, there must be uniformity of application of Community law throughout all the Member States. This will not occur unless all States accord priority to EU law. In fact, all new members of the Union must accept the principle of *acquis communautaire*, which requires them to accept not only the Treaties, but the whole body of Community and now Union law.

A final case provides guidance to national judges faced with a case that shows a conflict between a national law and EU law. In *Simmenthal SpA (No 2)*, an Italian judge was faced with a conflict between a Council regulation on the common organisation of the market in beef and veal and the Italian veterinary and public health laws. Under Italian law, domestic legislation contrary to EC regulations may be held unconstitutional, but only by the Constitutional Court and not by the ordinary courts. Should the Italian judge of first instance disregard inconsistent national legislation without waiting for its repeal or a declaration from the Constitutional Court making it invalid? The instructions given in answer to the **Art 288 TFEU** (then **Art 177**) reference were that a national court was under a duty to give full effect to Community law, even if there was a conflicting provision of national law, and without waiting for a higher court to rule on the matter. This is similar to the *Factortame* case in the House of Lords, where it was accepted that directly effective Community law must prevail over any inconsistent subsequent domestic legislation. Any incompatible national law is automatically inapplicable, because, unless EU law is given priority over conflicting national law at once, from the moment of its coming into force, there can be no uniformity of application throughout the EU.

Within a short space of time, the courts of the Member States, despite their different constitutional rules and traditions, have adapted to the principle of supremacy of EU law. This is perhaps due in part to the persuasive judgments of the ECJ and the attitudes of the courts of the Member States. They have accepted that European Union law, stemming as it does from the Treaties, has an independent source. It cannot be challenged by judicial process on the basis of any national provisions, however framed, without being deprived of its character as EU law and, more importantly, without the legal basis of the EU itself being called into question. The supremacy of European Union law stems from the Treaties and not from the national constitutions. The special and original nature of EU law requires that its supremacy over national law is acknowledged. The ECJ recognised the importance of this and, as Lord Bridge stated in the House of Lords' judgment in *Factortame (No 2)* (1991): 'If the supremacy within the European Community over the national law of the Member States was not always inherent in the **EC Treaty**, it was certainly well established in the jurisprudence of the Court of Justice.' The decision of the House of Lords was subsequently confirmed in *R v Secretary of State for Employment ex p EOC* (1994), when it was stated that in judicial review proceedings in UK courts, an Act of Parliament can be declared incompatible with EU law.

Aim Higher ★

Emphasise the more recent cases to show that supremacy is a topic which is still being challenged in the Member States. See the Commission's web pages.

QUESTION 10

Critically examine the development of the doctrine of direct effect.

How to Answer this Question

This is an important topic and it is very likely that in any question where advice is required on enforcing a Community right, it will be appropriate to discuss the topic of direct effect. This question is an essay question, but it is not uncommon for problem questions to be asked on this topic. The main points that should be discussed in this essay are:

❖ what is meant by direct effect;
❖ the difference between direct effect and direct applicability;
❖ the test for direct effect;
❖ the direct effect of Articles of the Treaty, regulations, directives and decisions; and
❖ the difference between vertical and horizontal direct effect.

Answer Structure

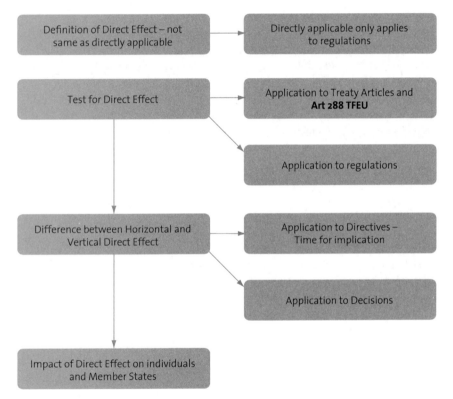

This diagram shows the key points to be discussed.

ANSWER

When a State joins the European Union, all EU law becomes part of its own legal system or, to use the international law phrase, 'directly applicable'. However, the ECJ has also developed a principle of direct effect whereby a provision of EU law may confer rights upon an individual which are required to be directly applied by national courts at the suit of individual litigants, without the need for domestic implementing legislation. Not all EU law is directly effective. This will depend upon the construction of a particular provision, its language and purpose, although there is often confusion because of the phrase in **Art 288 TFEU** which describes regulations as directly applicable. This does not mean that only regulations are capable of direct effect. Many categories of EU law are capable of direct effect as long as they satisfy the test established by the ECJ. This began with the case of *Van Gend en Loos* (1963), which concerned a preliminary reference made by a Dutch court about **Art 25** (now **Art 30 TFEU**) obliging Member States to refrain from setting new customs duties. The view of the Dutch Government and other Member States was that this was a matter which did not allow an individual to bring an action enforcing rights, but should rather be left to an enforcement action under **Arts 258** or **259 TFEU**.

The ECJ set out the basic requirements for direct effect to be identified when it said in *Van Gend*: '**Art 25** [formerly **Art 12**, now **Art 30**] sets out a clear and unconditional prohibition, which is not a duty to act, but a duty not to act. This duty is imposed without any power in the Member States to subordinate its application to a positive act of internal law. The prohibition is perfectly suited by its nature to produce direct effects in the legal relations between the Member States and their citizens.' However, the Court has not restricted direct effect to prohibitions. In *Alfons Lutticke's* (1966) case, which concerned **Art 90** (now **Art 110**), it was established by the ECJ that a positive obligation to repeal or amend discriminatory provisions was directly effective. The test for direct effect is that the following conditions must apply if the measure is to be enforced: the provision must be clear and unambiguous, it must be unconditional and its operations must not be dependent on further action being taken by the Union or national authorities.

Subsequent to this case, many Articles of the Treaties have been declared to have direct effect, thus giving the citizen the ability to claim and enforce a right under the Treaties which the government of the Member State concerned has failed to provide. A good example of this development is *Defrenne v Sabena (No 2)* (1976) . This case involved a claim made by a Madame Defrenne for equal pay with male stewards. She based her claim upon **Art 157 TFEU** (then **Art 119**). Whereas Van Gend was seeking to enforce a right against the Dutch State, Madame Defrenne was seeking to enforce a right against her employer, Sabena Airlines. This was an important point, because before it was thought that direct effect was limited to relationships with State bodies, that is, vertical effect. The judgment in *Defrenne* said that the direct effect of **Art 157** extends to all agreements which are intended to regulate paid labour collectively, as well as to contracts between individuals. Thus, many Treaty provisions have now been successfully invoked vertically and horizontally. The fact of their being addressed to States has been no bar to their horizontal effect.

It was more surprising for Member States when the ECJ took a similar line with directives. Under **Art 288 TFEU**, 'a directive is binding, as to the result to be achieved, upon each

Member State to which it is addressed, but shall leave to the national authorities the choice of form and methods'. They are not described as 'directly applicable', as are regulations. This, the Member States argued, was an indication that they should not produce direct effects. In addition, they required further action by the Member State and thus could not meet the test for direct effect indicated in *Van Gend*. However, in *Grad*, the ECJ ruled that a directive and a decision could be directly effective. The directive, in this case on VAT, specified a limit for its implementation, as is common with all directives. These directives, addressed to Member States, impose an obligation to achieve the required result. As the ECJ said in *Becker* (1982), another case involving VAT, 'wherever the provisions of a directive appear ... to be unconditional and sufficiently precise, those provisions may, in the absence of implementing measures adopted within the prescribed period, be relied upon as against any national provision which is incompatible with the directive or in so far as the provisions define rights which individuals are able to assert against the State'.

If the time limit given for the implementation of the directive has not expired, it cannot have direct effect, as was stated in *Ratti* (1979). Ratti was an Italian who ran a firm selling both solvents and varnishes in Italy. Two directives had been adopted covering the packaging and labelling of these products. Ratti complied with these directives, but they had not been implemented in Italy, with the result that he was prosecuted for failure to comply with the provisions of the Italian law. At the relevant time, the deadline for the implementation of one of the directives had expired, but that for the second had not. On an **Art 267 TFEU** reference, the ECJ held that the directive for which the time for implementation had expired was directly effective, but the other was not. This gave Ratti a defence to the charges relating to the packaging and labelling of the solvents, but not for those concerning the varnishes. It must be remembered that in all cases when an individual is seeking to enforce direct effect, the test must be satisfied.

Even if the Member State has introduced the required legislative act, it may be that what they have done is defective. In this type of situation, the directive may still be directly effective, as was held in the *Verbond van Nederlandse Ondernemingen (VNO)* case. However, unlike Articles of the Treaty, directives cannot have horizontal effect. They cannot have direct effect as against another individual or company. This type of horizontal direct effect is felt to be contrary to the principles of equality. This was stated in *Marshall v Southampton and South West Hampshire AHA* (1986), where Marshall was said to be employed by a 'public' body in the form of the Health Authority and thus able to enforce the direct effect of the **Equal Treatment Directive 76/207** (now **Directive 2002/73**). However, the ECJ in *von Colson* (1984) put an obligation on the courts of Member States to 'take all appropriate measures to ensure fulfilment of a directive'. Under the
von Colson principle, the courts of Member States should interpret national law so as to ensure that the objectives of the directive are achieved. In *Lister v Forth Dry Docks* (1990), the House of Lords took this line by interpreting the UK domestic regulation on

safeguarding employees whose employer's business was transferred on the basis that it had been introduced for the purpose of complying with an EU directive. This has obviously greatly extended the possibility for an individual to obtain the benefits of the direct effect of a directive, even though the State (or any emanation of the State) is not the defendant to the action. In the *Marleasing* case, the ECJ took the *von Colson* principle a step further when it held that the principle could be applied, even if the necessary national legislation had not been introduced to comply with the directive.

As in other circumstances where the ECJ has developed the scope of its interpretation, there is one important limitation to the *von Colson* principle. This is in relation to criminal proceedings, as in *Kolpinghuis Nijmegen*, where the Dutch authorities sought to prosecute Kolpinghuis for breach of a Water Purity directive which had not been implemented in the Netherlands. The ECJ held that, when interpreting national law to comply with Community law, regard must be had to the general principles of the Community, notably that of legal certainty and non-retroactivity (see *Arcaro* (1997)).

In addition to regulations and directives, the other source of law specified in Art 288 TFEU is decisions, which are legally binding on the person to whom they are addressed. The Court stated in the *Grad* case that these can have direct effect. With regard to international agreements, the ECJ has not taken a consistent approach. Some, like the GATT Treaty in *International Fruit Co*, were held not to be directly effective, whereas others were, such as the Yaounde Convention, under the ACP policy of the EU, in *Bresciani* (1976). It would appear that each agreement must be considered by the ECJ on its own merits.

The test for direct effect requires three criteria to be passed by the provision concerned. The provision must be sufficiently clear and precise; it must be unconditional; and it must leave no room for the exercise of discretion in implementation by the Member State or EU institution. Each criterion is given a broad interpretation by the ECJ, so some provisions which are not particularly clear or precise have been found to produce direct effects. The interpretation skills of the ECJ can always be used to clarify the meaning of the provision. It is also important to note that, if the provision should not yet have been implemented by the Member State, it will not have direct effect. Obviously, you cannot enforce an obligation until the time has expired for that obligation to have been fulfilled. However, the development of the doctrine of direct effect has been an important one for the EU, but more importantly for the individual.

QUESTION 11

'Directives are addressed to the governments of Member States and therefore cannot give rights to individuals of Member States.'

▶ Discuss.

How to Answer this Question

Although there are general questions on direct effect, like the previous question, the direct effect of directives is a topic which has dominated in the last few years. Problem questions are generally not asked specifically on this topic, but it does lend itself to being included in particular situations, for example, where an individual is seeking to enforce a right based upon a directive which has not been incorporated in national law. However, it is essay questions, like this one, which allow for a discussion of the diverse points arising from the development of the principle of direct effect as applied to directives. The specific areas that need to be discussed are:

❖ the doctrine of direct effect generally, based on *Van Gend en Loos* (1963);
❖ the application of direct effect to directives (*Van Duyn v Home Office* (1974));
❖ the response to the direct effect of directives (*Cohn-Bendit* (1979) case);
❖ the *von Colson* principle; and
❖ developments in State liability (*Francovich v Italian State* (1991)).

> ### Common Pitfalls ✖
>
> You should avoid being too descriptive in your answer. This is a discussion question so you need to make sure that you deal with both parts of the argument about directives having direct effect.

Answer Structure

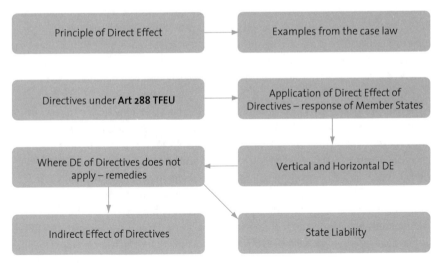

This diagram shows the key points to be discussed.

ANSWER

It is true that directives are clearly defined in **Art 288 TFEU** as being addressed to the governments of Member States, but the Article also adds that they are binding as to the result to be achieved. There is an obligation on the Member State to fulfil this requirement, even though it has discretion as to how this is achieved. Thus, directives are a source of European Community law and are part of the new legal order which developed with the establishment of the Community. As the ECJ stated in the important case of *Van Gend en Loos*, this new legal order is for the benefit not only of the Member States themselves, but also their nationals or citizens. The Court went on to say that, in this way, obligations and rights would be conferred on individuals. How does this apply to directives? Presumably, there is no problem if the government of the Member State receiving the directive fulfils it by selecting an appropriate domestic mechanism, such as an Act of Parliament or Statutory Instrument, to implement it. In this way, any rights associated with the directive will become available to the individual and recognised and enforced by the national courts. However, what if the government of the Member State fails to implement the directive, or does so in such a way as to deprive the individual of some of the rights associated with the directive? It is in this context that this statement has been made, and will now be discussed.

The principle of direct effect was established by the ECJ in the case of *Van Gend en Loos*, which concerned **Art 30 TFEU** (then **Art 12**). The judgment stated that, if certain criteria were satisfied, the provisions in question would give rise to rights or obligations on which individuals may rely before their national courts, that is, they would be directly effective. The criteria are that the provision must be clear and unambiguous, it must be unconditional and it must take effect without further action by the EU or Member State. Could this principle apply to directives? There are obvious questions to be asked because, by definition, directives do require further action, in that Member States have the choice as to the form and methods to be used to implement the directive. The Court did not find this a hindrance.

In the case of *Van Duyn v Home Office* (1974), the ECJ held that provisions of directives could be directly effective on their own. Before this case, questions about directives were always linked with Articles of the Treaty or decisions, so no clear principle could be established. In the *Grad* case, involving a decision and the directive introducing the VAT system, the Court held that, although regulations under **Art 288** (then **Art 189**) were directly applicable, it did not follow that other categories of administrative acts could not have similar effects. They added that this was particularly the case where the Community had imposed an obligation on Member States to act in a certain way, as *l'effet utile* of such a measure would be weakened if they did not fulfil that obligation. It would mean that the nationals of that State would not be able to invoke it before the courts, and the national courts would not be able to consider it as part of Community law.

In *Van Duyn*, the Court had to consider in an **Art 267 TFEU** (then **Art 177**) reference whether a private individual could invoke an Article of a Council directive dealing with the personal conduct of an individual and the derogation allowed to a Member State on the grounds of public policy – specifically, whether the UK Government could refuse leave to enter the UK to a Dutch Scientologist because of the UK Government's policy towards the Church of Scientology. The Court repeated its judgment in *Grad*, only making the specific reference to directives instead of a decision, as it had done in that case. Thus, Van Duyn could ask the national courts to enforce the individual rights given to her by the directive.

This judgment did not go without criticism, notably by the French *Conseil d'Etat* in *Cohn-Bendit* (1979). Cohn-Bendit wished to challenge a decision taken by the French Minister for the Interior expelling him from French territory on the grounds of **Directive 64/221** (now **Directive 64/221**). An Article in this Directive requires the person against whom such measures are ordered to be informed of the reasons, for example, public security, public policy, etc. In *Rutili* (1975), this Article had been declared by the ECJ to be directly effective. However, even though the minister had subsequently decided not to oppose Cohn-Bendit's entry into France and thus remove the substance of the case, the *Conseil d'Etat* went on to give judgment. They had not made an **Art 267 TFEU** (then **Art 177**) reference, but gave their clear view that directives cannot be invoked by the nationals of Member States, that is, they cannot have direct effect when challenging an administrative decision of the State. This was completely contrary to the case law of the ECJ.

The judgment in *Cohn-Bendit* prompted the European Court to clarify its ruling on the possibility of individuals involving the provisions of directives. It considered that if a Member State had not adopted the implementing measures required by a directive in the prescribed periods, that State should not be able to rely upon its own failure to deprive individuals of seeking to enforce rights before the national courts. This was clearly stated in *Ratti*. However, direct effect as applied to directives was to have some limitations. Unlike Articles of the Treaty and, to a certain extent, regulations, directives were to be limited to vertical direct effect and not encompass horizontal direct effect. If it was the government which had not fulfilled its obligations arising from the directive, it should be against the government that rights arising from the directive should be enforced. In *Becker* (1982), a German credit broker successfully claimed the benefit of a provision of the sixth **VAT Directive** against the German VAT authorities. However, it was also made clear in this judgment that there was no question of a directive being involved to impose obligations on individuals, or to have an incidence on mutual relations between individuals, that is, horizontal direct effect. The contrast between the UK cases of *Marshall* (1986) (who was employed by an area health authority) or *Foster* (1990) (who was employed by the pre-privatisation British Gas corporation) on the one hand, with *Duke* (1988) (employed by GEC Reliance Ltd, a public company) on the other, clearly shows how a right can be enforced by some, but not by others, under the principle of direct effect of directives. It would appear, therefore, that unless the individual is able to show that there is some relationship with the State, the quotation forming this question is correct.

It is also correct that every directive involves a timescale for implementation. This period, normally two years, is to give the government of the Member State time to formulate and pass the appropriate domestic measure. Until this period has elapsed, the directive cannot, as was confirmed in *Ratti*, have direct effect.

In *Emmott v Minister for Social Welfare* (1991), Mrs Emmott brought an action against the Irish Minister for Social Welfare on the basis that she received less benefit than a man would have done in equivalent circumstances. Under a directive issued in 1979, all discrimination on the grounds of sex in matters of social security is prohibited. The directive should have been implemented by 1984, but was not implemented in Ireland until 1988. Mrs Emmott brought her action in 1987, when another case before the ECJ had led to it declaring that the directive had direct effect. The vertical relationship between herself and the Irish Government satisfied the case law of the Court. The Irish Government, however, claimed that her action was statute-barred, because it had not been brought within the three months required by Irish law for judicial review. Could this national procedural requirement be used to deny Mrs Emmott a remedy? The Court held that directives had a particular nature, imposing an obligation on Member States to adopt, within the framework of their national legal systems, all the measures necessary to ensure that the directive is fully effective. Thus, Community law precludes the competent national authorities from relying on national procedural rules relating to time limits to stop an action by one of its citizens seeking to enforce a right that that Member State has failed to transpose into its domestic legal system. The time limit does not run until the date when the national implementing legislation is correctly adopted.

In *Francovich v Italian State* (1991), the ECJ extended the impact of the law regarding directives by stating that 'Community law lays down a principle according to which a Member State is liable to make good damage to individuals caused by a breach of Community law for which it is responsible'. Mr Francovich was owed 6 million lire by his insolvent employers. However, because he was unable to enforce a judgment against them, he brought an action against the Italian Government for compensation. Under a Council directive aimed at protecting employees in the event of the insolvency of their employers, Member States were required to ensure that payment of employees' outstanding claims arising from the employment relationship and relating to pay was guaranteed. Unfortunately, the Italian Government had not set up any Italian system to act as a guarantor in these circumstances, hence his claim against them. The ECJ held that, subject to three conditions, damages are available against the State for failure to implement EC directives. The conditions specified are that the result required by the directive includes the conferring of rights for the benefit of individuals; the content of those rights is identifiable by reference to the directive; and, lastly, there exists a causal link between the breach of the State's obligations and the damage suffered by the person affected.

The ECJ has further developed this idea of indirect effect in its judgments in *Brasserie du Pêcheur* (1996) and *Dillenkofer* (1996). It is clear now that failure by a Member State to take any measure and transpose it as required into national law will constitute a serious breach of Community law per se. It will give rise to a right to damages for those individuals who suffer injury and there is a causal link between the breach of the State's obligation and the loss and damage suffered.

The ECJ has continued to evolve its principles with regard to providing the individual with the possibility of enforcing a right derived from a directive. In the *von Colson* and *Harz* cases in 1984, the Court developed an approach to interpretation based on Art 20 TEU (then Art 5), which requires Member States to take all appropriate measures to ensure fulfilment of their Community obligations. Under this principle, the national courts should interpret national legislation so as to ensure that the objectives of the directive are achieved. This assists those litigants who are unable to satisfy the test for direct effect, or who are bringing an action against a private employer, rather than the State or an emanation of the State. This method of interpretation has maximised the impact of directives for individuals. As a further development of the *von Colson* principle, the Court held, in *Marleasing* (1990), that the principle could be applied even if the necessary national legislation had not been introduced to comply with the directive.

The development of the ECJ's approach to directives conferring rights upon individuals has continued throughout the last 20 years. It has been a true reflection of the comments made by the Court in *Van Gend en Loos* and subsequent cases that, when establishing the European Community, the Member States were creating a new legal order which has given rights to the citizens of the Member States and which must be recognised by their courts. In some circumstances, the Court has applied the principle of direct effect to achieve this and in others it has extended its approach to interpretation. It is clear that although directives are addressed to the governments of Member States, they do confer rights on those who live within the Community.

QUESTION 12

Critically review whether the English courts have given effect to EU directives by following the precedents of the ECJ?

How to Answer this Question

Essay questions are quite common for this topic but they are not exclusive as some problem questions are set to test the student's knowledge and understanding of this important topic in European law. The English judges have had some difficulties in assimilating the principles of EU law with the common law tradition with which they usually apply. You should cover the following points:

❖   direct effect of directives – *Marshall* (1986);
❖   vertical and horizontal effect of directives;
❖   European Communities Act 1972;
❖   *von Colson* (1984);

❖   *Marleasing* (1992);
❖   *Pickstone v Freemans plc* (1989);
❖   *Lister v Forth Dry Dock and Engineering Co Ltd* (1990);
❖   *Francovich* (1990); and
❖   the *Brasserie du Pêcheur* and *Factortame* cases (1996).

Answer Structure

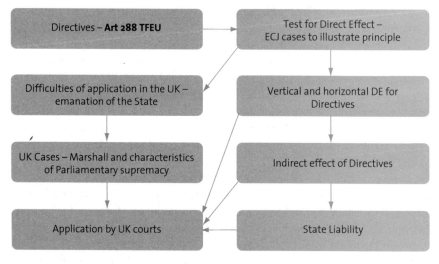

This *diagram shows the key points to be discussed.*

ANSWER

The supremacy of Union law over national law is a principle which was well established by the ECJ jurisprudence before the UK became a Member of the EU in 1973. The *acquis communautaire* requires a Member States to be bound by Union law and to fulfil all the obligations arising from the Treaties and other binding sources of EU law as stated in Art 20(4) TEU. This is achieved by accepting that Union law overrides any conflicting national law (*Simmenthal* (1978)). These laws also include the case law of the ECJ and it is here that the principle of direct effect of directives was established. The important principle of direct effect is that it has been held by the ECJ that individuals can enforce the legal rights arising from these laws in the courts and tribunals of the Member States. Thus the individual does not have to attempt to take their case to the Luxembourg court where there will be delay, additional expense and often no *locus standi* to bring the case. Articles of the Treaty and regulations have been held by the ECJ to have direct effect in both vertical and horizontal terms (see *Defrenne (No 2)* (1976)). Thus, in such circumstances, the individual can enforce the right against the government (as with vertical direct effect) or another individual (which is horizontal direct effect). However, the other common source of Union law, directives, was in a much weaker position, even though such measures are important in creating rights under Union law. The ECJ has sought to redress this imbalance by making directives come within the principle of direct effect. In *Van Duyn* (1975), the ECJ relied on the binding effect attributed to a directive under Art 288 TFEU (then Art 189 EC), coupled with the civil law doctrine that a legal measure must be presumed to have an *effet utile*, or useful effect. Furthermore, the Court thought it was inequitable to allow a Member State to rely on its own failure to implement a directive as a defence (*Ratti* (1979)). This view was strengthened by Art 20 TEU (then Art 10 EC), which requires a Member State to take all appropriate measures to ensure fulfilment of the obligations arising out of the Treaty or resulting from action taken by the institutions of the Union. In this way, it became impossible for the Member State to evade an obligation imposed by a directive and very often the enforcement happened faster in the national courts than would have occurred if a case had been before the ECJ.

To the Member States the right action that should be taken if they were not fulfilling EU law was an enforcement action by the Commission under Art 258 TFEU or by another Member State under Art 259 TFEU. However, this was unlikely to provide any redress to the individual who suffered as a consequence, although the *Francovich* (1990) principle would now be able to assist with this. Direct effect requires that certain conditions be met to identify direct effect, such as the measure being precise and unconditional. The main problem, which still remained, was that an individual could only use direct effect against the State and not another individual or company (*Marshall* (1986)). The ECJ has a good imaginative approach to developing the law and often sees what it is possible to achieve at a particular time as being a good way to proceed. Thus the Court limited the impact of this extension of the principle of direct effect to directives by limiting it to vertical relationships. The individual who was employed by the State or an emanation of the State (see *Marshall* (1986) and *Foster v British Gas* (1990)) could enforce a right arising from Community law in a national court and obtain the appropriate remedy. Those who could not prove such a relationship with the government were unable to do either, as was confirmed in the case of *Kampelmann* (1997) involving the Employee Directive 91/533. *Duke v GEC Reliance* (1988) provides a good example of the division that vertical and horizontal application of direct effect of directives brought about. Unlike Mrs Marshall or Mrs Foster, Mrs Duke was unable to enforce her rights under the Equality Directives because she was not employed by the State, but by a private employer.

A difficulty encountered in the UK that was not found in most other Member States was that there was a potential conflict between the doctrine of parliamentary sovereignty in UK law and the principle that Union law takes priority over inconsistent national laws. The European Communities Act 1972 attempts to deal with this problem by making all provisions of Union law which are directly effective part of English law. The European Union Act 2011 states in Section 18 that directly applicable or directly effective EU law falls to be recognised and available in law in UK only by virtue of that 1972 Act. Lord Denning, in *Macarthys Ltd v Smith* (1979), suggested that English courts would give effect to a directly effective provision of Community law, notwithstanding any subsequent enactment by Parliament, unless Parliament had made it clear that it intended to override any inconsistent provisions of Community law. Lord Diplock, in *Garland v BREL* (1982), stated that the words of a statute passed after the adoption of a Community measure dealing with the same subject were to be interpreted, if they were reasonably capable of bearing such a meaning, as being intended to carry out the UK's obligations under the Community measure and not as being inconsistent with it. Thus the judges were required to enforce Union law within the UK and as the *Factortame* case showed in 1996, in extreme circumstances this may mean not enforcing a UK statute that has been properly passed.

Mrs Duke in 1988 maintained that the Equal Treatment Directive, as interpreted in *Marshall*, required Member States to prohibit discrimination in relation to retirement ages and that s 6(4) of the Sex Discrimination Act 1975 had to be interpreted in a way that was consistent with that requirement. Lord Templeman, giving the main judgment in the House of Lords, rejected this argument. He held that, although the Equal Treatment Directive had been adopted subsequent to the 1975 Act, s 2(4) of the European Communities Act 1972 did not require the courts to give it priority over the 1975 Act in Mrs Duke's case, because the directive was not directly effective as between her and her former employers. Section 2(4) only required the court to construe an Act of Parliament in accordance with directly effective provisions of Community law. This judgment has been criticised as taking too narrow a view of the European Communities Act. However, in *Pickstone* (1989), Lord Templeman made the point in his judgment that the Sex Discrimination Act had not been passed to give effect to the directive. But, in *Pickstone*, the 1983 Regulations had been introduced to meet the obligations of the directive and the rulings of the Court against the UK Government. Thus by following the precedents of the ECJ on this matter the English courts were denying a remedy to an individual because of the legal status of their employer and not their right under the Directive.

The division between vertical and horizontal direct effect of directives was circumvented by the ECJ in its judgment in *von Colson* (1984). This required national courts to construe national law to give effect to the provisions of a directive. In this way, the provisions entered into domestic law and could be relied upon before national courts. The provisions of the directive become an aid to construction of the national law and in this way are enforced by the national court. The *Marleasing* judgment (1992) extended this principle by requiring a national court to construe national law in the light of the wording and purpose of any relevant Community directive, whether the national law originated before or after the adoption of the directive. The UK courts have taken up this approach. In *Pickstone v Freemans plc* (1989), the House of Lords said that English courts must adopt this interpretation, even if to do so would involve departing from the normal canons of construction. This could amount to reading certain words into the relevant national legislation in order to achieve a result compatible with Community law. The Court of Appeal encountered difficulties in the appeal by Mrs Webb against her dismissal by her employer when she became pregnant (*Webb v EMO Air Cargo (UK) Ltd* (1992)). The national legislation that the Court of Appeal had to interpret was the Sex Discrimination Act 1975. Judgments of the ECJ on the Equal Treatment Directive appeared to indicate that dismissal on the grounds of pregnancy was automatically contrary to the directive. However, the Court of Appeal held that the Sex Discrimination Act did not automatically forbid the dismissal of a woman on the grounds of pregnancy and to give it that meaning would be to distort, rather than construe, English law! On the subsequent appeal to the House of Lords, it was indicated that national law had to be open to an interpretation consistent with the directive if the duty of construction were to apply. Following a further reference to the ECJ, it was stated that Mrs Webb's dismissal could not be justified on the grounds of pregnancy (1994).

The judgment in *Pickstone* was cited with approval by the House of Lords in *Lister v Forth Dry Dock and Engineering Co Ltd* (1990), where a claim had been made against a private party. The judgment suggests that, where legislation has been introduced specifically in order to complement an EC directive, UK courts must interpret domestic law to comply with the directive. In some circumstances, this may require supplying the necessary words by implication, in order to achieve a result compatible with EC law. In the *Lister* case, no reference was made to the fact that the directive in question was not directly effective. However, there is some inconsistency in approach. The judgment in *R v British Coal Corp ex p Vardy* (1993) indicated a reluctance to apply the *Marleasing* principle. In this case, Glidewell J found it impossible to follow the House of Lords' approach in *Lister* since the wording of the statute, the Trade Union and Labour Relations Act 1992, was clearly at odds with the Directive. In such circumstances, the wording of the statute approved by Parliament was to be followed. An action by the European Commission under Art 258 TFEU would have seemed until recently to be the only possibility. However, the ECJ has developed a remedy by stating that it is a principle of Community law that the Member States are obliged to make good any loss and damage caused to individuals by breaches of Community law for which they were held responsible (*Francovich* (1990)). In the *Brasserie du Pêcheur* and *Factortame* cases in 1996, the ECJ held that, provided the conditions for State liability were satisfied, the principle could and did apply to all Community law as a whole, whether or not directly effective. Therefore, if there is not a manifestly serious breach by the Member State, it is not required to compensate for any loss suffered (*R v HM Treasury ex p BT* (1996)).

The English courts have also followed the precedents of the ECJ when it comes to awarding damages to compensate breaches of EU law on the same basis as any other action in national law (*Sutton v Secretary of State for Social Security* (1997)). In *Levez v Jennings* (1999), the UK rule that damages for sex discrimination should not go back further than two years was considered. Although the rule itself was not criticised, the ECJ indicated that there may be circumstances where its application would be incompatible with the principles of EU law, for example, where there had been deceit by the employer. In the House of Lords' judgment in *Factortame 4* (1999), the UK's breach of its Community obligations was sufficiently serious to entitle the Spanish owners of the vessels to substantial damages. The English courts have given effect to EU directives by following the precedents of the ECJ as the judges share the same objective – to enforce the law from whatever legitimate source. If the date for the implementation of a directive has passed and the other conditions of direct effect have been satisfied then the directive will be enforced against the State. If the defendant is an individual or a company the courts will look towards the *Marleasing* guide to interpretation to assist them and enforce the right of the individual. In certain circumstances this will involve damages from the State under the *Francovich* approach where the State has failed to implement a directive or to implement it correctly. Judges do not always agree with the outcome when they apply EU law, like any other law, but they have a duty to apply it. In C-487/07 *L'Oréal SA & others v Bellure NV & others* Jacob LJ stated in a case about the **Trade Mark Directive 89/104** that: 'My duty as a national judge is to follow EU law as interpreted by the ECJ . . . As I have said I do not agree with or welcome this conclusion – it amounts to a pointless monopoly. But my duty is to apply it.'

Judicial Remedies and Review (1): Direct Actions

4

INTRODUCTION

As part of their jurisdictions, the ECJ and the General Court can hear cases brought before it by individuals, EU institutions or governments of Member States. These actions must be brought under specific Articles of the Treaty and are heard solely by the Court, hence the term direct actions as compared with indirect actions or preliminary references made under Art 258 TFEU. These are covered in the next chapter. This area of Community law lends itself to both problem and essay questions, as the 'popular' areas are suitable for both question formats.

Checklist ✔

You should have a general knowledge of how the European Courts and in particular the Court of Justice operates. In particular, you must be familiar with the following areas:

- enforcement actions brought by the European Commission under **Art 258 TFEU**, including both the formal and informal stages of the procedure;
- enforcement actions brought by Member States under **Art 259**;
- the remedy available by **Art 260** to actions under **Arts 258** and **259**;
- the action for annulment under **Art 263**, especially the question of *locus standi* and grounds for annulment;
- the possible action under **Art 265** and its relationship with **Art 263**;
- the remedies provided for under **Arts 263** and **265**; and
- the plea of illegality – **Art 277**.

QUESTION 13

What enforcement actions are available against a Member State in breach of its obligations? Are such actions effective?

How to Answer this Question

This is typical of questions set on this topic. It should be noted that it is in two parts, both of which must be answered in the essay that follows if good marks are to be gained. It is not sufficient merely to describe the possible actions, as some evaluation must also be included. The main points to be raised are:

- ❖ direct actions under Arts 258 and 259 TFEU;
- ❖ the remedies available under Art 260 TFEU;
- ❖ the role of the Commission under Art 258 TFEU; and
- ❖ possible action available in a Member State.

Common Pitfalls ✗

Make sure that your answer deals with evaluation of enforcement actions being effective because many students ignore this part of the question and forgo the marks they would otherwise gain.

Answer Structure

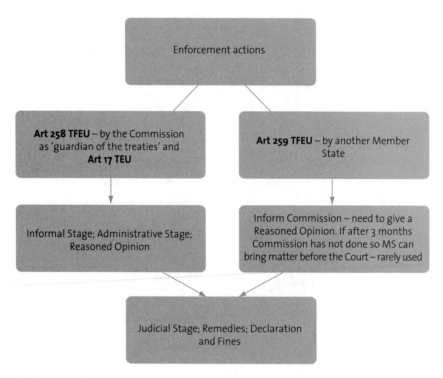

This diagram shows the key points to be discussed.

ANSWER

The TFEU Treaty allows two types of direct enforcement action under Arts 258 and 259 TFEU. The most usual action taken against a Member State is by the European Commission under Art 258. Although Member States have a possible action under Art 259, which allows them to take another Member State before the ECJ, as in *France v UK (Re Fishing Net Mesh Sizes)* (1978), this is rarely used. It is therefore Art 258 which is the predominant enforcement action used against Member States that are in breach of their obligations, although it is possible for action to be taken in the national courts of the Member State in certain circumstances.

It is appropriate that Art 258 should give the Commission power to bring an action against a Member State in breach of its obligations, as it has a duty to make sure that Community law is applied. This duty is found in Art 17 TEU, which lays down the general duties of the Commission. The instigation of the Art 258 procedure may be due to an act or omission, such as national legislation contrary to Community law or a failure to implement Community law. Therefore, a Member State's failure under the Treaty can be sufficient grounds, as can an action contrary to Community law. However, the procedure under Art 258 is lengthy and does not provide a speedy process for getting the breach rectified. Whether it is a failure of a positive or negative act, the consequence of a successful action under Art 258 is for a declaration by the Court under Art 260 requiring the Member State to take action to fulfil its obligations and the possible imposition of a fine.

The first stage of the Art 258 procedure is often described as the administrative stage. The ECJ has stated that the purpose of this stage is to allow the Member State either to comply with its obligations under Community law or to put forward an effective defence to the complaints made by the Commission. Initially acting on a complaint, perhaps from a trade association, MEP or another government, the Director General responsible for that sector of Community policy will write to the Member State concerned. These informal communications with the Member State will attempt to ascertain the facts and if possible reach a settlement. They are conducted with discretion, so as to avoid any embarrassment that might result for the Member State. The Commission, having fully investigated the possible breach, will consider whether there is sufficient evidence to justify the commencement of formal proceedings. If the Commission has taken the view that a Member State is in breach of its obligations, the Commission will write to the Member State under its powers in Art 258, indicating the breach and inviting the Member State's observations. The Member State then responds to this letter with its own view, which is generally that they are not in breach of this particular obligation. If a settlement acceptable to the Commission is not possible, this administrative stage of Art 258 will end with the Commission issuing a Reasoned Opinion. This Opinion is very important, as it provides the Member State with a final opportunity to remedy its failure and to this end informs the Member State of what, in the Commission's view, needs to be done to accomplish this. If the Commission decides to go on to the judicial stage of the Art 258 procedure, the Opinion defines the matters which the Court will be requested to adjudicate on.

It could be argued that the matter could end before the judicial stage, especially as the number of contraventions of Community law is large. To take all the matters further under the procedure would require a large staff. There is also the fact that many Member State governments resent the initiation of the formal enforcement procedure. Does the Commission have to take the matter further? Some writers argue that the Commission has a discretion as to whether it takes further action. However, this ignores the duty given to the Commission under Art 17 TEU to ensure that Community law is applied. This duty requires the Commission to take the most appropriate action in the circumstances to ensure compliance with Community law. In the EURATOM case of *Commission v France* (1971), Advocate General Roemer indicated that, in some circumstances, the Commission might be justified in not initiating the enforcement procedure. These included situations where an amicable settlement may be achieved if formal proceedings were delayed, or where a major domestic political crisis could be aggravated if proceedings were commenced concerning matters of secondary importance.

An attempt is made to reach a satisfactory settlement without resorting to litigation and in the great majority of cases this has proved possible. If this is not possible, an action by the Commission can be brought before the European Court. The aim of the action is to obtain a declaration that the Member State has failed to fulfil its obligation. The Member State will be bound under Art 260 TFEU to take the necessary measures to comply with the judgment. At one time, the only sanction available to the Commission was to institute a further action against the Member State if it did not comply. The Maastricht Treaty made an important amendment to Art 260 in relation to an action brought under Art 258. This now allows the Court to impose a lump sum or penalty payment on any Member State failing to fulfil its obligations, based upon a sum specified by the Commission when it brings the matter before the Court. The basic penalty is fixed at €5,000 per day multiplied by factors reflecting the gravity and duration of the non-compliance as applied in the case of *Commission v Greece* (2000).

A common form of infringement by Member States has been the adoption of measures that restrict the free movement of goods within the Community, contrary to Art 260. Such measures are against one of the fundamental principles of the Community and are often disguised under legitimate derogations allowed by Art 36. Action taken by the Commission in these circumstances is seeking effective rather than purely formal compliance with the Treaty obligations, that is, with the spirit rather than just with the letter. For example, in *Turkey* (1982), the UK Government had imposed a ban on the importation of poultry not vaccinated against Newcastle disease. Although ostensibly to protect animal health, which is possible under Art 36, its effect was to protect the British poultry industry against imports, notably from France. Although the Court held that such restrictions were contrary to the UK's obligations under the Treaty, the measure did give the British poultry industry some limited protection before the UK Government complied with the Art 260 (then Art 171) order. There are many such examples involving all Member States where, perhaps for domestic political reasons, national measures have been adopted, only to be repealed when the Court has given judgment against them. In this sense the Art 258 action is ultimately effective, but it does take time.

The action available to a Member State under Art 259 is very similar to that used by the Commission under Art 258. However, the Member State must inform the Commission, which is given three months to investigate the matter and deliver a Reasoned Opinion. Here, the Commission is acting more as an umpire and conciliator than an accuser. After the Reasoned Opinion has been given by the Commission, or if three months have elapsed without its doing so, the complainant Member State can bring the matter before the Court. The burden of proof is on the complainant Member State, with the Commission intervening in support of one side or the other. This procedure is very unpopular with the Member States, who generally leave such enforcement actions to the Commission, unless there is a strong political or other reason for them to do otherwise.

In the early years, the Commission did not pursue defaulting Member States with vigour. However, in 1977, the Jenkins Commission decided that, in future, more rigorous use would be made of the Art 258 TFEU procedure. Nevertheless the volume of work places a heavy burden upon the staff of the Commission, which now encourages complainants to seek remedies in the national courts where appropriate. In the landmark case of *Van Gend en Loos* (1963), the Court had recognised that individuals should be able to protect their rights themselves in addition to relying on the Commission. This has become much easier with the development of the principle of direct effect. For example, in *Schoenenberg* (1978) and *Meijer* (1979), individuals were able to claim that national legislation was contrary to obligations imposed by the Treaty in the Member State concerned. This was achieved by the courts concerned using the preliminary reference procedure provided by Art 267 TFEU (then Art 177). This happened at the same time as the Commission was taking action against the Member State under the Art 258 (then Art 169) procedure. However, while the Art 258 procedure has its value in bringing the Member State into line for the future, action in the national courts coupled with an Art 267 reference does concentrate the mind of the Member State involved! Developments in the law relating to the award of damages have given new emphasis to the possibility of using the national courts for enforcement purposes. In *Francovich v Italian State* (1992), the European Court stated that: 'Community law lays down a principle according to which a Member State is liable to make good damage to individuals caused by a breach of Community law for which it is responsible.'

It can be seen that, although the Treaty only specifies enforcement action under Arts 258 and 259 TFEU , these are not the only possibilities. Action under Art 258 by the Commission does achieve the desired result, but its main drawback is the time it takes to achieve this, although it is possible to obtain interim measures under Art 259 where proceedings are being taken under Art 258 against a Member State. For example, both the UK Government, in relation to a temporary subsidy to pig farmers, and the Irish Government, over its fisheries conservation measures, were brought before the Court in 1977 and appropriate orders were made to stop their infringements immediately. However, the most effective actions are those indirect actions brought in the courts of the Member State concerned.

QUESTION 14

In response to calls to encourage healthy eating among young children, Vegnon has developed a process to puree vegetables to make them attractive to children. They are one of only five producers in the EC to produce such a mixture of vegetables in puree form, and anticipate huge demand from both the private purchaser and also the public sector from schools, hospitals, etc. To meet this demand Vegnon has opened a new plant in Scotland to handle the range of bottled and tinned pureed vegetables.

Last month the Council, following representation from the meat extract industry, adopted a regulation to reduce the quantity of vegetables going forward for pureeing. In an annex to the regulation there was a list of the five producers, including Vegnon, who were subject to the regulation and limiting their production to that of the last year. This meant that the production anticipated for the Scottish plant could not now take place and would result in a big financial loss to Vegnon.

Vegnon seek your advice as to how they may challenge this regulation and what remedy would be available.

How to Answer this Question

This problem question is the kind of practical scenario question often set on this topic, regardless of the actual product or process used to provide the framework. This question requires you to advise Vegnon, who wish to challenge this regulation. Keep to the points raised in the question and do not merely describe all you know about the subject! Questions on Art 263 often cause difficulty for students, but one way of solving this is to break the problem down into a number of small questions, pose them and then answer them as if you were advising someone in front of you.

The main points to be raised for Vegnon are:

- ❖ the procedure under Art 263, including the time limit;
- ❖ whether the measure is a 'true' regulation (what is a 'true' regulation?);
- ❖ the Court's interpretation of 'direct and individual concern';
- ❖ possible action in the national courts if *locus standi* for Art 263 is not accepted by the European Court; and
- ❖ possible action for damages under Arts 268 and 340.

Answer Structure

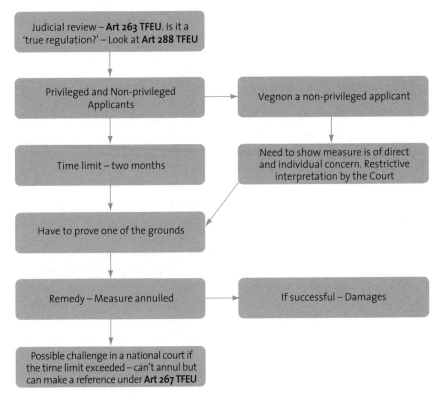

This diagram shows how to apply the law under Art 263 TFEU for judicial review for Vegnon.

ANSWER

Vegnon wishes to challenge the regulation so that it can be declared invalid. There are two ways under Community law that this can be done. The Treaty allows for actions for annulment or judicial review under Art 263 but there is also the possibility for a challenge to be brought before a national court. If the challenge under Art 263 is successful, the remedy provided by the Treaty will be the annulment of the regulation, thus allowing Vegnon to bring the Scottish plant into production. There may also be the possibility of a claim for damages against the Council under Arts 266 and 340. However, it is very rare that a successful action can be brought under Art 263 by non-privileged applicants like Vegnon. In order to advise Vegnon, careful consideration must be given to the wording of Art 263 and the interpretation given by the ECJ.

Under Art 263, any legal person may bring an action against a decision addressed to that person or against a decision which, although in the form of a regulation or a decision addressed to another person, is of direct and individual concern to the former. For Vegnon it is a regulation that they wish to challenge, and to do this they must show that it is not a true regulation but a 'bundle of decisions'. When approaching this question, the ECJ is not restricted by the title of the Community measure as merely because it is called a regulation is not conclusive. In *Calpak* (1980), it was pointed out that this is to prevent Community institutions choosing to issue a decision in the form of a regulation so as to deny the opportunity to an individual to challenge the measure. In *Royal Scholten-Honig v Intervention Board for Agriculture* (1978), the ECJ said: 'In examining this question (re Regulation) the Court cannot restrict itself to considering the official title of the measure, but must first take into account its object and context.' A starting point is the definitions given to various Community measures in **Art 288**, where regulations are described as the main legislative instrument of the Community.

A regulation under **Art 288** should apply to objectively determined situations and produce legal effects with regard to categories of persons regarded generally and in the abstract. This means that it should have a 'normative' character. As long as the regulation maintains these objective characteristics it will still be considered a regulation, even though the number or even identity of the persons to whom it applies can be ascertained. In *Royal Scholten-Honig* the Court insisted that an individual cannot challenge a true regulation, so Vegnon must get over this hurdle if the proceedings at the ECJ are to be admissible. It is not always easy to state clearly that a particular Community measure is a true regulation but, in the *Fruit and Vegetable* case in 1962, the Court said: 'A measure which is applicable to objectively determined situations and which involves immediate legal consequences in all Member States for persons viewed in a general and abstract manner cannot be considered as constituting a decision, unless it can be proved that it is of individual concern to certain persons within the meaning of **Art 263**.' There have been relatively few cases where the applicants have satisfied the Court on this point.

A case which may assist Vegnon is *CAM SA v Commission* (1975), where a fixed number of traders were held to be individually concerned because of a factual situation which differentiated them from all other persons and distinguished them individually. Here there were a fixed and known number of cereal traders, because the regulation affected those who had already applied for export licences. This factual situation differentiated them from all other persons and distinguished them individually from others affected by the regulation. Thus the action was admissible, since he was individually concerned because the applicant was one of a fixed and identifiable category. Vegnon may only challenge a regulation if the 'regulation' is really a decision. Decisions are characterised by the limited number of persons to whom they are addressed. In order to determine whether or not a measure constitutes a decision, one must inquire whether that measure concerns specific persons. Can this be linked to the named five producers in the regulation? In Vegnon's case the number of producers is limited and in fact they are named. They can be said to be directly concerned, in that the regulation leaves the Member State no discretion in implementation, but are they individually concerned as is required by Art 263? Applicants can only claim to be individually concerned if the decision being challenged affects them by reason of certain attributes which are peculiar to them, or by reason of circumstances in which they are differentiated from all other persons, and by virtue of these factors distinguishes them individually, just as in the case of the person addressed. It will not be sufficient for Vegnon to prove that its business interests will be adversely affected. In the cases where it has been successfully pleaded, such as *Toepfer* (1965), the decision being challenged referred to a fixed list of importers which could not be amended. In Vegnon's case there is not this fixed list, although the companies are named in the regulation. However, it could be argued that anyone could enter this business activity, so the requirement of 'individual concern' in Art 263 is not met. In *Zuckerfabrik Watenstedt* (1968), a producer of raw beet sugar asked for an Article of a regulation to be declared void, with no success. The Court said that a regulation does not lose its characteristics as a regulation simply because it may be possible to identify the persons to whom it applies, as long as it fulfils the objectivity of a regulation.

More importantly the ECJ has taken a very narrow view of what is meant by individual concern and follows the principles stated in the *Plaumann* (1962) case. In that case involving clementines, the ECJ stated that the applicant must show that it was affected by reason of certain attributes or circumstances which differentiated if from all others and which distinguished it as individually as if the decision had been addressed to it. There have been exceptions such as in the *Japanese Ball Bearing* (1997) cases, where four major Japanese producers of ball bearings were held entitled to challenge a regulation. Although the measure was of general application, some of the Articles specifically referred to the applicants. Even a 'true' regulation can be of individual concern to some persons if it is referable expressly to their particular situation, either alone or as a member of a known or closed class: for example, the Japanese manufacturers. However, this seems to have been an exception to the general approach of the Court. The ECJ in *Union de Pequeños Agricultores* (2002) reaffirmed its case law on the conditions for access of individuals to an action under Art 263. Vegnon must fulfil all the criteria if the action is to be admissible. As it cannot challenge a regulation, it must prove that it is a decision which is of direct and individual concern to it.

The fact that Vegnon is listed makes it, arguably, directly and individually concerned, as there is a close and specific relationship between it and the measure being challenged. However, the ECJ has not always been consistent on this point. The Court has laid more emphasis on the requirement of individual concern. If the Court can be satisfied on this, the requirement of direct concern is often assumed.

All this advice has centred on the question of *locus standi*, as this is the major hurdle for any applicant in Vegnon's situation. It must be remembered that the proceedings under Art 263 must be instituted within two months from the date of publication of the regulation, and from the facts in the problem this is still possible. Having obtained the Court's agreement that the action is admissible Vegnon would have to prove one of the grounds for annulment specified in Art 263. There are four such grounds, covering lack of competence, infringement of an essential procedural requirement, infringement of the Treaties or of any rule of law relating to their application and finally, misuse of powers. It is not clear from the problem which particular grounds Vegnon may plead, but the most general one is infringement of the Treaties or of any rule of law relating to their application as this would include general principles of Community law such as legitimate expectations. If successful, the remedy under Art 264 is for the regulation to be declared void or *erga omnes*.

It is possible to challenge the validity of a regulation in the national courts of a Member State. However, if a company knew that it had a right under Art 263 and failed to take up that right, the ECJ may refuse to give a preliminary reference on validity (*TWD Textilwerke Deggendorf GmbH v Germany* (1994)). Assuming that this is not the situation for Vegnon, it would have to be a party to an action in a Member State and the court hearing the case would have to make a request for a preliminary ruling under Art 267(1) concerning the validity of the regulation. As Vegnon will suffer financially because of the regulation they may bring an action for damages for 'normative injustice' where the regulation constitutes a sufficiently flagrant breach of a superior rule of law protecting individuals under Art 340. In *Schoppenstedt* (1971), the Court held that the plaintiff company could sue the Council for damages on the basis of an allegedly illegal regulation even though as a 'natural or legal person' they would have no *locus standi* to seek its annulment under Art 263. The advantage of an action under Art 340 is that it is not restricted to the two-month time limit which applies to challenges under Article 263. The disadvantage is that the Court has adopted a very restrictive view of the three elements identified in the *Schoppenstedt* case as being necessary to satisfy for Community liability in tort to be imposed.

QUESTION 15

Critically review the ability of an individual to challenge the validity of a Community Act under Art 263(4) TFEU.

How to Answer this Question

This essay question reflects the discussion that is taking place with regard to the remedies provided by the Community Courts for individuals. Although the national courts can make a request for a preliminary ruling under Art 267 TFEU, the restrictive tests used by the ECJ have raised criticisms from academics and practitioners. This developing area of EU law gives rise to many discussion questions and it is important to deal with the basic principles but then go on to discuss the issues.

The main points to be raised are:

* the procedure under Art 263 TFEU;
* the ECJ's interpretation of 'direct and individual concern';

❖   the *Plaumann* test;
❖   the challenges to the case law of the ECJ on Art 263 TFEU .

Answer Structure

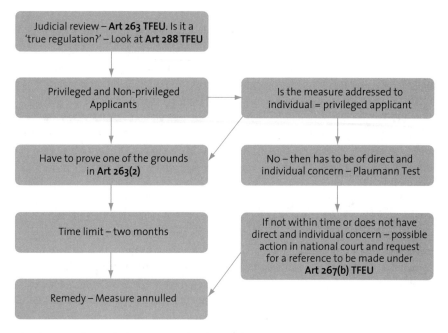

Judicial review – **Art 263 TFEU**. Is it a 'true regulation?' – Look at **Art 288 TFEU**

Privileged and Non-privileged Applicants

Is the measure addressed to individual = privileged applicant

Have to prove one of the grounds in **Art 263(2)**

No – then has to be of direct and individual concern – Plaumann Test

Time limit – two months

If not within time or does not have direct and individual concern – possible action in national court and request for a reference to be made under **Art 267(b) TFEU**

Remedy – Measure annulled

This diagram shows the key points to be discussed.

ANSWER

The case law of the ECJ acknowledges the principle that an individual who considers himself wronged by a Community measure must have access to a remedy and be able to obtain complete judicial protection. There are a number of ways in which this can be achieved, including an action for annulment under Art 263 TFEU . There is also a possible action for damages under Arts 268 and 340 TFEU or an action before a national court where the question of validity can be raised.

However, there is an argument that proceedings before the courts of a Member State may not provide effective judicial protection for individual applicants because such courts cannot declare Community Acts invalid. Where an applicant can raise the question of validity before a national court, that court may make a request for a preliminary ruling from the ECJ. Advocate General Jacobs in *Union de Pequeños Agricultores* (2002) argued that this strictly limited competence of national courts does not provide the individual with the rights identified in the European Convention on Human Rights and the **Charter of Fundamental Rights. Article 6** of the **European Convention** requires a fair trial and **Art 13** refers to an 'effective remedy'. More recently, the **Charter of Fundamental Rights** states in **Art 47** that 'everyone whose rights and freedoms guaranteed by the law of the Union are violated has the right to an effective remedy before a tribunal'.

Also, under **Art 267** the right to make a request for a preliminary ruling is with the court and not the parties to an action. Therefore, the national court may, using its discretion, refuse to make a request for a ruling and delay may occur if the individual appeals that decision through his national legal system. If no implementing legislation is required of the national authorities of a Member State, there may be no basis for an action before the national courts. Even if there is such legislation, Advocate General Jacobs stated in his Opinion in *Union de Pequeños Agricultores* (2002) that it is wrong to expect someone to 'breach the law in order to gain access to justice'. Such actions are both expensive and time-consuming for the individual who wishes to challenge a Community Act.

On the other hand, there is the advantage under an **Art 263** challenge that the institution that adopted the measure in dispute is a party to the proceedings from the beginning. However, the difficulty arises in the question of *locus standi*, or the right to bring the action before the Court. If individuals wish to challenge a decision addressed to themselves there is no problem, other than meeting the time requirements under **Art 263(5)**. Given the substance of most Community measures that may be challenged, it is desirable for reasons of legal certainty that this happens as soon as possible. Where the decision is addressed to another, or where the challenge is against a decision disguised as a regulation, the individuals must show that the measure is of direct and individual concern to them.

This has been very restrictively interpreted by the ECJ, and it was in this context that the remarks of Advocate General Jacobs arose in *Union de Pequeños Agricultores*. The Union de Pequeños Agricultores, a trade association that represents and acts in the interests of small Spanish agricultural businesses, wished to have annulled a regulation that set up a common organisation in olive oil. As the regulation in question had the normative characteristics associated with a regulation, it could not be challenged by the Union under **Art 263(4) TFEU**. This follows the case law identifying that the general rule to be applied is that if a decision is not of individual concern to an undertaking, that undertaking cannot challenge it even though it may be adversely affected by it (*Plaumann v Commission* (1962)). If that condition is not satisfied, then a natural or legal person does not have, under any circumstances, the standing to bring a challenge before the Community Courts (*CNPAAP v Council* (1996)). Is there a compelling reason to read into **Art 263(4)** a requirement that individual applicants must be differentiated from all others, in the same way as an addressee? In Jacobs' opinion, the key factor is whether an individual is likely to be adversely affected by the measure. Such an interpretation would improve judicial protection and greatly simplify the application of **Art 263(4)**, but it was rejected by the ECJ.

In *Jégo-Quéré et de SA v Commission* (2002), the Court of First Instance had to consider whether the plaintiff could challenge a regulation concerned with the size of fishing nets used off the Irish coast. The regulation established emergency measures to protect fish stocks and as such it would be hard to show it to be of individual concern under the case law of the ECJ. However, taking up the points made by Advocate General Jacobs in *Union de Pequeños Agricultores* (2002), the CFI said that the interpretation of **Art 263(4)** should be reconsidered in the context of the EC establishing a complete system of legal remedies and procedures so that the Community Courts could review the legality of measures adopted by the institutions.

However, the ECJ has rejected these requests to reconsider the way that **Art 263(4)** is applied. The ECJ has taken the view that individual applicants in such cases may challenge general measures in the form of regulations as in *Extramet* (1991). The Court has also recognised that a factual situation may arise which differentiates the applicant from other persons and may be regarded as individually concerned, as in *Codorniu* (1994), but the Court will not go further. In the discussions leading up to the **Treaty of Amsterdam**, the Court itself raised the issue of whether **Art 263(4)** is sufficient to guarantee effective protection against infringements of fundamental rights arising from the legislative activity of the institutions.

In this context, though, the view of the ECJ is that it is for the Member States to establish a system of legal remedies and procedures, which ensure respect for the right to effective judicial remedy. For the ECJ to adopt the views of the Advocate General in the case would go beyond the jurisdiction conferred by the Treaty on the Community Courts. However, the ideas in the courts of the Member States on increasing the ability of an individual to bring an action for judicial review have not been mirrored by the ECJ when applying **Art 263(4)**. However, there has possibly been some progress in the Lisbon Treaty to assist the individual. In the **Lisbon Treaty Art 263(4) TFEU** was amended to allow an individual to challenge a 'regulating act' by only showing direct concern. the impact of this change will become clearer in the future when cases arise. Under the **Treaty on the Functioning of the EU**, it will be the General Court that will generally hear actions for annulment, subject to the possibility of appeal to the European Court of Justice, and that may maintain the pressure for reform.

Aim Higher ★

In this question remember that there have been suggestions in the past for the interpretation and application of judicial review to be relaxed. For higher marks emphasise this in your discussion.

QUESTION 16

Critically discuss the development of State liability in damages in the national courts for violation of EU law.

How to Answer this Question

This essay question is looking at the availability of damages in actions before a national court. This is in contrast to Art 340, which is more restrictive. The main thrust of any answer is the *Francovich* case of 1992, and the implications of the case in future proceedings before national courts. The ECJ has developed the principles of State liability since this case and this development needs to be analysed.

Answer Structure

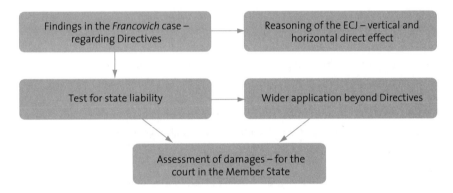

This diagram shows the key points to be discussed.

ANSWER

The ECJ recognised, in *Francovich* (1992), that individuals may have a right to damages in the national courts against the national authorities where they have suffered loss as a result of the non-implementation of a directive by a Member State. The *Francovich* case involved Directive 80/987, which provided for the approximation of the laws of the Member States relating to the protection of employees in the event of the insolvency of their employer. The Italian Government had not implemented the directive, with the result that, when Francovich's employer became insolvent, the employees had substantial arrears of salary.

Consequently, the parties brought an action against the Italian State for failing to fulfil the obligations incumbent on it under Directive 80/987. The European Court, responding to an Art 267 TFEU reference, developed its analysis of direct effect of directives from *Costa v ENEL* (1964) to deal with the question of damages. It identified three criteria which would have to be satisfied. The Court began by restating the criteria for the application of direct effect. These are that the provision must be clear and unambiguous, it must be unconditional and, finally, its operation must not be dependent on further action being taken by Community or national institutions. In applying these criteria to the facts of the *Francovich* case, the provisions of the Directive were insufficiently precise and were not unconditional, and so did not have direct effect. Thus, Francovich and the other employees involved could not rely on the Directive as against the Italian Government in order to recover their lost wages.

In the *Francovich* case, the ECJ considered the question of the circumstances in which a Member State could be held liable in damages for its violation of Community law. Until this case, the approach taken by the Court had been to state that it was left to national law to determine in which courts an action could be brought and what procedural rules should govern the action. On this basis, the general rule was that Community rights were to be treated no less favourably than analogous domestic law rights. In this way, it was assumed that domestic law would fully protect Community rights by providing a remedy obtainable in national courts. The Court stated that the effectiveness of Community law could be called into question, and the protection of rights would be weakened, if individuals could not obtain compensation when Community rights were undermined by violation of Community law.

The Court emphasised the principle that national courts are obliged to give full effect to Community law to protect rights which individuals derive from Community law (*Simmenthal* (1978), *Factortame* (1991)). It also referred to the obligation imposed on a Member State by Art 20 TEU (then Art 5) to take all appropriate measures to ensure fulfilment of Community law. Arising from these considerations, the Court stated that, as a general principle, Member States are obliged to make good damage caused to individuals by a violation of Community law for which they are responsible. In those cases where there has been a failure to implement a directive, three conditions are required to be satisfied. These are that the contents of the directive were intended to confer rights on individuals, that the contents of the rights can be identified from the provisions of the directive and, lastly, that there was a causal link between the damage suffered by the individual and the State's breach of its obligations. It was for national law to determine the courts dealing with such claims and the procedures to apply.

In his Opinion, Advocate General Mischo had given weight to the fact that the European Commission had already taken action against the Italian State under Art 258 TFEU (then Art 169) for its failure to implement the Directive. This had resulted in a declaration by the Court against Italy under Art 260 (then Art 171). However, the Court did not make this point in its judgment. The ECJ held that all the conditions necessary to give a right of action in damages for non-implementation of the Directive were present and, therefore, Francovich and the other applicants had a right to compensation from the Italian State.

Directives only have vertical direct effect and can be enforced only against the State. In the *Francovich* case, the applicants could not rely upon the principle of direct effect as against the State, as the State was not the body responsible for protecting the substantive right to payment of unpaid wages. However, if the Directive had been implemented, the Member State would have designated a body responsible for respecting the substantive right. Italy had failed to implement the Directive, and the Court recognised a right of action based on the responsibility of the Member State for damage caused by its failure to give effect to substantive Community rights in its legislative capacity.

Although *Francovich* involved the non-implementation of a directive, a broad interpretation of the Court's judgment could be that there is a general right to compensation where an individual has suffered loss as a result of a breach of Community law. Thus, the right to damages in the future might be understood as extending more broadly than the facts of *Francovich* would suggest. For example, in *Kirklees MBC v Wickes Building Supplies Ltd* (1992), the House of Lords held on the basis of *Francovich* that if the ECJ considered s 47 of the **Shops Act 1950** to be invalid as being in conflict with **Art 34** (then **Art 30**), the UK might be obliged to make good the loss caused to the individuals by the breach.

In *Bourgoin SA v Minister of Agriculture, Fisheries and Food* (1986), the Court of Appeal was dealing with a situation where a public authority had exercised its public law powers in a way that contravened Community law. The minister had imposed a ban on the import of turkeys contrary to **Art 28** (then **Art 30**), which was directly effective. The Court of Appeal had held that the appropriate remedy was a public law remedy, obtainable by way of judicial review. Only if the public body had been guilty of misfeasance in a public office would the public body be liable in damages. This is difficult to prove and would result in damages not being available. In *Kirklees*, the House of Lords doubted whether, in the light of *Francovich*, the *Bourgoin* case was correctly decided and considered that the UK might be potentially liable in damages for a breach of **Art 28** (then **Art 30**).

Francovich clearly represents a further development in Community law on remedies. Further references were made to the ECJ under **Art 267** (then **Art 177**), in order to obtain clarification of the implications for individuals who have suffered loss through a breach of Community law. The ECJ subsequently elaborated on the *Francovich* criteria in *Brasserie du Pêcheur* and *Factortame (No 3)* (1996), where the Court developed the prerequisites for the application of the principle of State liability. The Court held that, provided the conditions for State liability were satisfied, the principle applied to all Community law as a whole, whether or not it was directly effective. In *Dillenkofer* (1996), there had been a total failure to implement a directive and the question of discretion was raised. The ECJ held that the Member State had manifestly and gravely disregarded the limits on its discretion, which gave rise to an individual right to a claim for damages provided the stated preconditions were satisfied. The Court took the view that difficulty in implementation of a directive was no defence.

In *Sutton v Secretary of State for Social Security* (1997), the ECJ stated that it is up to the national court to assess the amount of damages, provided that the domestic law does not treat breaches of EU law less favourably than similar domestic claims. In *Factortame (No 4)* (1999), the Court of Appeal held that the breaches of Community law identified in *Commission of the EC v UK* (1989) were sufficiently serious to give rise to liability for any damage that might subsequently be shown to have been caused to individuals. As a result of this judgment, it is likely that Spanish trawler owners will receive in excess of £80m in damages. In the *Köbler* case (C-224/01) in 2003 the claimant was unsuccessful but the ECJ extended the principle of state liability to courts of last instance which infringed Union law obligations. It would seem that State liability as a principle can be seen as an effective mechanism for safeguarding the rights of individuals who can meet the three criteria.

> ### Aim Higher ★
> There are now more successful actions against Member States so to gain extra credit look to mention the more recent cases that can be identified at the Commission's website.

QUESTION 17

Analyse TWO of the following cases which came before the ECJ and explain their importance in the development of Community law:

(a) *Plaumann* – Case 25/62;

(b) *Roquette Frères v Council* – Case 138/79;

(c) *Schoppenstedt* – Case 5/71.

How to Answer this Question

When approaching a question like this, the temptation is to produce too descriptive an answer. The facts are important, but are only one element of the answer. You should deal with the following:

❖ The facts, the legal points raised and the decision of the Court.

❖ The kind of case it was? – whether a preliminary reference or a direct action and which Article of the Treaty it was based upon.

❖ The cases chosen for this type of question have usually played their part in developing or reinforcing European Court judgments – what part has this case played?

Answer Structure

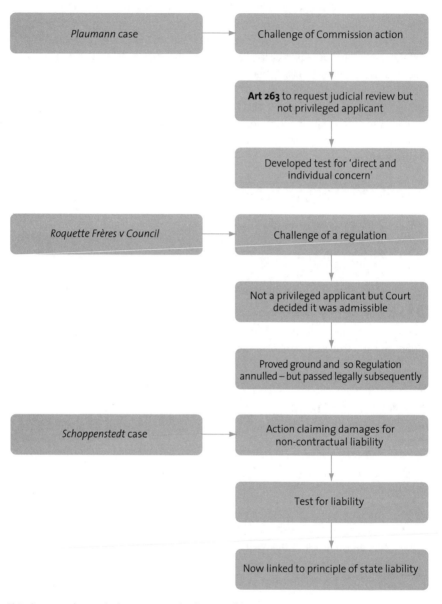

This diagram shows the key points to be discussed.

ANSWER

(A) *PLAUMANN v COMMISSION* – CASE 25/62

This was an action by one of 30 German importers of clementines against a refusal by the Commission to grant a request by the Federal Republic of Germany for permission to suspend the customs duties on the import of fresh clementines from non-EC countries. The refusal by the Commission had been made in a decision under the now repealed Art 25(3). The implication for Plaumann was that it had to pay a customs duty of 13%, whereas the German Government had asked the Commission to reduce it to a 10% duty.

The main importance of this case was concerned with whether Plaumann could challenge this decision by the Commission. It was open to the German Government to challenge the decision because it was addressed to them. But could Plaumann as a 'private individual' bring the matter before the ECJ? An action for annulment can be brought under Art 263 TFEU, but as far as individuals are concerned this Article has been restrictively interpreted by the Court. It is possible to challenge a decision addressed to oneself, but if it is addressed to another, the applicant must show that it is of direct and individual concern to them.

The Commission contested the case by claiming that it was inadmissible under Art 263 (then Art 173(2)) because the decision addressed to the government of a Member State was of a special nature and therefore not susceptible to challenge by private persons. It also said that Plaumann was not directly and individually concerned. Thus, the argument before the Court concentrated on this issue of inadmissibility.

The Court accepted that Art 263 TFEU (then Art 173(2)) does allow an individual to bring an action against decisions addressed to another person if they are of direct and individual concern, but the Article neither defines nor limits the scope of these words. The words should be given their natural meaning and the broadest interpretation. As the provision provides a right for interested parties to bring an action, it must not be interpreted restrictively. Therefore, the Commission's argument was not considered to be well founded.

On the question of 'direct and individual' concern, the Court decided to look at whether the applicant was individually concerned, because if the answer is negative it will be unnecessary to inquire whether he is directly concerned. On this question of 'individually concerned', the decision must affect applicants by reason of certain attributes which are peculiar to them, or there must be certain circumstances which differentiate them from all other persons. As a result of these factors, the applicant is distinguished individually, just as if they were the person to whom the decision was addressed.

In the *Plaumann* case, the decision affects Plaumann as an importer of clementines, a commercial activity which may be practised by any person. Thus, he is not distinguished sufficiently to show individual concern. Therefore, the Court declared the action for annulment to be inadmissible on the second point put forward by the Commission. This case was followed by a number of cases decided on a similar basis, to the detriment of the applicants – for example, *Spijker Kwasten BV v Commission*, which involved a six-month import ban on Chinese brushes where Spijker was the sole importer into the Netherlands. Although attempts have been made to make the 'individual concern' more flexible, as in *Jégo-Quéré et de SA v Commission* (2002), this was rejected by the ECJ. However, the change in the Lisbon Treaty with regard to Art 263(4) as it applies to 'regulatory acts' may assist future litigants.

(B) *ROQUETTE FRÈRES v COUNCIL* – CASE 138/79

This case arose in the wake of a successful challenge to Regulation 1111/77 in the *Isoglucose* case of *Royal Scholten-Honig* (1978). The result was that the regulation was declared to be invalid on the ground of discrimination. The regulation had sought to control the sugar market. Isoglucose is a direct substitute for liquid sugar, of which there was a surplus. As this surplus had to be exported at a loss, it was felt that the isoglucose manufacturers should contribute to export costs by paying a levy. As the regulation imposing the levy was invalid, no such levy was being collected. Therefore, a new regulation was needed which imposed a levy, but did not discriminate between the producers. Under the Common Agricultural Policy, such a regulation required that the Parliament should be consulted before being adopted by the Council.

The problem was a matter of time. The new regulation was needed to come into force at the same time as the sugar scheme, namely July 1979. By March 1979, the Commission had drafted the regulation, which was based on the one which applied to sugar. Therefore, the new regulation did not discriminate between the two products. However, the regulation contained an annex which gave precise methods of calculation.

The draft regulation came before the Parliament in April, but no final decision was made. June 1979 was the first time that direct elections were to be made to the European Parliament. The old Parliament 'died' before it could give its opinion, although the specialist Agricultural Committee was in the process of reconsidering the regulation. The regulation was urgently needed, but there was no Parliament. In the recitals to any regulation the words 'having regard to the opinion of the European Parliament . . .' are usually included. This regulation said that the Parliament had been consulted, but had not delivered its opinion! The Council believed that the judgment of the Court in the *Isoglucose* case had to be implemented before too long and that the regulation be adopted before the beginning of the sugar year on 1 July 1979.

Who could challenge the regulation? At that time, the Parliament was considered not to have *locus standi* under the then Art 173 (now 263 TFEU), although, following *Les Verts v Parliament* (1983), this would not be the situation today. Therefore, the only possibility was for an individual to bring an action for annulment under Art 263 (then Art 173(2)).

However, no individual can challenge a true regulation. There was something special about this regulation, in that it contained the annex which applied the scheme set up by the regulation to particular firms. Therefore, as far as these firms were concerned, the measure affected them 'like a decision'. Such firms could also count on the Parliament intervening in the action on their support, as they are entitled to do under the Court Statute.

The Council challenged the firms' action under Art 263 TFEU (then Art 173), but the Commission observed that if the action was declared inadmissible, there would surely be a reference on the matter under Art 237 from a court of a Member State. The Court agreed that the action was admissible. The ground under Art 263 (then Art 173(1)) which was successfully pleaded was the breach of an essential procedural requirement, in that the Parliament had not been consulted. This raised the question as to what amounted to consultation? As the Parliament had received the draft regulation, was this sufficient? The Court found that it was not, as Parliament was allowed, under the Treaty, to play an actual part in the legislative process. This reflects the fundamental democratic principle of the Community.

Having found that the regulation was faulty, the Court had to declare it void under Art 264 TFEU (then Art 174). This case provides a good example of a decision which, although in the form of a regulation, is of direct and individual concern under Art 263 TFEU. The importance of the case goes further in its effects on the balance of power of the Community institutions. Since the case, the Single European Act 1986 introduced the co-operation procedure for certain policy areas followed by the co-decision procedure of the Maastricht Treaty until we now have the ordinary legislative procedure of the Lisbon Treaty where the EP has equal role to that of the Council. This case is a landmark as it shows that the Court recognised the importance of the democratic principle and the role it gives to the European Parliament.

(C) *SCHOPPENSTEDT* – CASE 5/71

The undertaking Aktien-Zuckerfabrik Schoppenstedt brought an action in 1971 on the basis of Art 340 TFEU (then Art 215(2)), claiming damages from the Council caused by Regulation 769/68. This regulation laid down the measures needed to offset the difference between national sugar prices. The European Court is given jurisdiction in disputes relating to compensation for damage by Art 268 TFEU. However, this jurisdiction is linked to Art 340 TFEU, which states that, in the case of non-contractual liability, the Community shall make good any damage caused by its institutions. The case is to be judged in accordance with the general principles common to the laws of the Member States.

The Council contested the admissibility of the application on the grounds that the applicant was claiming compensation for the removal of the legal effects arising from the contested regulation and not for any wrongful act or omission. Second, if the action was recognised as admissible it would undermine Art 263 TFEU (then Art 173), under which individuals are not entitled to bring applications for the annulment of regulations.

On the substance of the case, the Court said that the non-contractual liability of the Community presupposes at the very least the unlawful nature of the act alleged to be the cause of the damage. No non-contractual liability will arise involving measures of economic policy unless a sufficiently flagrant violation of a superior rule of law for the protection of the individual has occurred. Having set this principle, the Court had to decide whether such a violation had actually occurred in this case.

Analysing this sentence, 'a superior rule of law for the protection of individuals' includes any general principle of Community law. This would include such examples as equality or proportionality. The requirement that there should be a 'sufficiently flagrant' or serious violation has been narrowly construed by the Court. In the case of *Bayerische HNL Vermehrungsbetriebe GmbH v Council and Commission* (1978), the Court stated that no liability would be incurred by the Community institutions unless the institution concerned had manifestly and gravely disregarded the limits on the exercise of its power. In subsequent cases, the Court's view has been that the breach must be both serious and inexcusable.

The applicants contended that by adopting different criteria for the right of compensation of sugar producers, the regulation infringed the then Art 37(3). However, the Court rejected this argument, as prices must be governed by market forces. Therefore, the applicant's action failed on the substance, because the condition mentioned above was not satisfied. The impact of the case has been the test set by the Court in actions under Art 340 TFEU in the field of legislative economic policy. In the case of C-352/98 *Bergaderm v Commission* (2000) the ECJ stated that in the absence of a particular justification, the liability for damage due to breach of Community law cannot differ from state liability.

Judicial Remedies and Review (2): Indirect Action – Preliminary References

INTRODUCTION

This type of action has proved very important for the development of Community law. It has been used by the Court of Justice (ECJ) as a vehicle for establishing many of the fundamental principles covered in other chapters of this book. It is very important, therefore, to have a good understanding of this topic, which can arise in both problem and essay questions.

Checklist ✔

You should have a general knowledge of the reasons for such a procedure being incorporated into the Treaty and, in particular, you must be familiar with the following areas:

- the matters for referral under **Art 267 TFEU**;
- the difference between interpretation and validity questions;
- what is a court or tribunal within the Article;
- the difference between courts which have a discretion and those which have an obligation to refer;
- the impact of the *CILFIT* case;
- the guidelines and procedures used in English courts; and
- the impact of a reference on the parties and subsequent cases.

QUESTION 18

What are the objectives of the system of preliminary references? Has the ECJ extended the use of Art 267 TFEU beyond these objectives?

How to Answer this Question

This type of essay question allows you to use your knowledge of areas of Community law to illustrate how the ECJ has extended the role of Art 267 within the Community. The following points should be covered:

❖ objectives of the Art 267 TFEU procedure (formerly Art 177; new numbering should generally be referred to, as in this answer);

❖ the relationship between the ECJ and national courts under the procedure;

❖ the role of policy in the ECJ;

❖ the extension of the scope of Art 267 TFEU;

❖ the development of direct effect;

❖ the development of *acte clair* in the context of Art 267 TFEU.

Answer Structure

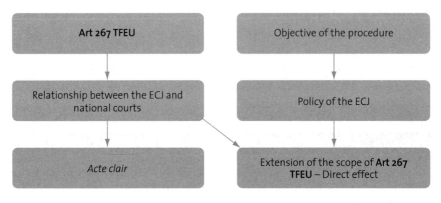

This diagram shows the key points to be discussed.

ANSWER

In the early stages of the European Community, the ECJ made it clear that a new legal order had been established. It was recognised by the authors of the Treaties establishing the Community that a court was necessary to ensure that there was a uniform interpretation and application of Community law throughout the Member States. It would undermine the new Community if the effect of its law varied from one Member State to another, especially in the economically sensitive areas associated with the European Economic Treaty (1957). It was necessary to give ultimate authority to one court, whose jurisdiction extended over the whole Community. This was the ECJ. However, the relationship between the ECJ and the national courts was not to be on a hierarchical appellate basis associated with national court structures. It was important that the relationship should be seen to be based on co-operation, with the shared objective that all courts wished to apply the law, whether it be of national or Community origin. The ECJ was granted the power to give definitive judgments on the validity and interpretation of Community law.

Thus, from the beginning, there were seen to be two clear differences between the procedure under Art 267 TFEU and the action of appellate courts. First, it is the parties to an action who normally decide whether to appeal or not. Second, when a case goes to appeal in a national context, it is normally the appeal court that decides the case and it may uphold, amend or overturn the decision of the lower court. Neither of these applies to the Art 267 TFEU procedures. It is the national court that decides whether a reference should be made, and only specific issues are referred to the ECJ in the form of questions. Once the ECJ has answered these, they are sent back to the national court for a final decision. This suggests that national courts are not subordinate to the ECJ, but co-equal. In reality it means that they have different functions with Art 19TEU specifying the ECJ role.

Given this need for uniformity in the Community, Art 267 TFEU specifies the initial boundaries of the role of preliminary references. Under Art 267, the Treaty specifies that references can be made requesting: (a) interpretation of the Treaty; and (b) the validity and interpretation of acts of the institutions, bodies, offices or agencies of the Union. It is in both (a) and (b) where the important developments have been made in Community law by the use of Art 267 references. In the early cases of *Van Gend en Loos* (1963) and *Costa v ENEL* (1964), the ECJ took the opportunity to stress the relationship between national law and Community law and the legal implications of the transfer of sovereignty when Member States established the Community. Both of these very important cases were brought before the Court via Art 267 TFEU references from their national courts. However, perhaps the best example of how the Court has used Art 267 to develop Community law is direct effect. Having established the supremacy of Community law over national law, the ECJ introduced the concept of direct effect. This was the result of the Court's view that a new legal order had been established with the Community and that this gave rights to individuals which their national courts had to uphold. Subject to three requirements being satisfied, this meant that an individual could claim a right under the Treaty, administrative act or other act treated as *sui generis* by the Court. This very important development was not expressly mentioned in the Treaty, the primary source of Community law. It was implied by the ECJ under its powers of interpretation and within its role in explaining what Community law was. Thus, it was possible to identify three issues which could be referred for a ruling under Art 267 TFEU, namely, interpretation, validity and direct effect.

As a policy decision, the Court has developed the principle of direct effect of Treaty Articles, regulations and directives. However, this is not the only example of how the ECJ has extended the jurisdiction of Art 267. As mentioned above, the Court has extended 'acts' of the institutions to include not only those specified in Art 288 TFEU, but also those acts that are *sui generis*. In *ERTA* (1971), the Court held that such acts of the Council could be an act for the purposes of judicial review under Art 263 (then Art 173) and thus likely to fall within Art 267 procedures. This was taken further in *Haegeman* (1974), where the Court held that the Association Agreement between the Community and Greece was covered by Art 263 TFEU (then Art 177(1)(b)). As agreements between the Community and non-Member States are normally concluded by the Council, this was sufficient grounds for the Court to regard such agreements as Community Acts. It could be argued that, as the agreement was concluded by means of a Council decision, this was correct. However, it was not the decision which was interpreted by the Court, but the agreement itself. Obviously, the non-Member State was not bound by the Court's interpretation, but Member States were. As international agreements between the Community and non-Member States are part of Community law and binding on Member States, it is clearly important that uniform interpretations should be given to the agreement throughout the Community. The agreement had to be brought within Art 267 TFEU if it was to be interpreted by the Court. Thus, the Court said that the agreement constituted an act of a Community institution in so far as it concerned the Community. Even if the agreement between the Community and a non-Member State is a mixed agreement in that there is a shared authority between the Community and Member States, this does not seem to have affected the ECJ's view of its jurisdiction to interpret the agreement. This approach is another example of the Court's policy-orientated interpretation, which has extended Art 267 TFEU .

There are other examples of the impact of Art 267 references on Community law as its scope has been broadened by the ECJ. It is seen by the Court as the best way of moving Community law forward within the teleological interpretation of the Court. The flow of cases on the direct effect of directives is perhaps a clear example of this, culminating in the Francovich (1992) judgment. However, the constitutional impact of references on Member States should not be ignored. In the UK, the Factortame case challenged long-standing constitutional principles. However, if the objectives of the preliminary references system are to ensure uniformity and not to allow disparities due to legal traditions, it would appear that the ECJ is seeking to fulfil them. As the scope of Community action has increased, it is to be expected that the matters coming within Art 267 references will also increase. How else can the ECJ provide the interpretation and validity necessary for uniform application throughout the Community? If the ECJ did not provide these, there would be no focus for the Member States and a danger of various interpretations undermining the Community itself.

Another objective of Art 267 was to distinguish between those courts which have discretion to refer under Art 267(2) and those which had an obligation to refer under Art 267(3) . Courts under the latter paragraph are those against whose decisions there is no judicial remedy under national law. This does not automatically mean the highest court in the judicial structure of a Member State, but the highest court hearing that particular case (Costa v ENEL (1964)). In the UK, some judges, such as Lord Denning, consider that only the House of Lords comes within the category of Art 267(3) .

However, whatever the arguments on this point, the ECJ has taken a policy decision to limit the obligation of such courts to refer. The CILFIT case of 1982 is the most important development in this respect, where the ECJ held that final courts are in the same position as other national courts in deciding whether they need to refer a question of Community law before giving judgment.

If, for example, the ECJ had already given an authoritative interpretation under Art 267 TFEU , there is no purpose in a further reference, although it could be made. However, the Court went further, to say that the correct application of Community law may be so obvious as to leave no scope for any reasonable doubt as to the manner in which the question is raised, thus enabling the Art 267 court to refrain from making a reference. This echoes the principle of *acte clair*, so familiar to the French legal system. The ECJ may have felt that the national legal systems were now so well schooled in the principles of Community law that this development could take place. It may be that they felt this was a reasonable way of reducing the workload of the Court or to further the co-operation on which the relationship with national courts is based. However, to ensure that national courts did not remove this obligation as a matter of course, the Court indicated the special characteristics of Community law which had to be considered, for example, the linguistic nature of the Court's jurisdiction, the special terminology and the contextual approach of the ECJ. Only if the national court could satisfy itself on these matters could the obligation to refer be removed.

Given that the preliminary procedure was designed to deal with the danger of divergences in the interpretation of Community law in Member States (*International Chemical Corp* (1981)), it can be seen that the ECJ has extended the interpretation of Art 267 itself. This is in three respects, namely, the scope of Community law covered, direct effect and the mandatory nature of Art 267 . However, there have been limitations on this development, as can be seen in *Firma Foto-Frost* (1988) , where the ECJ reiterated that national courts could not declare a Community Act invalid, but had to make a reference under Art 267 . In the *IATA* case C-344/04 (2006) the ECJ said that such a national court was not required to make a reference simply because there was a challenge to the validity of a measure. They only had to refer if the national court considered that the challenge was well founded.

QUESTION 19

Christine is a secretary with Welch's Import Agency. On a recent visit to Amsterdam, Christine collected a number of boxes at the request of her employer and brought them back with her to England in her car. She was stopped by customs officials at Dover and her car was searched for drugs. Although no drugs were found, the boxes belonging to her employer were opened and were found to contain pornographic films and magazines, much to the embarrassment of Christine. She was subsequently charged with a criminal offence under the Obscene Publications Act 1959 .

At the Crown Court hearing, Christine's counsel stated that the case raised a question of European law and requested that a reference be made to the ECJ. The judge said that he would make no reference, as the law was clear in his eyes and he did not wish to delay the case.

Can the judge refuse this request? What guidelines have been developed to assist English judges when deciding whether to make a reference?

How to Answer this Question

This problem question on Art 267 TFEU requires the application of basic principles, including:

- ❖ the procedure under Art 267 TFEU;
- ❖ the difference between Arts 267(2) and 267(3) TFEU;
- ❖ implications of *acte clair* and *CILFIT* (1982);
- ❖ English guidelines produced by senior judges;
- ❖ the *Rheinmuhlen* (1974) case.

Common Pitfalls ✘

Students often get diverted by the facts of the problem question. Remember that the key part for you in the examination is the last paragraph. That is what you have to answer.

Answer Structure

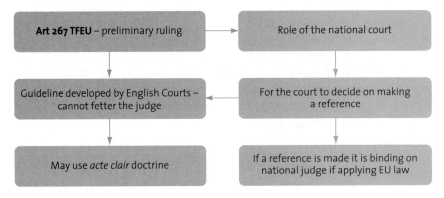

This diagram shows how to apply the law under Art 267 TFEU for Christine.

ANSWER

Christine's counsel has asked about a possible reference by the Crown Court judge to the ECJ. Under Art 267 TFEU, it is possible for any court or tribunal to request a preliminary ruling from the ECJ on a matter of Community law in order for the national court to give a judgment in the case before it. This request can be on a question of interpretation of the Treaty, interpretation or validity of acts of the Community institutions or whether the principle of direct effect applies. The purpose is to provide the means for a definitive statement from the Court that will ensure that Community law is applied uniformly across all Member States. Thus, the Crown Court comes within the category of court which **Art 267** was designed for. However, within **Art 267**, there are two categories of court. Under **Art 267(2) TFEU**, courts or tribunals have a discretion in that they may make a reference.

Article 267(3) indicates that those courts or tribunals in Member States against whose decision there is no judicial remedy under national law have an obligation to make a reference. This obligation has been qualified by the case law of the ECJ, such as the *CILFIT* case. As Christine's case is being heard before the Crown Court, **Art 267(2)** clearly applies. However, in either instance, it is the court or tribunal which decides and not the parties to the action. Therefore, the judge hearing Christine's case can refuse the request for a preliminary ruling under **Art 267** to the European Court of Justice.

Given the importance of the decision to make a reference to the Court, a number of guidelines would appear to be desirable to assist a judge hearing a particular case to decide whether to exercise discretion to make a reference or not. The European Court itself has refrained from producing guidelines as to the circumstances in which this step should be taken, but it has indicated that it is essential for the national court to 'define the legal context' (*Irish Creamery* (1981)). However, national judges have attempted to fulfil this need. The first judge to do so in the UK was Lord Denning, in the first case to come before the Court of Appeal involving Community law. This case was *Bulmer v Bollinger* (1974), an action over the use of the term 'champagne' when describing an alcoholic drink called Babycham. In this case, Denning indicated what he considered to be important factors. Perhaps the most important was that the point of Community law must be conclusive, in the sense that the case must turn on the point of Community law involved. In other words, if Community law was 'x', then the plaintiff would succeed, but if, on the contrary, it was 'y', then the defendant would defeat the action. It may be that, after hearing the evidence, the case could be settled on national law, thus making the reference unnecessary. The other factors he specified were associated with the time it took to get a ruling from the European Court, which required a stay of the English proceedings, which may have unfortunate results for the parties. Obviously, there was the expense of obtaining the ruling and the danger of overloading the European Court with too many references. He also felt that the wishes of the parties should be taken into account. Clearly, Christine wants a reference made, but this is not conclusive.

These guidelines have been criticised, in that they may fetter the English judge, contrary to the principle that national law cannot constrain the judge in the exercise of his discretion. This principle was stated by the ECJ in the German case of *Rheinmuhlen* (1974). In this case, the Court held that the power of a lower court to make a reference cannot be abrogated by any rule of national law. It also reiterated the importance of the **Art 267** procedure by stating that it is essential for the preservation of the Community character of law and ensuring that the law is the same in all Member States. However, the Court did recognise in *Rheinmuhlen* that, although the widest discretion was given to national courts regarding when to refer, **Art 267** does not preclude a decision to refer from remaining subject to the normal national law remedies. Thus, it would still be possible to appeal in these circumstances through the national court structure. Although in subsequent English cases, judges have been influenced by the words of Denning in *Bulmer v Bollinger*, they have repeated that they are only guidelines and do not fetter the discretion of the judge. However, one important point made by Lord Denning and repeated by subsequent English judges and the European Court itself is that it is important to ascertain the facts first, before the discretion to make a reference is considered.

In some civil cases, the facts may be agreed by the parties but, in criminal cases, such as Christine's, it is normally only after the case has been argued that conclusions can be drawn on the facts of the case. This is apparent in the context of deciding whether the point of Community law is conclusive. It may be that the case can be settled on the basis of national law. However, more importantly, it has a crucial role in framing the questions to be put to the ECJ in the request for a preliminary ruling.

MacPherson J, in *R v HM Treasury ex p Daily Mail and General Trust plc* (1987), provided a useful list of factors which consolidate those of previous English judges. His last point, that he did not find the point raised free from doubt, brings the wording of **Art 267** back into focus. The judge hearing Christine's case has the discretion to make a reference if he considers it necessary to enable him to give judgment. Although Christine's counsel has stated that a question of European law has been raised by the case, the judge clearly feels that he has the answer. This may be gleaned from the case law of the Court itself on the point raised, which was recognised in *CILFIT* (1982). However, in *R v Henn and Darby* (1981) English judges were warned by Lord Diplock that just because the meaning of the English text seems plain, it does not mean that no question of interpretation arises. Where this is necessary, the ECJ, as Bingham J pointed out in *Commissioners of Customs and Excise v Samex ApS* (1983), is far better equipped than national courts to resolve issues of Community law. Later, as Sir Thomas Bingham MR, he confirmed this view and added that if there was any real doubt a court should make a reference (the *Stock Exchange* case of 1993).

It may be different for Christine if the hearing is before magistrates and thus without a jury to decide on questions of fact. In such courts, once questions of facts have been decided, it may be appropriate for the magistrates to make an **Art 267** reference if the guilt of the defendant turns on the interpretation or validity of Community law. This was followed in *R v Pieck* (1980), where the incompatibility of English law with Community law led to the defendant having the prosecution against him dropped. However, in *R v Plymouth JJ ex p Rogers* (1982), the Divisional Court dismissed the argument of the prosecution that no court or tribunal could refer questions to the Court of Justice unless all the facts had been admitted or found, because this would mean that, in criminal cases, there would not be an opportunity to request a ruling on the basis of no case to answer unless all the facts had been settled. On the other hand, it was better to call all the evidence so that there was no question of the defendant being acquitted on the facts, thus saving the expense and delay of a reference. A case before a judge and jury in a Crown Court highlights the problem of delay associated with making a preliminary reference. Lord Diplock stated in *Henn and Darby v DPP* (1981) that it can seldom be a proper exercise of a judge's discretion to hold up the proceedings for over nine months. The delay caused by a reference being made now would probably be at least double this length of time. The better course, he suggested, was to decide the case at first instance and allow an appeal against conviction through the hierarchy of national courts. This approach was subsequently adopted by the judge in *R v Tymen* (1981).

It would appear that the judge hearing Christine's case has complete discretion, but is there any appeal available to her? As mentioned above, the European Court recognised in the *Rheinmuhlen* case that **Art 267 TFEU** references are subject to the normal appeal processes. If a reference had been made under the Crown Court equivalent of the High Court procedure in Civil Procedure Rules (CPR) Part 68, there would be a two-week period before the reference was sent to the ECJ to allow for an appeal by one of the parties. However, in Christine's case, it is the decision not to make a reference that she is unhappy with. In these circumstances, the judge's refusal is interlocutory and leave to appeal is necessary either from the judge or from the Court of Appeal.

QUESTION 20 --

What is the role of preliminary references in the EU legal order? Has it been successful in fulfilling this role?

How to Answer this Question

Questions on this topic are very often asked at all levels of assessment. Sometimes it takes the form of a problem question, but very often there will be an essay question like this to give the candidate more opportunity to discuss the law. It allows you to draw upon other parts of the syllabus to demonstrate your knowledge and to look critically at the impact of the preliminary reference procedure. The main points to cover are:

❖ purpose of **Art 267**;
❖ the *Foglia* cases;
❖ guidance provided by the ECJ;
❖ changing relationship with the national courts;
❖ the *CILFIT* judgment and *acte clair*;
❖ specific examples drawn from the English or UK cases.

Answer Structure

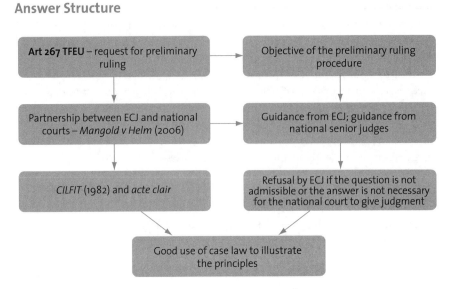

This diagram shows the key points to be discussed.

ANSWER

The most important source of EU law can be found in the Treaties. The recent Treaty of Lisbon has meant that there are now two important Treaties in the EU: the Treaty on European Union and the Treaty on the Functioning of the European Union. However, under the Treaties other types of administrative acts such as Regulations and Directives under Art 288 TFEU (formerly Art 249 EC) are used to make EU laws. The legal order of the EU is also made up of the judgments of the ECJ and to a lesser extent the General Court. These judgments have developed and enforced principles of great importance such as supremacy of EU law over national law and direct effect. The mechanism of preliminary rulings has been present in the legal order since the original treaties establishing the then European Economic Community in 1957 and can now be found in Art 267 TFEU. The role of preliminary rulings is to provide a means by which definitive judgments can be given on questions of EU law so that there is consistency across the 27 legal systems of the Member States. The European court providing the responses to request for preliminary rulings is the European Court of Justice but since the Treaty of Nice the General Court can also give such rulings where requested to.

Art 267 TFEU is different from previous treaties in that in Art 267(1) the scope of the jurisdiction of the ECJ keeps the wording of the important themes of interpretation of the Treaties and the validity and interpretation of acts of the institutions without specifically mentioning the European Central Bank or other bodies. There is also a new Art 267(4) TFEU which relates to situations where individuals are in custody, in which case the questions asked by the national court should be answered with the minimum of delay. The ECJ is already able to expedite the procedure for preliminary rulings but this change in the Treaties perhaps reflects the widening of the scope of EU law in the area of criminal law. Any court or tribunal can make use of the procedure under Art 267 TFEU as long as it meets the requirement that it is fulfilling a judicial function, regardless of what it is called in the Member State. It has to have the ability to give binding determinations affecting the legal rights and obligations of individuals. This gives an indication of the wide scope of the institutions that can and have utilised the procedure.

Under Art 267(2) TFEU a court or tribunal can use the procedure if it wishes to, where it needs a definitive answer to a question on interpretation or validity of a Community law or for interpretation of the Treaties. It does not have to make a reference because it may feel that previous judgments of the ECJ has made the need for a reference redundant or where it can make the decision for itself without making a reference to Luxembourg. Those courts or tribunals against whose decisions there are no appeals in national law were thought to have to make a reference because of the wording of Art 267(3) TFEU but this view has been changed due to the judgments of the ECJ itself. Some have argued that the relaxation of the interpretation of Art 267(3) TFEU was long overdue as the situation seemed strange that the senior courts in the Member States, such as the Supreme Court, had to make a reference even though their judges were the most experienced and able in that Member State.

The relaxation of the application of Art 267(3) TFEU was signalled in the case of *CILFIT* (1982) where the principle of *acte clair* was said to apply to EU law and specifically the preliminary ruling procedure. The concept of *acte clair* is taken from French administrative law and applies where the interpretation is so obvious as to leave no scope for any reasonable doubt. This puts the courts, which before were obliged to make a reference, in the same situation as those that had the discretion. The important wording being that a reference is made 'when it is necessary'. The ECJ judgment did give some words of caution as a warning to courts not to ignore the opportunity of making a reference, such as that something which is 'obvious' to them has to be accepted in all the official languages of the EU. However, the case did signal that the ECJ considered that important principles of EU law, such as supremacy and direct effect, had been accepted in the Member States so it was possible to progress towards a more even partnership given that the shared responsibility of all courts is that the law should be applied correctly.

This does not mean that the ECJ will consider all cases that come before it under the preliminary procedure without applying Art 267 TFEU. The cases involving *Foglia v Novello* in 1980 and 1982 were considered by the ECJ not to reflect a real dispute between the parties and were in fact an opportunity for hypothetical questions to be put to the Court. These requests were refused because the 'answers were not necessary to enable a court to give judgment'. Also in *Bacardi-Martini v Newcastle United FC* (2003) a request under Art 267 TFEU was refused because a court in England was asking about the compatibility of another Member State's (France) law with EU law. The answers were not necessary for that court to give judgment. There have been other cases where the ECJ has not given a ruling, such as where it considered that the questions were not relevant as in *Meilicke* (1992). Although normally in these situations the ECJ will do all it can to identify for itself what is relevant there is always the danger that the national court may feel that in doing so the ECJ has exceeded its role under **Art 267 TFEU**, as happened in *Arsenal Football Club v Reed* (2002).

There are other circumstances where the ECJ may refuse a reference such as where the questions are not articulated clearly enough for the Court to give any meaningful legal response, as in *AGS Assedic Pas-de-Calais v Dumon & Froment* (1995). Although the ECJ may tease out the real question the national court is asking, in this case they thought that it would be wrong to alter the substance of the questions asked. Lastly, the ECJ may refuse a reference where the facts are insufficiently clear for the Court to be able to apply the relevant legal rules. In *Telemarsicabruzzo* (1993), the Italian court referred two questions to the ECJ concerning the compatibility of national provisions on the distribution of TV frequencies with EC competition law. The national court provided almost nothing by way of explanation for these questions and therefore the Court decided that there was no need to answer the questions. In the recent Bulgarian case of C-27/11 *Vinkov v Nachalnik Administrativno-nakazatelna deynost* (2012) the Court declared a reference inadmissible as a purely internal affair as it concerned a traffic offence that had resulted in a fine and deduction of points. His claim under the Charter of Fundamental Rights failed.

The Court has recognised that there are limitations to its power to decline to take a reference and in fact has rejected very few. In *ICI v Colmer* (1996) the ECJ stated that 'A request for a preliminary ruling from a national court may be rejected only if it is manifest that the interpretation of Community law or the examination of the validity of a rule of Community law sought by that court bears no relation to the facts or the subject matter of the main proceedings'. The relationship between the national courts and the ECJ and General Court is said to be one of partnership and that is why it has been successful. The relationship is not one of an appeal court and inferior courts because all courts have specific functions in the administration of justice. However, it could be argued that there is a form of hierarchy but not in the sense of the diagram showing the various courts within a Member State and their jurisdictions. Rather it is a vertical relationship between national and Union law, which means that the latter has supremacy over the national law. The court that can give the definitive judgments on EU law must obviously have superiority in that function. There cannot be more than one court where the final judgment on questions of EU law is given, let alone allowing 27 supreme courts from Member States to fulfil this role!

There is a dialogue between the national courts and the Union courts because they all share the same objective mentioned above. Case C-144/04 *Mangold v Helm* (2006) is an example of the highest court in a Member State accepting that a judgment under **Art 267**

TFEU means that national law cannot be applied because it is contrary to EU law. In 2010 the German Constitutional Court accepted that EU court decisions can only be re-examined 'if the breach of EU competences by the EU authority is obvious and the act in question leads to a structurally significant shift in the arrangement of competences between the member states and the European Union to the detriment of member states'. The acceptance of the principles of supremacy, direct effect, indirect effect and state liability into the *acquis communautaire* are all examples of the success of the system of preliminary rulings as part of the EU legal order.

> ## Aim Higher ★
> For extra marks you could give some more details on the cases associated with supremacy, direct effect, etc which are all cases brought under the **Art 267 TFEU** procedure for preliminary rulings.

QUESTION 21

Crinkley plc are a large producer of potato crisps in the UK. Like all companies who are involved in manufacturing potato products, Crinkley have to purchase their potatoes from a national marketing organisation, as required by EU legislation. Under a recent Community regulation, all purchasers have to submit a tender together with a deposit of 10% of the total value of the tender.

Subsequently, Crinkley failed to take up all the supplies they had tendered for and were informed that they would, under the regulation, forfeit their deposit. This amounted to a substantial amount to Crinkley and could force them into liquidation. As a result, they are seeking to challenge the validity of the regulation, on the basis that it is contrary to the principle of proportionality. They are also suing the national potato marketing organisation to recover their deposit.

▶ Advise Crinkley plc.

How to Answer this Question

This problem question is seeking the application of Arts 263 and 267 TFEU as a means of challenging a Community Act. In particular, the following points should be stressed:

- ❖ the requirements under Art 263 TFEU for *locus standi* and the grounds for annulment;
- ❖ the procedures under Art 267 TFEU and specifically the power of the ECJ under Art 267 TFEU on questions of validity; and
- ❖ remedies.

Answer Structure

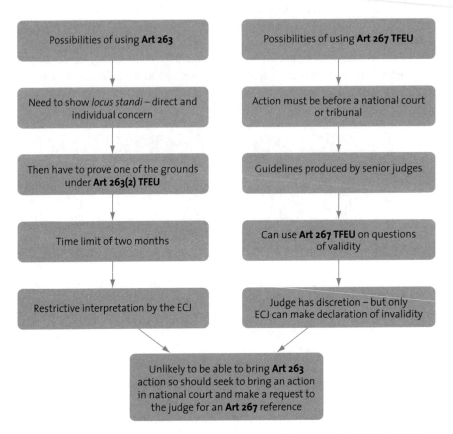

This diagram shows how to apply the law under Art 267 TFEU or Art 267 TFEU for Crinkley.

ANSWER

There are two ways open to Crinkley to challenge the regulation which has affected them. One possibility is a direct action under Art 263 TFEU, whereby they will bring an action before the ECJ and ask them to annul the regulation.

If they are successful, the Court could declare, under Art 264 TFEU, the regulation *erga omnes* or, if appropriate, merely declare void that part of the regulation which is contrary to Community law and leave the rest of the regulation as lawful. Such a declaration would have an immediate impact on everyone within the Community. The alternative possibility is for Crinkley to seek to challenge the validity of the regulation in the English courts, probably in the action against the national potato marketing organisation to recover the deposit. In this situation, a successful challenge using the Art 267 TFEU preliminary ruling procedure would have an immediate impact on Crinkley.

In order to bring an action under Art 263 TFEU, it is necessary to satisfy the ECJ with regard to *locus standi*. Under Art 263, it is possible for an individual or company to institute proceedings against a regulation if it is in fact a decision and is of direct and individual concern to the individual or company. The measure in this problem is titled a regulation, although the name of the measure is not decisive in the view of the Court. A regulation under Art 288 is of general application and has direct applicability throughout the Community. It is thus the main legislative or normative measure of the European Community. The main characteristic of a regulation is that it applies generally and objectively to categories of persons, whereas a decision binds those named individuals to whom it is addressed.

As far as the Court is concerned, a true regulation may not be challenged by an individual, as it stated in *Calpak* (1980). The problem for Crinkley is that the measure they are seeking to challenge does appear to satisfy the requirements of a regulation. Merely because it has had this financial impact on Crinkley, as against its effect on other potato product manufacturers, does not stop it being a regulation. In some cases, the Court has looked at the other requirements of Art 263 TFEU, namely, that the measure is of 'direct and individual concern' to the applicant and, having concluded that it is, they have held that it cannot be legislative in character, that is, not a true regulation (*Sgarlata* (1965)). To satisfy the 'direct' requirement, it is merely necessary to show that there has been no exercise of discretion on the part of national authorities (*Toepfer v Commission* (1965)). However, 'individual concern' has been restrictively interpreted by the Court so as to make it very difficult for an individual to satisfy the Court on this matter.

In *Plaumann* (1963), a case involving the importation of clementines, the Court gives a good idea of the factors to be taken into account in deciding the criterion of 'individual concern'. If Crinkley could satisfy the requirement of *locus standi*, it would still have to satisfy the Court as to the ground for annulment specified in Art 263 TFEU. Crinkley has already indicated that it wishes to challenge the regulation on the basis of proportionality. This is one of the general principles of Community law, initially derived from German law but now firmly recognised as being a Community principle. One of the most widely used grounds for annulment is 'infringement of this Treaty or of any rule of law relating to its application', which encompasses the claim that the principle of proportionality has been breached. The principle of proportionality requires that the means used must not be excessive in the context of the aim which it is intended to achieve. It has been successfully pleaded in a number of cases, including the *Skimmed Milk* case in 1977. In this case, the ECJ had declared an EC regulation which compelled producers of animal feeding stuff to add milk powder to their products in place of soya invalid.

As an action under Art 263 TFEU looks unlikely to materialise because of the problem of *locus standi*, it is necessary to look at an alternative possibility before the national courts. In order for Crinkley to use Art 267, a case must be brought before a court. This will be possible if the action is brought against the potato marketing organisation in an English court, probably the High Court. The judge hearing the action will have the discretion as to whether or not to make a reference to the ECJ. Under Art 267, the Court can give definitive answers to questions of interpretation and validity of Community Acts, which includes regulations. As the Court hearing the case will come within Art 267, the judge will have a discretion as indicated above. There are guidelines from previous cases heard in the UK to assist the judge in deciding whether to make a reference or not. The main one, which is supported by the European Court, is that it is important to ascertain the facts first. The Court prefers any reference to be set in the appropriate legal context. With regard to other factors, Lord Denning suggested, in *Bulmer v Bollinger* (1974), that time, cost, the workload of the European Court and the wishes of the parties should be taken into account. A number of references have been made by UK courts to the European Court on the validity of Community Acts, including regulations. In *R v Intervention Board for Agricultural Produce ex p ED and F Man (Sugar) Ltd* (1985), a large firm of sugar traders brought proceedings for judicial review of a decision based upon a Commission regulation. The grounds for the review included that the regulation was contrary to the principle of proportionality. On an Art 267 reference, the Court answered that the regulation did contravene the principle and, to that extent, was invalid.

Does it make a difference to Crinkley that they probably do not have *locus standi* under Art 263 TFEU? In the *Berlin Butter* case of *Ran v BALM* (1987), the Court stated, in response to an Art 267 reference on the validity of a decision addressed to the German Government, that it is irrelevant whether the plaintiff would have *locus standi* under Art 263, or if, in fact, such an action had been initiated. Thus, it should not influence the judge in deciding whether to make a reference or not that an Art 263 action is not possible. Is it possible, therefore, for the judge hearing the case in the national court to declare the regulation invalid without an Art 267 reference? In the case of *Sugar* (1985) mentioned above, the Divisional Court recognised that it could not make an order that the regulation was invalid. This view was clearly stated by the ECJ case of *Firma Foto-Frost* (1988). In this important case, the Court held that national courts could reject an argument based on invalidity of a Community measure, but they could not declare a measure invalid. National courts had the discretion whether or not to make a validity reference, but only the ECJ was competent to declare invalid the acts of Community institutions. One of the reasons given by the Court for this was that under the rules of procedure of the Court, Community institutions whose acts were being challenged were entitled to participate in the reference proceedings before the Court. Thus, they had the chance to defend their action before the Court before the measure was declared invalid. This approach was confirmed in the recent case of C-344/04 *IATA* (2006).

What if the Court considers that Crinkley's view is well founded and agrees that the regulation is invalid? A special feature of invalidity rulings is the immediate consequence they may have outside the context of the actual case in which the question of validity is raised. In *International Chemical Corp SpA v Amministrazione delle Finanze dello Stato* (1981), the European Court held that, once an act had been declared void, a national court could not apply the act without creating serious uncertainty as to the Community law applicable. Therefore, although a judgment of the ECJ under Art 267 declaring a regulation void is directly addressed only to the national court which referred the question, it is sufficient reason for any other national court to regard that act as void for the purposes of a judgment which it has to give. Thus, Crinkley will recover their deposit under national law if the regulation is declared invalid. However, the Court may decide to limit the retrospective effect of its rulings in order to leave previous transactions unaffected. The Court claimed jurisdiction to do this in proceedings under Art 267, by analogy with the power conferred upon it by Art 264, whereby the Court may state which of the effects of the regulation it has declared void (*Maize* and *Starch* cases in 1980).

My advice to Crinkley is that there is a presumption under Community law that a regulation is valid. Therefore, in order to defeat this presumption, an action must be brought which allows the European Court the opportunity to deliver its view on this matter. As an action under Art 263 is unlikely, given its restrictive nature, a reference by a national court under Art 267 seems the best way to challenge the regulation.

Although the national court under Art 267 has a discretion as to whether or not it makes a reference, if a *prima facie* case can be made out by Crinkley, it is probable that a reference will be made. In the *Firma Foto-Frost* case, the ECJ suggested that a national court might grant interim relief even pending a ruling on validity, as happened in *Factortame Ltd v Secretary of State for Transport (No 3)* (1991). It has to be remembered that the national court cannot declare the regulation invalid, but merely uphold its validity. This issue was raised in *R (on the application of British American Tobacco) v Secretary of State for Health* (2003). If a reference is refused, Crinkley will have to be prepared to appeal, in the hope that a court which comes within Art 267TFEU will be obliged to make a reference to the European Court.

QUESTION 22

Critically discuss the application of *acte clair* to Community law.

How to Answer this Question

As well as appearing in problem questions concerning cases before courts within the Art 267 TFEU definition, essay questions like this one can be set. You need to cover the following points:

❖ the role of Art 267 TFEU;
❖ the specific interpretation of Art 267 TFEU;
❖ the relationship between Art 267(2) and 267(3) TFEU courts (formerly Art 177(2) and (3) respectively, but referred to throughout this answer using the new, post-Amsterdam Treaty numbering);
❖ the doctrine of *acte clair*;

❖   the impact of the decision in *CILFIT* (1982); and
❖   the approach of UK courts.

Answer Structure

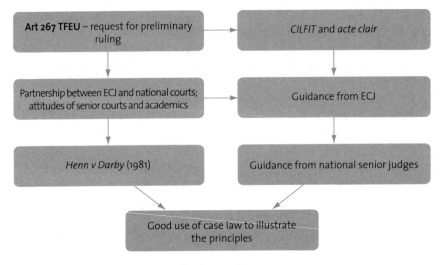

This diagram shows the key points to be discussed.

ANSWER

The principle of *acte clair* is derived from French law. Its origin lies in the principle that the ordinary courts must seek a ruling from the Ministry of Foreign Affairs where a question of Treaty interpretation arises, unless the point of Treaty interpretation is clear. In such circumstances, no question of interpretation arises. It was not surprising, therefore, that the first courts to apply the doctrine to Community law were the French *Conseil d'Etat* and the *Cour de Cassation*. In *Re Shell-Berre* (1964), the *Conseil d'Etat* was concerned with the application by some oil companies for the annulment of a ministerial decree affecting garages selling petrol, contrary to the-then **Art 31**. The *Conseil d'Etat* refused to make a reference under **Art 267**, because that would only happen if there was any doubt as to the meaning or scope of the Treaty as it applied to the facts of the case.

The ECJ has accepted that a national court of last resort is not under a duty to make a reference under **Art 267 TFEU** in certain circumstances. These are that the provision in question has already been interpreted by the Court, or where the correct application of European law is so obvious as to leave no scope for any reasonable doubt. This echoes the principle of *acte clair*. In *Da Costa en Schaake* (1963), the Court stated that the same question in this case had been referred in the case of *Van Gend en Loos* (1963) and had been answered to the effect that **Art 30** had direct effect. Therefore, the ECJ merely referred the Dutch administrative court to its previous decision. It went on to say that, if

possible misuse could lead to the misapplication or non-application of Community law by national courts. The case of *Cohn-Bendit* (1979) illustrates this point, where the *Conseil d'Etat* held, contrary to the case law of the ECJ, that a directive could not have direct effect. To counter such possibilities happening in Germany, the German Federal Constitutional Court emphasised in *Re Patented Feedingstuffs* (1989) that it will review any arbitrary refusal by a court subject to **Art 267(3)** to refer to the European Court.

Professor Rasmussen believes that the *CILFIT* judgment means something very different from what it *prima facie* establishes. For him, the real strategy of *CILFIT* is not to incorporate an *acte clair* concept into Community law, but to call the national judiciaries to circumspection when they are faced with problems of interpretation and application of Community law. 'The reins are not cut loose, although that might seem to be what the court ruled in *CILFIT*.' However, it must not be forgotten that, in all such circumstances, national courts and tribunals, including those in **Art 267(3)**, remain entirely at liberty to bring the matter before the ECJ if they consider it appropriate to do so. If the principle of *acte clair* is to be invoked in the context of European Community law, it must be on the basis of the criteria supplied by *CILFIT*.

The Free Movement of Goods

6

INTRODUCTION

This is one of the fundamental freedoms of the European Community and is perhaps the most important one as far as examination questions are concerned.

Examiners set both problem and essay questions on this area of Community law and it is one which you are strongly advised to revise thoroughly. The benefit of this hard work is that many important principles have been developed through cases associated with the free movement of goods, so that you can use them as examples in answering questions on other topics, such as preliminary references or general principles of Community law.

Checklist ✔

You should have a clear idea of the principles of a customs union (Art 28 TFEU) and the following specific points:

- prohibition of import duties on imports and exports within the EU and of all charges of equivalent effect (**Art 34 & 35 TFEU**);
- prohibition of discriminatory taxation (**Art 110 TFEU**);
- prohibition of quantitative restrictions and measures having equivalent effect on imports (**Art 34 TFEU**) and exports (**Art 35 TFEU**);
- the *Dassonville* formula and *Cassis de Dijon* principles; and
- derogation from **Arts 34** and **35** via **Art 36 TFEU**.

QUESTION 23

Critically review the role played by the European Court of Justice (ECJ) in the removal of non-pecuniary barriers to trade between Member States.

How to Answer this Question

This essay question requires an answer which covers the following points:

- ❖ Arts 34 and 35, as they affect barriers to trade;
- ❖ Directive 70/50 EC;
- ❖ the *Dassonville* formula;
- ❖ the first principle from *Cassis de Dijon* and the rule of reason and mandatory requirements; and
- ❖ the second principle of the *Cassis de Dijon* case on the marketing of goods in Member States.

Answer Structure

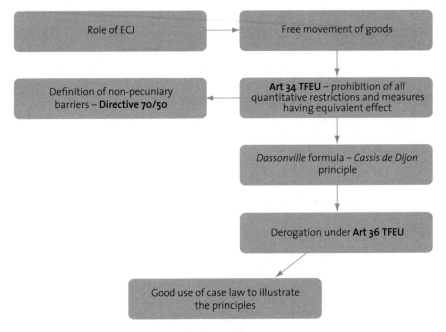

This diagram shows the key points to be discussed.

ANSWER

The European Community is based upon free trade between Member States, brought about by the abolition of customs duties and charges of equivalent effect. However, there are other barriers to trade of a non-pecuniary nature which have to be removed. Arts 34 and 35 TFEU are designed to eliminate these barriers. These Articles are addressed to the Member States, but neither the Community institutions nor individuals are free to act in breach of them. Even if the measure concerned is not binding, these Articles will apply. This was provided for by the European Commission in the Preamble to Directive 70/50 and confirmed by the ECJ in *Commission v Ireland* (1982). The most important one is Art 34, which prohibits quantitative restrictions and all measures having equivalent effect on imports. 'Quantitative restrictions' was interpreted by the ECJ in *Riseria Luigi Geddo v Ente Nazionale Rise* (1974) to include any measures which amount to a total or partial restraint on imports, exports or goods in transit.

Measures having equivalent effect to quantitative restrictions is a wider concept than that of quantitative restrictions. More importantly, the concept has been given a very generous interpretation by both the European Commission and the European Court. It has been held to include not just those measures which are overtly protective or applicable to imports or exports, which are referred to as distinctly applicable measures, but also measures which are applicable to imports, exports and domestic goods alike. These measures are called indistinctly applicable measures, and are often introduced for the most worthy of reasons. They range from regulatory measures designed to enforce a minimum standard, such as weight, size, quality, price or content for products, to tests and inspections or certification requirements to ensure goods conform to the set standard. They also include activity capable of influencing the behaviour of traders, such as promoting goods by reason of their national origin. This occurred in the case of *Commission v Ireland* (1987), where an agency of the Irish Government promoted a 'buy Irish' campaign to promote Irish goods within the Irish Republic, which was held to be contrary to **Art 34 TFEU**.

To assist Member States in the identification of measures having equivalent effect to quantitative restrictions, the Commission passed **Directive 70/50**. Although this Directive was aimed at the transitional period during which time such measures were to be abolished, the Directive has been seen as providing some non-binding guidelines to the interpretation of **Art 34 TFEU**. The Directive was not intended to provide an exhaustive list of measures capable of having equivalent effect to quantitative restrictions. The Directive used the terminology indicated above by dividing such measures into two categories. The first was distinctly applicable measures, which hinder imports which could otherwise take place, including measures which make importation more difficult or expensive than domestic production (**Art 2(1)** of the Directive). The other category covers indistinctly applicable measures (**Art 3** of the Directive), which are only contrary to **Art 34** 'where the restrictive effect of such measures on the free movement of goods exceeds the effects intrinsic to trade rules', or where 'the same objective cannot be attained by other measures which are less of a hindrance to trade'. Thus, such measures appear to be acceptable if they comply with the Community's general principle of proportionality.

The ECJ has developed its own definition of measures having equivalent effect to quantitative restrictions. This was first achieved in the case of *Procureur du Roi v Dassonville* (1974), and has been applied consistently by the Court. The *Dassonville* 'formula' is that all trading rules enacted by Member States which are capable of hindering, directly or indirectly, actually or potentially, intra-Community trade are to be considered as measures having an effect equivalent to quantitative restrictions. From this formula, it can be seen that it is not necessary to show that the measure is an actual hindrance to trade between Member States, as long as it is capable of such effects. It is necessary, however, to show some proof of a hindrance to trade, because a measure which is not capable of hindering trade between Member States will not breach Art 34 TFEU; for example, where the measure merely affects the flow of trade, as in *Oebel Belgian Bakery* (1981).

The measure in *Dassonville* was a requirement under Belgian law that imported goods should carry a certificate of origin issued by the State in which the goods were manufactured. Dassonville imported a quantity of Scotch whisky from France. Unfortunately, the seller did not have the required certificate, so he produced a 'homemade' one, and was subsequently charged with forgery. In his defence, he claimed that the Belgian law was contrary to Community law. The national court made a reference under Art 267 (then Art 177) to the ECJ, which applied the *Dassonville* formula and found that the Belgian measure was capable of breaching Art 34 TFEU (then Art 36).

The *Dassonville* formula was developed further in the *Cassis de Dijon* case, which identified two principles. Having applied the *Dassonville* formula to the facts of the case, the Court stated that obstacles resulting from disparities between the national laws relating to the marketing of products must be accepted in so far as they may be recognised as being necessary in order to satisfy mandatory requirements. Such requirements were listed as those relating to the effectiveness of fiscal supervision, the protection of public health, the fairness of commercial transactions and the defence of the consumer. This is known as the first *Cassis de Dijon* principle. Thus, certain measures may be within the *Dassonville* formula, but will not breach Art 34 TFEU if they are necessary to satisfy such mandatory requirements. This principle has come to be known as the 'rule of reason'. Before the *Cassis* case, it was assumed that any measure which fell within the *Dassonville* formula was a breach of Art 34, and could only be saved by the permitted derogation under Art 36 TFEU. Since *Cassis*, as far as indistinctly applicable measures are concerned, the rule of reason may apply and save them from Art 34. If the measure is necessary in order to protect mandatory requirements, it will not be a breach of Art 34. This is significant, since the mandatory requirements permitted under the *Cassis* principle are wider than the grounds provided under Art 36. For example, in *Commission v Denmark* (1986), regarding disposable beer cans, the protection of the environment was held to constitute a mandatory requirement. However, where the mandatory requirement falls under one of the specific heads of derogation provided by Art 36 TFEU, the Court may prefer to rely on the express provision of that Article. This happened in *Commission v Germany Re German Sausage* (1989), where the derogation was on health grounds. In the *Cassis* case itself, it was felt that the derogation was not necessary.

The word 'necessary' has been interpreted to mean no more than is necessary and is subject to the principle of proportionality. Other measures could have been used to protect the consumer regarding the alcoholic content of Cassis, such as labelling, which would have been less of a hindrance to trade. It would also have been fair to the domestic producer. The second principle from the *Cassis* case has far-reaching implications. It is suggested that there is no valid reason why, 'provided that goods have been lawfully produced and marketed in one of the Member States, they should not be introduced into any other Member State'. This principle gives rise to the presumption that goods which have been lawfully marketed in another Member State will comply with the 'mandatory requirement' of the importing State. This can be rebutted by evidence that further measures are necessary to protect the interest concerned. It is hard to rebut this presumption. The burden of proving that the measure is necessary is a heavy one, particularly when, although justifiable in principle, it clearly operates as a hindrance to intra-Community trade. Any evidence submitted in support of the measure will be closely scrutinised by the Court. In the case concerning additives in beer (*Commission v Germany* (1985)), evidence was taken concerning the medical effect of such additives from the World Health Organization and the Food and Agriculture Organization.

The ECJ has played an important part in removing the barriers to trade associated with measures having an equivalent effect to quantitative restrictions. By the introduction of the 'rule of reason' to such measures and the extension of the two principles stated in the *Cassis de Dijon* case, the Court has to try to balance the need for applying Art 34 with the need to respect the mandatory requirements justified under Art 36. Instead of the slow process of seeking Community-wide standards under the harmonisation procedures, where the interests of Member States could delay progress, the case law of the Court moved the Community forward in the direction of achieving its goal of a common market.

QUESTION 24

Rodney is a farmer living in the Welsh mountains who specialises in breeding rare varieties of pigs and sheep. For some time Rodney sent the animals to the nearby market for sale to meat wholesalers, but he has now decided to change his marketing strategy. He felt that he was not getting the added value that his special sheep and pigs should command, so he decided to slaughter and market the animals himself, selling direct to the consumer. The internet has allowed him to sell a lot of meat in the UK and he has now been approached by consumers in France who wish to buy his vacuum-packed joints of meat and special sausages. However, he has received a letter from the French meat marketing board, which raises the following objections to his sales in France.

They claim that as his packs of meat are not labelled in French, they cannot be sold in France; the price list he included with the meat indicated that he was selling his meat below the minimum price set in France, and thus contrary to French law; the sausages contain additives which, although permitted under English law, are banned under French law; the pre-packed joints of meat do not comply with French standards of consumer protection with regard to weight, and finally that the selling of meat by post is contrary to French law.

Rodney feels that the French love of good food will provide a profitable market for his meat and sausages, so he seeks your advice as to the points raised by the French authorities.

How to Answer this Question

This question represents the typical problem associated with the free movement of goods. The approach you should take is to state the principles and then apply them to the individual aspects of the problem.

You should deal with the following points:

- ❖ Art 34 TFEU and barriers to trade;
- ❖ definitions and examples of quantitative restrictions and measures having equivalent effect;
- ❖ the *Dassonville* formula;
- ❖ the principles of *Cassis de Dijon*;
- ❖ the distinction between Article 34 TFEU and the categories of selling arrangements following the *Keck* case; and
- ❖ remedies.

Common Pitfalls ✗

Students often leave themselves insufficient time to deal with all parts of the problem. Plan your answer so that you do not have to repeat common points.

Answer Structure

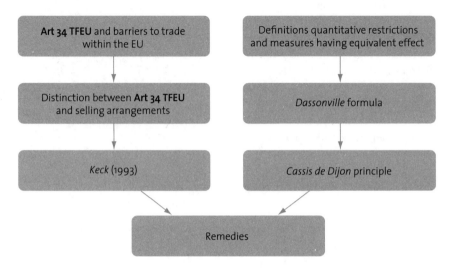

This diagram shows how to apply the law under Art 34 TFEU *for Rodney.*

ANSWER

Article 28 TFEU underlines the importance of the free movement of goods in the context of the four freedoms associated with the objectives of the Community. The internal market is identified as an area without internal frontiers in which the free movement of goods is protected and all obstacles to trade are removed. It has been relatively easy for the Community to deal with the more obvious barriers to trade, such as tariffs. It has been the non-pecuniary barriers or measures that are equivalent to quantitative restrictions, which are more subtle and disguised, that have caused problems, such as those experienced by Rodney. Article 34 TFEU provides that barriers to trade which amount to quantitative restrictions and all measures having equivalent effect are prohibited. Such quantitative restrictions were interpreted by the ECJ in *Riseria Luigi Geddo v Ente Nazionale Risi* (1974) to cover any measure which amounts to a total or partial restraint on trade between Member States.

The concept of measures having equivalent effect to quantitative restrictions has been given a wide interpretation by the ECJ. It is much wider than mere quantitative restrictions. To assist with the application of the concept, it is divided into those measures which are indistinctly applicable and those which are distinctly applicable. Indistinctly applicable measures are often introduced by governments for seemingly the most worthy of purposes. As such measures are applied to both imported and domestically produced goods alike, they are often thought by the government concerned not to discriminate in any way and not to fall within the prohibitions of Art 34. Such measures include regulatory controls designed to enforce minimum standards, such as price, which occurs in Rodney's problem. Distinctly applicable measures are those which are applicable only to imported goods.

In the problem, the French Government has introduced standards for packaging any meat product. This was introduced to protect consumers. This measure comes within the category of indistinctly applicable measures, as it applies to both French and imported products of this type. It was Directive 70/50 which introduced the categories of measures having equivalent effect to quantitative restrictions in order to help Member States to identify and eliminate such measures in the transitional period. Although this period has passed, the Directive is still seen as providing non-binding guidelines to the interpretation of Art 34 TFEU. It is Art 3 of the Directive which deals with indistinctly applicable measures. Such measures are said to be only contrary to Art 34 if they do not satisfy the principle of proportionality; that is, if the same objective cannot be attained by other measures which are less of a hindrance to trade.

However, it is the case law of the European Court which is of most importance to Rodney. Building upon the Directive, the Court has given some very important judgments in this area of Community law. The first case was *Procureur du Roi v Dassonville* (1974), which led to the development of the *Dassonville* formula. Dassonville had imported some Scotch whisky from France. Under Belgian law, it was necessary to have a certificate of origin from the State in which the goods had been manufactured. As the seller did not have such a certificate, he produced one of his own. When he was subsequently charged with forgery, he claimed that the Belgian law was contrary to Community law. The Belgian court made a request for a preliminary ruling under Art 267 TFEU. In its reply the ECJ referred to the *Dassonville* formula, which stated that the Belgian measure was capable of breaching Art 34. The formula is that all trading rules enacted by Member States which are capable of hindering, directly or indirectly, actually or potentially, intra-Community trade are to be considered as measures having an effect equivalent to quantitative restrictions.

In *Cassis de Dijon* (1978), the *Dassonville* formula was extended. In this case, a German law required the minimum alcohol content of Cassis to be 25%, whereas that imported from France was 15–20%. When it was challenged by the importer, the Court applied the *Dassonville* formula and held that the German law contravened Art 34 TFEU (then Art 36). In rejecting the claim that they were protecting public health and the consumer, the Court stated that this could be achieved by the alcoholic content of the different products being stated on the label. Under the first principle, certain measures may fall within the *Dassonville* formula, but will not breach Art 34 if they are necessary to satisfy mandatory requirements of the public interest. These include protection of public health and the defence of the consumer, and are wider than those listed in Art 36. This principle has become known as the 'rule of reason'. However, the national measure must be proved to serve a purpose which is in the general interest and has to take precedence over the requirements of the free movement of goods. Thus, if the measure is necessary in order to protect mandatory requirements, it will not breach **Art 34**.

The second principle derived from the *Cassis de Dijon* case gives rise to a presumption that goods which have been lawfully marketed in one Member State will comply with the 'mandatory requirements' of the importing State. This presumption can be rebutted, but it is very difficult to do so. The burden of proving that the measure is necessary to protect the interest concerned falls on the Member State which imposed it. Although the measure may be justifiable in principle, such measures clearly operate as a hindrance to intra-Community trade.

For his business to prosper, Rodney needs to challenge the French law and obtain a judgment that it is contrary to Community law. The most direct way to do this is to seek to sell a quantity of his meat and sausages in France and to be charged with contravening the domestic legislation. Once the case is before a court, he can request them to declare the legislation to be contrary to the provisions of Community law. The court will probably be reluctant to do this without a reference being made to the ECJ under **Art 267**. The discretion to make such a request under **Art 267** belongs to the court alone, but having raised the matter of Community law, the court can either decide the point itself or make a reference. It may be in Rodney's interest for the court to decide the matter itself, as a reference can take up to 18 months. Whatever the court decides to do, it is the principles of Community law outlined above which will be applied. It will be necessary to apply the principle of proportionality to ensure that the measures that go beyond what is strictly necessary to achieve the desired end are held to be contrary to Community law. It is therefore important to see how the ECJ has dealt with cases similar to Rodney's, because, as in *Greenham and Abel* (2004), the onus is on the French to show that their rules are necessary.

The first issue is the requirement that labelling should be in French. The ECJ in *Colim NV v Bigg's Continent Noord NV* (1997) made a distinction between linguistic requirements imposed by Community law and information required by national law with regard to labelling. Applying the second *Cassis* principle, Rodney's meat must be admitted to the French market, as it is marketed in the UK. The second point raised in the letter refers to the minimum selling price for meat in France, and following the case of *Keck and Mithouard* (1993) this would not be covered by **Art 34 TFEU** but would be seen as a selling arrangement. Such an arrangement would be outside **Art 34** if the rule applied indistinctly to all traders operating within the territory and affected the marketing of both domestic and imported products. The same point would be made about the sale of meat by post. In the case of *Deutsche Apothekerverband* (2003) the internet was used for the sale of pharmaceutical products by mail order. In clarifying its case law, the Court said that the application to products from other Member States of national provisions restricting or prohibiting certain selling arrangements was not such as to hinder directly or indirectly, actually or potentially, trade between Member States within the meaning of the *Dassonville* judgment. This was provided that those provisions applied to all affected traders operating within the national territory and affected them the same way, both legally and factually. Obviously those who wished to sell by mail order from outside the country were at a disadvantage.

Another point raised by the French official deals with the weight of the pre-packed joints of meat. This measure appears to be indistinctly applicable, and since the *Cassis* case, it is necessary for any court hearing the case to apply the rule of reason to Art 34 TFEU. Is the measure necessary to protect the mandatory requirement of consumer protection? If it is, then it will not breach Art 34 TFEU. However, the ECJ case law has shown that the word 'necessary' has been interpreted to mean no more than is necessary by applying the principle of proportionality. As indicated above, the German Government in the *Cassis* case did not succeed with their defence, because the consumer could have been protected by some other means. In *Commission v Germany* (1985), a case was brought against the German prohibition of additives in imported beer. The European Court held that the prohibition of marketing products containing additives authorised in the Member State of production, but prohibited in the Member State of importation, is permissible only if it complies with the requirements of Art 36. But, the Court emphasised the last sentence of Art 36, which states that such prohibitions should not constitute a means of arbitrary discrimination or a disguised restriction on trade between Member States. The Court concluded that the use of a specific additive which is authorised in another Member State must be authorised in the case of a product imported from that Member State. In *Commission v Germany* (1989), German law on the meat content of sausages could not be enforced against imported sausages where there was no threat to health to invoke the derogation allowed to Member States under Art 36. This was held to be in breach of Art 34 TFEU because the objective could have been achieved by other means, such as labelling, which would be less of a hindrance to trade. Here again, it would seem that Rodney can defeat any attempt by the French Government to justify the measures as being a mandatory requirement.

QUESTION 25

Empire Pharmaceuticals have been involved in the manufacture of pharmaceutical products for over 20 years and have successfully developed products that are now very popular and are among the market leaders. They have produced a new anti-aging cream which they have trade marked as Adolphene and have granted the right to sell it within the EU to a company in Sweden and another in Spain. In this way the EU market will be covered and Empire Pharmaceuticals themselves will concentrate on the very profitable markets of North America and Japan.

Unfortunately the plans of Empire Pharmaceuticals have recently been upset by Jackal Pharmaceuticals a company based in Scotland, who have started to aggressively promote their own products. They have produced their own anti-aging product under the Rejuvo label. They claim that this product is much cheaper and have produced a list of products that make claims for anti-aging, including Adolphene, and have sent these to retail outlets who sell these products. Adolphene is shown to be the most expensive anti-aging cream on the market.

A further problem for Empire Pharmaceuticals is that the Swedish company has reported that large quantities of Adolphene have been offered for sale to chemists by Amigo Supplies who purchased the Adolphene cream in Spain and Malaysia and are now offering it for sale in Sweden at a greatly discounted price.

Empire Pharmaceuticals ask for your advice as to what action they can take, if any, against Jackal Pharmaceuticals and Amigo Supplies to protect their trademark.

How to Answer this Question

As you read this question, you should mark those passages which you feel cover the facts and are relevant to the law, and make sure that you deal with them in your answer. The main points to cover are:

- ❖ Arts 34 and 35 TFEU, stating the policy of free movement for imports and exports;
- ❖ the principles from *Cassis de Dijon*;
- ❖ derogation under Art 36 TFEU;
- ❖ rights associated with trademarks;
- ❖ the Trademark Directive 2008/95 replacing 89/104/EEC.

Answer Structure

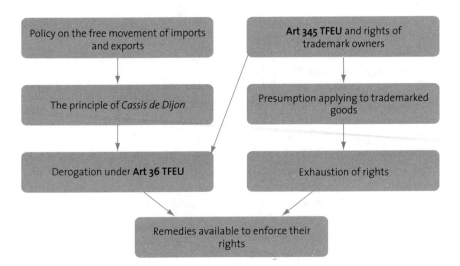

This diagram shows how to apply the law under Arts 34–36 TFEU for Empire Pharmaceuticals.

ANSWER

This question raises the issue of trademarks and the rights of the proprietor to benefit from their intellectual property. There is also a free movement of goods dimension because the European Union is founded on the principle of a customs union which allows for the free movement of goods, including those which have come from outside but have paid duties and are thus able to have free circulation in the EU. The free movement of goods applies to both imports (**Art 34 TFEU**) and exports (**Art 35 TFEU**). The European Union has made great efforts to remove barriers to the free circulation of goods so it does not take kindly to attempts by companies to institute their own barriers which may harm the interests of consumers and thus possibly be in breach of competition policy. However, in this problem the possibility of anti-competitive behaviour would not seem to be a factor as Empire Pharmaceuticals are not in a dominant position, which is covered by **Art 102 TFEU**, and there does not seem to be anti-competitive activity caught by **Art 101 TFEU**. Even though Empire Pharmaceuticals have consented to the Spanish and Swedish companies selling the Adolphene cream this is their right to do as the trade mark holders and judging from the problem there are a number of alternative suppliers. Therefore the advice to Empire Pharmaceuticals will concentrate on the rights of the trademark holder within the context of the principle of free movement of goods.

It is important to identify the rights of the holder of the trademark. All Member States have developed their own laws associated with intellectual property, including trademarks, and **Art 345 TFEU** states that the Treaty does not prejudice the rules in the

Member States governing the system of property ownership. As EU law recognises these rights the ECJ has developed a jurisprudence that draws a distinction between the existence of industrial property rights and their exercise. What rights does the trademark holder have? The intellectual property right means that they have the right to first put that product into the market so that they get their 'reward' for their endeavours. The trademark also provides an essential guarantee to the consumer about the origins of the goods (*Arsenal Football Club plc v Reed* (2002)). Article 5 of Directive 2008/95 deals with the rights conferred by a trademark and states that they confer on the proprietor exclusive rights which allows for all third parties not having his consent to be prevented from using the trademark in the course of trade. This was illustrated in the recent Supreme Court judgement in *Oracle America Inc v M-Tech Data Ltd* (2012) where Oracle stopped M-Tech importing and selling goods in the EU in breach of the Oracle trade mark. This would allow for the agreement with the Spanish and Swedish companies to stand but maybe a factor when considering the actions of Amigo Supplies.

Can Empire Pharmaceuticals take any action about the comparison lists produced by Jackal Pharmaceuticals, given that they have rights as the proprietor of the trademark? Their product has been identified in a way that will influence the purchases of the professional retailer and subsequently the consumer. This is known as comparative advertising. Article 2(2a) of Directive 84/450, as amended by Directive 97/55, states that comparative advertising means any advertising that explicitly, or by implication, identifies a competitor or goods or services offered by a competitor. Article 3a(1) then goes on to identify where such advertising is permitted. These conditions include that the advertising is not misleading, it does not create confusion in the market place, it does not discredit or denigrate the trademark of others, it does not take unfair advantage of the reputation of another's trademark and it does not present a product or a service as an imitation or replica of the trademarked goods or service (C-487/07 *L'Oréal SA & others v Bellure NV & others* (2009)). Empire Pharmaceuticals are a market leader so is the action of Jackal unfair and to the detriment of the Adolphene trademark? Would the retailer and consumer be influenced by such a list? Article 5(2) of Directive 2008/95, referred to as the Trade Mark Directive, establishes a wider form of protection for the benefit of trademarks with a reputation so that no unfair advantage is taken by competitors in a way that was detrimental to the mark. This Article does not require the existence of a likelihood of confusion for the protection to be implemented (C-102/07 *Adidas and Adidas Benelux* (2008)). What is necessary is for the degree of similarity between the trademark with a reputation and the sign used by a competitor to have the effect that the relevant section of the public establishes a link between the sign and the mark. If such a link exists in the mind of the public this constitutes a condition that is necessary to establish the existence of one of the types of injury against which Article 5(2) of Directive 2008/95 ensures protection for the benefit of trademarks with a reputation. Other factors are taken into account but the possible injury to the holder of the trademark is important. In the case of *L'Oréal SA & others v Bellure NV & others* (2009) the ECJ found in favour of the trademark owner, even though the Court of Appeal felt obliged to enforce that view even though it was a conclusion that they did not agree with. Thus it would seem that Empire Pharmaceuticals can successfully take action against Jackal Pharmaceuticals to stop them issuing the comparison list.

There is a presumption in favour of goods lawfully marketed in one Member State of the Community being accepted in another Member State. This was clearly stated in the second principle identified by the Court in the case of *Cassis de Dijon* (1978). If a company or State is seeking to rebut that principle, it must prove that the conditions are such that Art 36 is applicable. This Article gives a number of grounds that are only available to the government of a Member State, for example, where it is claimed that restrictions are justified on the grounds of public policy or public security. However, it is possible for a business to seek derogation under Art 36 on the ground of 'protection of industrial and commercial property'. This includes such intellectual property rights as trademarks, patents and copyright. This supports the recognition given in the Treaty that property rights have not been affected by the establishment of the EU. As mentioned above Article 345 TFEU states that the Treaty shall in no way prejudice the rules in the Member States governing the system of property ownership. However, how much protection will this Article give to them? In *Deutsche Grammophon (78/79)*, a case concerning copyright but also applied to trademarks, the ECJ stated that Art 36 TFEU (then Art 36) permitted prohibitions or restrictions on the free movement of goods only to the extent that they were justified for the protection of the rights that form the specific subject matter of the property. In other words, it is necessary to look at what the owner of the property right is seeking to protect. This is where the key point is not the right of the trademark owner but the way they are seeking to exercise it.

In the pharmaceutical case of *Centrafarm BV v Winthrop BV (16/74)*, a claim was made by Winthrop that their trademark had been infringed. The Court held that they had the exclusive right to use the trademark for the purposes of putting into circulation products protected by the trademark for the first time. They might either do this themselves or transfer that right to a third party by way of licences, etc. Once the protected product has been put onto the market in a particular State by or with the consent of the owner, he can no longer be allowed to rely on his national property rights to prevent the importation of that product from that State into other Member States. The rights that are associated with the trademark are exhausted. This doctrine of exhaustion of rights has been applied by the court to all types of property rights, including trademarks, patents and copyright – for example, see *Pharmacia & Upjohn SA v Paranova SA (379/97)*.

In this problem, Empire Pharmaceuticals are the owners of the trademark and therefore have the rights described above. They exercise these rights themselves in certain countries, but have consented to two companies exercising this right on their behalf in the EU. If a product like Adolphene has been lawfully put onto the market with the owner's consent in one Member State, the importation of that product into another Member State cannot be restricted. This will apply even if the purpose is to prevent parties taking advantage of price differences in different Member States. This is after all what was attempted in *Centrafarm v Winthrop*. (The emphasis in that case was to ask what makes a trade mark valuable – the reservation to the owner, through his exclusive right to put marked products into circulation, or the goodwill associated with the mark.)

However, the principle of 'exhaustion of rights' only applies within the European Union. The ECJ has been concerned that individual Member States cannot create their own rules regarding exhaustion of rights where the goods are imported from outside the EU. In the important case of *Silhouette International (335/96)*, the ECJ stated that the exhaustion of rights does not and cannot apply where goods placed on the market outside the EEA are brought into and sold within the EEA, which obviously includes the EU. The only exception to this appears to be where the trademark owner can be said to have consented to the importation, circulation and sale. This was the view applied by the High Court in *Zino Davidoff SA v A&G Imports Ltd (No 1)*. Therefore although no action would seem possible against Amigo supplies for the quantities of Adolphene cream purchased in Span and sold in Sweden this would not apply to those purchased in Malaysia as their rights have not been exhausted. They should take action to enforce their rights and seek damages as occurred in the cases of *Sebago Inc v GB Unie SA (173/98)* and *Bristol Myers Squibb v Parnova (427/93)*. As mentioned above they can stop Jackal Pharmaceuticals issuing the comparison list.

> ### Aim Higher   ✘
> If time allows try to bring in at least one example where a company like Empire Pharmaceuticals has been held to have acted against the EU's competition law.

QUESTION 26

Analyse TWO of the following cases which came before the ECJ, and explain their importance in the development of Community law:

(a) *Cassis de Dijon* – Case 120/78;

(b) *Commission v Ireland* – Case 249/81;

(c) *Centrafarm v Sterling Drug* – Case 15/74.

How to Answer this Question

When approaching a question like this, the temptation is to produce too descriptive an answer. The facts are important, but are only one element of the answer. You should try to deal with the following:

❖   the facts, the legal points raised and the decision of the Court;

❖   the kind of case it was – whether a preliminary reference or a direct action and which Article of the Treaty it was based upon;

❖ the cases chosen for this type of question have usually played their part in developing or reinforcing European Court judgments – what part has this case played?

Answer Structure

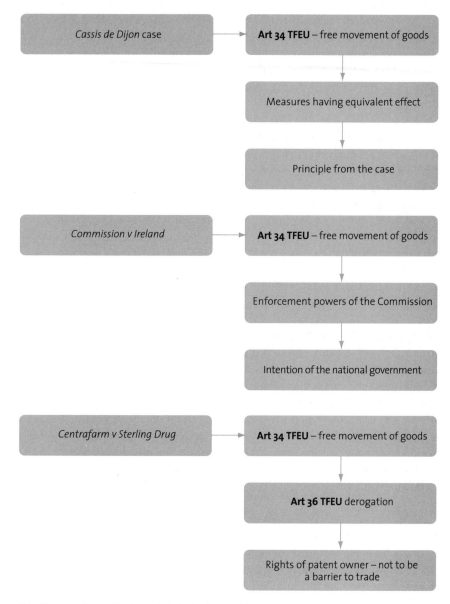

This diagram shows the key points to be discussed.

ANSWER

(A) *CASSIS DE DIJON* – CASE 120/78

This action was brought in a German court because of the application of a German law which forbade the marketing of liqueurs with a low alcohol content. The French liqueur called Cassis de Dijon had a maximum strength of 20% alcohol by volume, whereas German law required a minimum content of 25%. The French company claimed that the German law was contrary to Art 34 TFEU (then Art 30), as it interfered with the free movement of goods. Although the German authorities were not affecting the free movement of goods by imposing quotas, their actions were still covered by Art 34 TFEU (then Art 30). This is because the Article also forbids measures having an equivalent effect to quotas.

The German authorities claimed that the law did not discriminate against the French liqueur, as the same minimum content also applied to German producers. To allow the 'milder' French drink to be treated as a liqueur would lead to a reduction in alcohol content applied to German producers and thus a lowering standard. In order to avoid the application of Art 34 TFEU (then Art 30), the German Government had to plead Art 36 TFEU. This Article allows a government of a Member State to derogate from its obligations under Art 34 on such grounds as public policy, public morality, public security or the protection of the health and life of humans, animals and plants. Specifically, the German Government argued that its minimum standard law was inspired by the wish to protect the consumer from alcoholism, that is, public health. However, Art 36 ends by saying that it shall not be used as a means of disguised restriction of trade.

The ECJ said that, in the absence of common rules to the production and marketing of alcohol, it is for the Member State to regulate, in that they are necessary to satisfy fiscal supervision, the protection of public health, the defence of the consumer and the fairness of commercial transactions. These points were raised by the German Government. They said that public health was protected by fixing a minimum alcohol content, as beverages with a low alcohol content more easily induce a tolerance towards alcohol. There would be a general lowering of standards, as the lowest alcohol content permitted in any Member State would become the Community standard. This was rejected by the Court, as stronger beverages were generally consumed in a diluted form. They also rejected the claim that lower alcohol contents would lead to unfair practices against consumers.

As far as the Court was concerned, the requirements set by the German Government relating to the minimum alcohol content did not serve the general interest and interfered with the fundamental principle of the free movement of goods. It would be a much simpler matter to ensure that suitable information is conveyed to the purchaser by requiring the display of an indication of origin and of the alcohol content on the packaging of products.

(B) *COMMISSION v IRELAND* – CASE 249/81

Faced with economic problems, the Irish Government announced in 1978 a programme to create jobs in Ireland's manufacturing and service industries. The main platform for this policy was to persuade individuals to purchase Irish goods. Supported by public funds, a 'Buy Irish' campaign was launched, involving the Irish Goods Council and the use of a 'Guaranteed Irish' symbol. In 1981, the European Commission delivered its Reasoned Opinion that the campaign was equivalent to a quantitative restriction on imports and in breach of Art 34 TFEU (then Art 36). This Article prohibits all quantitative restrictions on imports and all measures having equivalent effect. The concept of measures having an equivalent effect has been interpreted very generously by the Court, to include any activity capable of influencing the behaviour of traders.

The Reasoned Opinion is a requirement when the Commission is seeking to exercise its powers under Art 258 TFEU against a Member State which is failing to fulfil its obligations under the Treaty. It is the final step in the administrative stage before the Commission decides whether to take the Member State before the ECJ. The Reasoned Opinion has to provide details of the failure on the part of the Member State, the action to be taken and the timescale in which this must be done.

The Irish Government argued that the campaign was not contrary to Art 34 TFEU (then Art 30). They did so by arguing that the prohibition only applies to measures which are binding. All that the campaign did was to give moral support and some financial aid for advertising the activities pursued by the Irish industries. The aid was compatible with Art 107 (then Art 92), which permits State aid to industry for such purposes as combating unemployment. They also claimed that there had been no restrictive effect on trade, as the campaign had failed. During the campaign, the proportion of Irish goods to all goods sold on the Irish market fell from 49.2% to 43.4%!

The Court rejected these arguments, because they believed that the Irish Government's considered intention was to substitute domestic products for imported products on the Irish market and thereby to check the flow of imports from other Member States. Even though the campaign did not have any significant success, the Court could not overlook the fact that the activities formed part of a government programme which was designed to achieve this substitution of domestic products for imported products and, as such, was liable to affect the volume of trade between Member States. The 'Buy Irish' campaign was discriminatory and had a potential effect on imports from other Member States as if it were one of a binding nature.

A measure like this cannot escape the prohibition laid down in Art 34 TFEU solely because it is not based on decisions which are binding on businesses. Even measures which are not binding may be capable of influencing the conduct of traders and consumers and thus of frustrating the aims of the Community set out in Arts 2 and 3. The action of the Irish Government was a restrictive practice which represented the implementation of a programme defined by the Government and which affected the economy as a whole by encouraging the purchase of domestic products. Given that the Irish Government had provided some financial funding for the campaign, they were in breach of their obligations under the Treaty. The judgment in this case should not have come as a surprise to the Irish Government, as they had already been the subject of an Art 258 TFEU (then Art 169) action by the Commission in Case 113/80. In that case, the Court had held that the Irish Government had breached Art 34 TFEU (then Art 30) by imposing a legal requirement that imported 'souvenirs of Ireland' should bear either the name of their country of origin or the word 'foreign'.

(C) *CENTRAFARM v STERLING DRUG* – CASE 15/74

Sterling Drug was the parent company holding a number of patents in several countries, including the Netherlands and the UK, for a treatment of infections of the urinary passages. The trade mark Negram is used for this product. In the UK, the trademark was the property of Sterling-Winthrop Group Ltd and, in the Netherlands, Winthrop BV, a subsidiary of the UK company.

Centrafarm imported into the Netherlands from England and Germany some of the medicinal preparations manufactured according to the patent method and put onto the market by subsidiaries of Sterling Drug, some of which carried the trademark Negram. They did this without the agreement of Sterling Drug. By importing from the UK, Centrafarm had been able to take advantage of a considerable price differential. This was almost 50% of the price charged in the Netherlands.

In June 1971, Sterling Drug submitted an application to a Dutch judge sitting in chambers requiring Centrafarm to refrain from any further infringement of their patent. The judge refused, on the basis of his interpretation of the patent law. Sterling Drug succeeded on appeal, and the case finally came to the Dutch Supreme Court on appeal by Centrafarm. This Court used the preliminary reference procedure of Art 267 TFEU (then Art 177) to ask certain questions on patent rights in relation to the provisions of the Treaty.

The European Court accepted that the main issue was whether the Treaty rules on the free movement of goods prevented the patentee from ensuring that the product protected by the patent is not marketed by others. It referred to Art 34 TFEU (then Art 30) and the prohibition on quantitative restrictions on imports and all measures having equivalent effect. However, it recognised that Art 36 TFEU did allow such restrictions or prohibitions on the grounds justified for the protection of commercial or industrial property, which would include patents. This had to be read in conjunction with the last sentence of Art 36, which states that such restrictions shall not constitute a means of arbitrary discrimination or a disguised restriction on trade between Member States.

Given that the EC Treaty does not interfere with property rights, the Court looked at the exercise of those rights. Article 36 allows for the derogation from one of the fundamental principles of the Community, but only where the derogation is justified for the purposes of safeguarding rights which constitute the specific subject matter of the property. What are these rights in relation to patents? The Court answered that the specific subject matter of a patent was the guaranteed right of the patentee, as a reward for its creative effort, to manufacture and put into circulation its product for the first time. This could be done directly by the company or by the grant of licences to third parties. In relation to this right, the patent holder could seek enforcement of its rights.

What the Court was concerned to do was not to allow the exercise of a patentee's right to interfere with the development of the Community. If the patentee could prevent the importation of protected products marketed by him or with his consent in another Member State, he would be able to partition off national markets and thereby restrict trade between Member States. Therefore, the action of Sterling Drug, given that it was not necessary to protect their exclusive rights flowing from their patent, was incompatible with the Treaty provisions concerning the free movement of goods. This principle has been applied in subsequent cases, especially where drug companies have sought to use their property rights to block parallel imports from other Member States.

Competition Policy

INTRODUCTION

The competition policy of the European Union is seen as a very important safeguard to its development. Many of the questions set on this topic are of the problem type, notably on the application of Arts 101 and 102 TFEU. However, there are possible essay questions on the main principles, as illustrated by some of the questions in this chapter. It is also possible for questions to be set which have a competition element and relate to the free movement of goods, for example, the Robson Pharmaceutical problem in Question 25. In such circumstances, you can either split your answer between the topics or indicate the possible involvement of one but concentrate on the other.

Checklist ✔

You should have a clear knowledge of the differences between **Arts 101** and **102** and the role each plays in the competition policy of the EU. More specifically, you should understand the following points:

- the type of agreements dealt with by **Art 101 TFEU**;
- the possible exemptions under **Art 101 TFEU**;
- the meaning of dominant position under **Art 102 TFEU**;
- the control of mergers within the EU;
- the sanctions for anti-competitive behaviour;
- the control of public anti-competitive behaviour under **Arts 107** and **108 TFEU**;
- the role and powers of the European Commission; and
- the remedies available, including those provided by the national courts.

QUESTION 27

Dicero plc have been purchasing large quantities of manopull textiles from Smart International, a German company, for five years. They are the only manufacturers of this product and they control world sales by a system of licensing agreements.

Two years ago, they began imposing retail prices on all purchasers, including Dicero, and restricted the distribution areas any company could control. Dicero were allocated the UK market, whereas companies in France and Italy were given their domestic market plus a share of the world market.

For the last 12 months, Dicero have had discussions with Smart International to try to obtain some of the necessary export markets to allow for viable production levels. They have conceded nothing. In fact, they have stated that, unless Dicero sign a new agreement with them, they will give the UK market to the French company.

▶ Advise Dicero.

How to Answer this Question

This traditional problem question requires the application of Art 101TFEU, and the following specific points:

❖ the relationship between Community and national competition law;
❖ a definition of 'dominance' within the meaning of Art 102 TFEU;
❖ factors associated with dominance in fact;
❖ abuse of a dominant position; and
❖ remedies.

Answer Structure

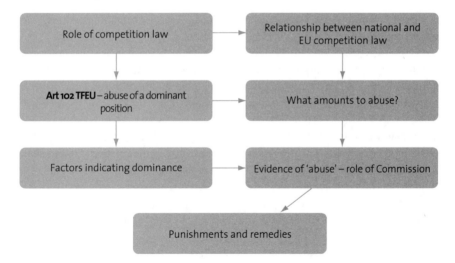

This diagram shows how to apply the law under Art 102 TFEU for Dicero.

ANSWER

This problem is concerned with one undertaking, Smart International, acting in a way which appears to be anti-competitive. The EU, having as one of its objectives the removal of barriers to trade between Member States, takes a strong policy against any undertaking which seeks to exercise economic power in the market in a way which sets up barriers to such trade. Under Art 102 TFEU, monopolies in themselves are not prohibited, but it does prohibit certain anti-competitive conduct by such organisations. The Article applies to either goods or services and has a scope that is not limited to those businesses which are established in the EU.

It would seem that Dicero plc may have a remedy under this provision of the Treaty. If they can prove that Smart International are acting in breach of Art 102 TFEU, such action is prohibited by the Article. In order to satisfy Art 102 TFEU, three essential ingredients must be proved. The undertaking must have a dominant position in the market, there must be an abuse of that position and that abuse must affect trade between Member States. If this last requirement is not met, the matter is left to be dealt with by the national competition laws of the Member State concerned.

In order to prove that Smart International are in a dominant position, Dicero need to satisfy the definition of dominance laid down by the ECJ in *United Brands Co v Commission* (1976). This case involved United Brands' position in the banana market. The Court said that dominance means a position of economic strength enjoyed by an undertaking which enables it to prevent effective competition in the relevant market because its strength allows it to act independently of its competitors, customers and ultimately its consumers. The Commission added to this, in *AKZO Chemie BV* (1986), that it may also involve the ability to eliminate or seriously weaken existing competitors, or to prevent potential competitors from entering the market.

Although this is the principle of dominance, it has to be looked at more closely if the rules of the Court are to be satisfied. It may be possible to say that this is the way that Smart International are acting, but are they in a dominant position?

Specifically, what is the market in which Dicero are claiming that Smart International are dominant? This is not as straightforward as it may appear, as the European Commission has found when seeking to apply Art 102. It is necessary to identify the relevant market. As far as the Court and Commission are concerned, this is a matter of product substitution. In the *Continental Can* case in 1972, a large Dutch packaging company was being taken over by a subsidiary of the Continental Can company based in the USA.

The Continental Can company was a large organisation in the packaging industry, controlling 86% of a German metal containers company, which it intended to transfer to the Dutch company if it acquired it. This would have meant that Continental Can would have had significant market power in Europe and specifically in Germany. However, although the Court agreed with the Commission that the takeover could be an abuse, the Commission had not looked at the relevant market. It had not taken into account product substitution. In other words, alternative suppliers of cans could adapt their production to produce cylindrical cans suitable for fish or those who purchased the cans could swap to a different shape or design. Such product substitution can be assessed by reference to the characteristics of the product, its price or the use to which it may be put. Are there any substitutes for manopull? What market is it in?

Although the Commission got the market wrong in *Continental Can*, in the bananas case of *United Brands* it satisfied the Court that the banana market was distinctive. In that case, United Brands had argued that the correct market was the fresh fruit market, in which they were not dominant. However, by means of information about buying habits of consumers and the special characteristics of bananas, the Commission was able to defeat this argument. Could Smart International argue that the consumer had alternative textiles to select from and therefore would not be disadvantaged by their actions? In the *Commercial Solvents* case in 1974, the Court stated that Art 102 TFEU (then Art 86) was concerned not only with abuses which prejudiced consumers directly, but also those abuses which impair the competitive structure of the market and thus affect consumers indirectly. It would appear that Smart International's action falls into this type of category. The Commission, supported by judgments of the Court, takes a hard line in seeking to protect competition in manufacturing and, in particular, to prevent smaller firms suffering at the hands of more powerful competitors. We are not told the size of Smart International or Dicero, but even where the relevant market has been quite small, as in the *Hugin Cash Registers* case, Art 102 has been applied, provided an undertaking has been dominant in the particular market.

If it is assumed that it is possible to identify the relevant market is Smart International behaving in a way that does not need to take into account its competitors, purchasers or consumers? In other words, is it dominant in fact? This requires a wide-ranging economic analysis of the market and Smart International. Following previous Commission decisions, four factors are taken into account. The first of these, and the most important, is market share. How big a share of the market does Smart International have? Second, how long has Smart International held this position in the market? Obviously, the longer the period of time, the greater the barriers to entry for new competitors or entrants to the market will be. Thirdly, the financial and technological resources of Smart International: can it use its resources to undercut potential rivals using predatory pricing or to maintain its technological advantage? Lastly, access to raw materials and outlets may give Smart International more power. Does it control not only raw materials and production, but also applications or retail outlets? This form of vertical integration within the business will be evidence of a dominant undertaking.

Finally, in order to come within Art 102 TFEU, it must also be proved that Smart International is dominant within the common market or in a substantial part of it. We are told that Smart International control sales worldwide but, more importantly, within the European Community, by means of licensing agreements. It is clear, therefore, that this criterion is satisfied.

Having identified that there is a dominant position, this does not mean that Art 102 has been satisfied. It is not sufficient to show that an undertaking is in a dominant position; Dicero must show that there has been an abuse. Article 102 TFEU provides a number of examples of abuse but this list is not to be considered exhaustive. It does illustrate what Dicero could prove. The problem states that Smart International is restricting the distribution area of each company granted a licence. More importantly, Smart International has threatened to refuse to supply Dicero if they refuse to sign the agreement. The refusal to supply in *United Brands* was found to be an abuse. In *Commercial Solvents*, the anti-competitive refusal to supply also amounted to an abuse. This will not always be the situation if the refusal is based on objective criteria and is non-discriminatory. It does not appear that this would be the case with Smart International.

If an undertaking is found to be abusing its dominant position, there is no possibility of exemption as there is with restrictive practices under Art 101. Fines can be imposed by the Commission for breach of Art 102 TFEU. ranging from €1,000 to €1 million, or 10% of the undertaking's turnover. The large fines can be illustrated by the 1.06 billion euros imposed in 2011 on Intel for having abused its dominant position by employing conditional rebates and imposing restrictions. The threat over Dicero may make them reluctant to wait for action to be taken by the European Commission against Smart International. Article 102 TFEU is directly effective and can be applied in the national courts. There has been some reluctance in national courts to do this, because of the detailed economic analysis indicated above, which is often necessary in Art 102 cases. However, breach of Art 102 should lead to the application of the same remedies as are available for similar breaches of national law. Therefore, it would be appropriate for Dicero to seek an injunction or a declaration in interlocutory proceedings. In the case of *Courage Ltd v Crehan* (2002) the ECJ recognised the right of an individual to claim damages before a national court for breaches of Art 102, and this could provide another remedy for Dicero.

QUESTION 28

Bakers is a successful chain of supermarkets with 55 stores in the north-west region. It has recently expanded the range of cosmetics and hopes to complement this by adding perfumes.

Unfortunately for Bakers, it has been refused supplies of exclusive brands by Ouvert, producers of one of the most popular ranges of French perfumes. This could damage the success of the new venture by Bakers, so it has contacted the marketing director at Ouvert requesting an explanation as to why their orders to various Ouvert distributors have been refused. The explanation given by the French company was that Bakers was not on the list of exclusive outlets used by Ouvert because they cannot provide the personal service required for Ouvert brands, and last Christmas they had sold the Ouvert perfumes obtained from a third party at a cut price, causing complaints from recognised Ouvert outlets in the region.

Bakers has written to Ouvert stating that its legal advice is that the refusal to supply them is a breach of EU competition law and that a complaint will be made to the European Commission and legal action taken if necessary to obtain supplies of the perfumes. In response to this letter Ouvert replied that they received a letter from the European Commission some years ago about their exclusive distribution agreements and this informed them that no action would be taken as there was no breach of Art 101, and the Commission considered the matter closed.

▶ What advice can you provide to Bakers with regard to what action, if any, it can now take in this matter?

How to Answer this Question

This question concerns Art 101 TFEU and the kinds of restrictive practices which have been identified under EC competition policy as being anti-competitive. You should cover the following points:

❖ the relationship between Arts 101 and 102 TFEU;
❖ types of agreements covered by Art 101 TFEU;
❖ the effect of Art 101 TFEU;
❖ possible exemption under Art 101 TFEU;
❖ guidance letters (previously comfort letters);
❖ the role of the national courts;
❖ remedies.

Answer Structure

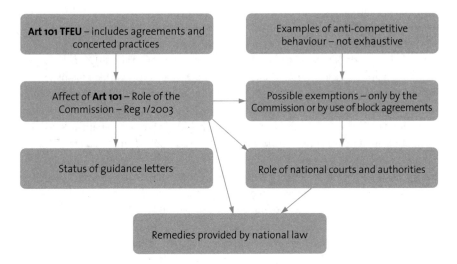

This diagram shows how to apply the law under Art 101 TFEU for Baker.

ANSWER

The Community is very concerned to safeguard legitimate competition undertaken by businesses such as Bakers. This is achieved by Treaty articles which deal specifically with restrictive trade practices (Art 101 TFEU) and monopoly situations (Art 102 TFEU). For Art 102 to be involved there has to be 'an undertaking which is in a dominant position' in the market for particular goods and abuses that position. Although Ouvert may have an exclusive range of perfumes, there are alternatives, indicating that it does not have a dominant position in the market for perfumes generally so it would seem that Art 101 dealing with restrictive trade practices is the area of competition policy that could be involved. If Ouvert is in breach of Art 101 TFEU, its action will be considered anti-competitive and therefore contrary to EU law, subject to the possibility of exemption under Art 101(3) TFEU.

Article 101 covers agreements which have as their object or effect the prevention, restriction or distortion of competition within the common market. A fundamental question: is there is an agreement between Ouvert and its distributors which is making it difficult for Bakers to obtain supplies of the perfumes? The agreement does not have to be a formal written one to fall within Art 101, because it also covers concerted practices, which include 'gentlemen's agreements'. In *ICI v EC Commission* (1972), the ECJ defined such practices as a form of co-ordination between enterprises that has not yet reached the point where there is a contract in the true sense of the word, but which in practice consciously substitutes a practical co-operation for the risk of competition. Therefore, because there are a number of recognised distributors for Ouvert perfumes, there must be an agreement between the parties, even if we are not told what form it takes.

It is clear that such agreements entered into by Ouvert are within the scope of Art 101, but are they amongst those identified as being incompatible with the common market? Article 101 lists a number of examples of such agreements which impede the free movement of goods or services throughout the Community and thus distort competition within the market. The list is not exhaustive, but it does include one which seems to apply to the situation facing Bakers. This is where the agreement directly or indirectly fixes purchase or selling prices, or any other trading conditions. It would seem from this that there is one aspect of the problem facing Bakers which is covered: namely, selective distribution agreements. This is the term used by the European Commission for sales conducted through a network of authorised dealers or outlets. Only certain selected dealers are admitted to the network, and only they may receive supplies. This type of agreement is often very attractive to manufacturers because, quite legitimately, it gives them control over the way in which their product is sold, and can help them maintain an upmarket image and sell their goods at a premium retail price. It is stated in the problem that one of the reasons for Ouvert refusing to supply Bakers is the fact that they had previously sold their products at below the price indicated by Ouvert, generating complaints from other outlets in the region. If an agreement comes within Art 101 it is automatically void. This means that the agreement can only be implemented at the risk of the parties to it. It can also mean that if action is taken by the European Commission under Regulation 1/2003, the parties to the agreement, notably Ouvert in this problem, could be heavily fined by the Commission. The fine could amount to €1 million, or 10% of the company's worldwide turnover, whichever is the greater. In the Vitamins Cartel the Commission imposed a fine of over 855 million euros.

However, although Art 101 states that all such agreements are void, it gives the Commission the power to grant exemptions. What the Commission looks for in the agreement is a contribution to the improvement of production or distribution of goods, or the promotion of technical or economic progress, with the proviso that customers are allowed a fair share of the resulting benefit. It is also necessary that the restrictions in the agreement go no further than is necessary for the objectives to be achieved and it does not provide the possibility of eliminating competition in respect of a substantial part of the products in question. If Ouvert had sought an individual exemption, it would have had to prove that the agreement with the outlets met these conditions; obtaining an individual exemption is a lengthy process and Ouvert does not indicate that it had entered into an exemption application with the Commission, or tried to conform to any block exemption. However, Ouvert does indicate that it entered into some correspondence with the Commission about their distribution agreements, but what is the status of the letter it received? Was it what is known as a 'guidance letter', a device used by the Commission following informal discussions based on information provided by an undertaking and indicating that in their view no infringement of Art 101 TFEU was taking place? Such letters do not grant exemption and were a means by which the Commission attempted to reduce its workload, as confirmed by the ECJ in the *Perfume* cases in 1980. They were merely an administrative letter and were not binding on the Commission, who could reopen the file at any time, or the national courts which could consider a complaint for breach of Art 101. However, a new framework for competition law was established in Regulation 1/2003, and the Commission no longer issues such 'comfort letters', although it may issue a 'guidance letter' covering novel questions concerning Arts 101 or 102 TFEU. The outcome for Bakers is that the letter referred to by Ouvert is not legally binding and does not provide any defence to its refusal to supply the perfumes.

It would seem that the refusal by Ouvert to supply Bakers is contrary to Art 101. Is there any action open to Bakers? It would be possible to complain to the European Commission on the expectation that they will utilise the machinery under Regulation 1/2003 to enforce Art 101. However, this would be a lengthy business, and a speedier remedy should be considered. Bakers has threatened legal action, so this may be a possibility. As the letter from the Commission mentioned by Ouvert is not legally binding, it is not possible to go to the ECJ to seek its annulment under Art 263 in an action for judicial review, but national courts are required to apply Art 101 as it is directly effective (*BRT v SABAM* (1974)), thus providing the best course of action for Bakers. The national court will be able to use the conditions listed in Art 101(3) to decide amongst other things whether the agreement affords the undertakings the possibility of eliminating competition in respect of a substantial part of the products in question, namely the Ouvert perfumes (*M6 & Others v*

Commission (2001)). If the agreement is found by the court to be incompatible, then it is void, because only the European Commission can grant an exemption, not the court. Thus the remedies available in national courts for breach of Art 101 are those remedies available for similar breaches of national law (*Rewe-Zentralfinanz* (1976)), although the court will not have the power to order fines. In the case of Bakers the remedy will be an injunction or a declaration in interlocutory proceedings, and possibly damages. In the UK, the possibility of the court awarding damages for breach of Art 101 remained uncertain following the case of *Garden Cottage Foods Ltd v Milk Marketing Board* (1984), but this has been cleared up by the case of *Courage Ltd v Crehan* (2002). In this case the ECJ recognised the right of an individual to claim damages before a national court for breaches of Art 101.

QUESTION 29

Why does the EU need a competition policy? How effective is it?

How to Answer this Question

This straightforward essay-type question requires the following points to be covered:

- ❖ the basis of EU competition policy;
- ❖ Arts 101, 102, 107 and 108 TFEU;
- ❖ procedures under Regulation 1/2003;
- ❖ power to issue decisions and levy fines by the European Commission and the system of appeals to the CFI; and
- ❖ control of the Commission's exercise of powers via actions for annulment (Art 263 TFEU) and damages (Art 340 TFEU).

Answer Structure

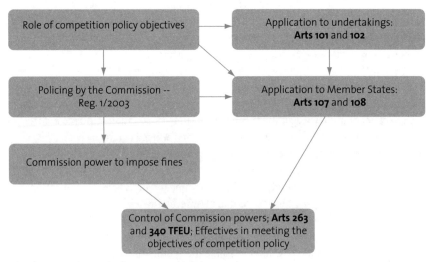

This diagram shows the key points to be discussed.

ANSWER

The EU is based on the acceptance by the Member States that they will operate free market economies within the territory of the Union. Article 3 TEU refers to a high degree of competitiveness because competition is the best stimulant of economic activity since it is said to guarantee the widest possible freedom of action. The Treaty does not define the concept of 'competition' but refers to certain measures which interfere with competition and are therefore prohibited, subject to exemptions granted by the Commission. Thus Art 3 sets as one of the objectives of the Community, the institution of a system ensuring that competition in the common market is not distorted. Competition policy is another instrument which the Community can use to ensure that objectives set out in the Treaty are obtained. For example, that economic integration will take place to produce 'one common market'. In this way the growth in the standard of living and quality of life of the citizens of the Union should be achieved.

The Treaty applies to all competitive activity whether undertaken by individuals, businesses or governments. The chapter of the Treaty dealing with competition contains mainly two sets of rules, reflecting this private and public economic activity which takes place. Articles 101 and 102 apply to enterprises which might be involved in restrictive practices or which are abusing a dominant position within the market. Articles 107 and 108 cover aid granted by Member States. However, in addition to the Treaty specifying anti-competitive activity there needs to be a means of policing and enforcing it. Each Member State has its own policies and agencies that deal with competition because there is some 'domestic or national' anti-competitive activity that does not come within the dimension of European law because it is minor or does not have the potential to affect trade between Member States. The competition agencies in Member States work closely with the European Commission but it is the Commission that is charged by the Treaty with enforcing Community competition policy. It has the power to issue decisions which are binding upon those to whom they are addressed under the definitions in Art 288 TFEU.

The Commission's powers relate to four main areas. It has the power to collect information, to grant exemption under Art 101, to impose fines and to make interim measures. The powers it has and the procedures it must follow are laid down in Regulation 1/2003. These substantial powers are necessary if the Commission is to fulfil its role. However, the procedural requirements are strict under Regulation 1/2003 and there is a general duty of confidentiality because they are dealing with commercially sensitive information. A breach of these duties or procedures can result in an action being brought under Art 263 before the Court of Justice, and ultimately the Commission decision can be annulled. It is also possible for an action for damages to be brought against the Commission, as happened in *Adams* (1986). Adams brought an action under the-then Art 288 EC (now Art 340 TFEU) against the Commission for breach of confidentiality when they allowed it to be disclosed to his employers, Hoffman-La Roche that he had assisted them.

Article 101 deals with restrictive practices such as price fixing, refusal to supply or limiting the market. Here the Commission's task is to monitor agreements with a view to granting negative clearance or exemption. To do this the Commission needs information supplied by the applicant and other parties. The Commission has the power to impose fines not exceeding 1 per cent of turnover where applicants intentionally or negligently supply incorrect or misleading information. The power of granting exemption under Art 101(3) is only given to the Commission. Before doing so the Commission must publish a summary of the relevant application or notification and all interested parties must be invited to submit their comments. If the final decision is adverse to the applicant, the Commission must give him an opportunity to be heard on the matters to which he objects. Due to the need to speed up the process of considering applications for exemption, the Commission has issued a number of block exemptions which allow undertakings to arrange their business affairs so as not to be in breach of competition policy.

In order to make a decision related to Community competition policy under Art 102, the Commission normally needs further information in order to come to an opinion on the legality of the behaviour in question. There are two basic ways to obtain this information, by either investigations or written requests for information. For example, if the Commission is investigating the behaviour of a dominant firm, it may write not only to the company concerned but to the smaller undertakings that have dealings with the company. If the replies from the undertakings are incorrect or incomplete the Commission has the right to impose fines. On some occasions it is necessary to undertake detailed market analysis and to this end the Commission has been given exhaustive powers. The Commission may conduct general enquiries into whole sectors of the economy if economic trends suggest that competition within the common market is being restricted or distorted. Additional information may be requested from governments or competent authorities in Member States. In all these instances the Commission can request any information which it considers 'necessary' to enable it to carry out its tasks. In addition to requesting information, the Commission can seek it by carrying out on-the-spot investigations. These include the power to enter premises, examine books or business records, to copy such records and to conduct oral examinations. These investigations may be 'voluntary' or 'compulsory'. Where they are compulsory, Commission officials are required to produce a decision specifying the subject matter and purpose of the investigation. Normally, the Commission will resort to an unannounced visit where a serious risk exists that the undertakings, if forewarned of the inspection, will destroy any incriminating evidence. In *National* (1980), a 'dawn raid' had taken place at National Panasonic's offices, with a search and seizure operation having taken place before the company's lawyers could arrive. National claimed that although the raid was authorised by a decision under Regulation 1/2003, some prior warning should have been given. The Court of Justice, hearing an action under Art 263 to have the decision annulled, disagreed. They held that under the regulation the Commission was entitled to undertake such investigations as are necessary to bring to light any breaches of Arts 101 and 102 (formerly 85 and 86). However, it is for the Court to control the investigative powers of the Commission as was stated in another case involving a 'dawn raid' (*Hoechst* (1989)). In some instances the Commission may request the competent authority of the Member State, such as the Office of Fair Trading, to carry out necessary investigations on its behalf. All undertakings are bound to comply with the legitimate demands of the Commission even if the information is self-incriminating. If they fail to co-operate or give false or misleading information they are liable to penalties.

The Commission has the power to impose fines of up to €1 million or 10% of the world annual turnover of the undertaking, whichever is the larger, where Arts 101 or 102 TFEU have been infringed. This applies whether the infringement has arisen intentionally or negligently. The amount of the fine will depend upon the seriousness of the behaviour, its duration and the size of the undertaking involved. A deliberate infringement will normally deserve a heavier fine than where an undertaking has been purely negligent. The Commission has not been hesitant in using its power to impose fines. In the Vitimins Cartel in 2001, a fine of over 855 million euros was imposed for breach of Art 101 TFEU and in 2011 a fine of 1.06 billion euros was imposed on Intel for a breach of Art 102 TFEU. Any fine levied is paid to the Commission and no amount of it goes to the injured victim of the anti-competitive practice. They must seek a remedy in their national courts. The General Court, under Art 261 TFEU, has unlimited jurisdiction with regard to fines. Where the amount of the fine is being challenged, this will normally be done by way of proceedings under Art 263 TFEU to annul the decision imposing it.

In relation to the competition policy of the European Union, the Commission does have very wide powers because the policy raises complex issues which may take up to two years before they are resolved. In some instances such a delay may cause irreparable damage to some of the undertakings. To deal with this possibility the Commission is given the power to take immediate action in the form of interim measures to stop objectionable behaviour. These measures are of a temporary nature aimed at safeguarding the status quo, as in the *Camera Care* case in 1980. In the exercise of all these powers the Commission is subject to the law of the Community, including the general principles of Community law which have been identified by the Court. The Court of First Instance has the power to confirm, reduce, cancel or increase fines and penalty payments imposed by the Commission. As all legally binding actions by the Commission are required to be made by decisions, these can be challenged before the Court of Justice via an action under Art 263 TFEU (formerly Art 173). There is, therefore, clear judicial control of the Commission to ensure that it exercises its powers within European Union law. Given the identified need in Art 119(1) TFEU for the Union to have an open market economy with free competition, the powers given to the Commission are necessary to achieve this. The Commission is only concerned where the competition rules have been abused or infringed. It recognises that European companies have to compete in the global market but the Commission wants to see a balance between the need for profits and the benefits to the consumer. As the competition policy of the EU has extraterritoriality and is imposed on all companies trading within the EU regardless of their country of registration, the policy has been very effective in maintaining that balance.

NOTE

This answer concentrates on the powers associated with Arts 101 and 102. It would be possible to concentrate more on Arts 107 and 108 as there are an increasing number of actions being taken by the Commission against the governments of Member States who are attempting to shield sectors of their economies from competition.

> ### Aim Higher ★
> The first part of this question is quite straightforward so to gain the extra marks concentrate on developing your answer to the 'effective' part of the question.

QUESTION 30

What is meant by 'an abuse of a dominant position'?

How to Answer this Question

This is a very popular type of question. It is straightforward, but you should cover the following points:

- ❖ Art 102 TFEU and the EU competition policy;
- ❖ the role of the Commission;
- ❖ definition of 'dominant position' from *Continental Can* (1972); and
- ❖ the decision in *United Brands*-Case 27/76.

Answer Structure

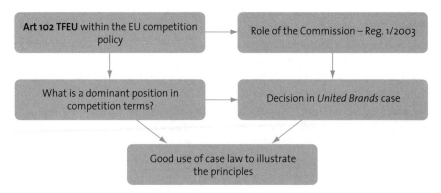

This diagram shows the key points to be discussed.

ANSWER

The term 'dominant position' is associated with Art 102 and the policy against anti-competitive behaviour by businesses. There is nothing in Community law which does not allow for a dominant position to be established. What Art 102 TFEU is concerned with is the abuse of that dominant position within the common market or a substantial part of it. It is designed to restrain the conduct by a dominant firm that harms those with whom it deals. Such an abuse is prohibited, in so far as it may affect trade between Member States.

In *Continental Can* (1972), the Commission defined its view of a dominant position. It said that undertakings are in a dominant position when they have the power to behave independently without taking into account their competitors, purchasers or suppliers. This arises due to the undertaking's share of the market or because of the availability of technical knowledge, raw materials or capital in addition to market share. It does not mean that there should be an absolute domination, in the sense that the undertaking can eliminate all other competitors. It is enough that its market strength allows it an overall independence of behaviour. The concept of dominance was developed further in *AKZO Chemie BV* (1986), in which the Commission stated that the ability to eliminate or seriously weaken existing competitors or to prevent potential competitors from entering the market may be involved in a dominant position.

In *Continental Can*, the Court insisted that the Commission analyse an undertaking's market power in two steps. First, it needed to define the relevant market and, second, it should assess the undertaking's dominance within that market. This is not an easy exercise, because markets are not always easy to identify. If the market is given a narrow definition, perhaps ignoring the possible substitutes available, it may indicate a large market share, which overstates the market power of the undertaking's product. If a wide definition is given to the market, the undertaking's market share is understated. The Court is quite stringent in requiring the Commission to define the relevant market and to give reasons for its definition. In the *Continental Can v Commission* case, the Commission's finding that the Continental Can company was in a dominant position over the supply of cans and closures used for meat and fish products was not accepted by the Court.

The main problem was that the Commission had not paid sufficient attention to substitute products. The meat and fish suppliers could turn to glass or plastic containers, or the manufacturers of cylindrical cans could move towards the production of the flat cans traditionally used for meat and fish products. In the *United Brands* case, the company sought to prove that the Commission had got the market wrong once more. However, the Court accepted that the Commission was right in identifying the relevant market as that of bananas. Although United Brands said that the relevant market was that of fresh fruit, in which they were not dominant, the Commission showed that bananas were consumed particularly by the very young, the old and the sick and were little affected by the pricing and consumption of other fruit.

It is clear that establishing dominance within a particular product market requires detailed economic analysis. From this analysis, a number of factors are used to determine dominance. The market share held by the undertaking is a crucial factor when determining dominance. In the *Continental Can* case, for example, the company had 80% of the German market. *United Brands* had 45% of the banana market, so it is possible to see the wide variation in market share which can be involved. The Commission considers that a share of between 20% and 40% may amount to dominance in certain markets. The period of time in which the undertaking has held its position in the market will be important. What are the financial and technical resources of the 'dominant' undertaking? Can it eliminate competitors by intensive advertising campaigns or by predatory pricing? The access to raw materials and markets can also be important. In the *United Brands* case, the company was vertically integrated, owning plantation, shipping, storage and distribution businesses for bananas. In *Commercial Solvents*, the company, which refused to supply another Italian company with aminobutanol, had a near-monopoly in its production. The refusal to supply in this case is an example of the final factor which may determine dominance, namely, the behaviour of the firm. A firm's behaviour may indicate that it is dominant within the definition given above from the *Continental Can* case, that is, it is able to act independently of its competitors, customers and, ultimately, consumers. Another example would be the discriminatory pricing system used by United Brands.

Article 102 TFEU is only infringed where dominance is within the common market or a substantial part of it. It is not entirely clear how large an area, or what proportion of supply, amounts to a 'substantial part of the common market'. In *Sugar* (1975), the Court stated that the pattern and volume of the production and consumption of a particular product as well as the habits and economic opportunities of vendors and purchasers must be considered. The Commission provided some useful guidance on the relevant geographical market in its Notice on Agreements of Minor Importance, where it noted that the cost of transport is particularly important. It is also necessary to consider the temporal aspect when looking at the question of dominance. The time of year can have a large impact on a particular market, especially when looking at fresh produce.

As indicated earlier, it is not the dominance in fact which **Art 102 TFEU** is designed to deal with, but the abuse of that dominant position. What amounts to an abuse under **Art 102**? The Article itself does give some examples of anti-competitive behaviour, but the list is not intended to be exhaustive. There are two main categories of abuse: exploitative and anti-competitive. Exploitative abuses arise where the dominant undertaking takes advantage of its position by imposing harsh or unfair trading conditions. The most common examples of these are unfair prices, unfair trading conditions, discriminatory treatment and refusal to supply. Unfair price was defined in *United Brands* as a price which bears no reasonable relation to the economic value of the product. Although the Court did not state its opinion on the point, the Commission argued that United Brands were charging excessively high prices for their Chiquita brand of bananas. When United

Brands refused to allow importers to sell the bananas when they were still green, they were found to be imposing unfair trading conditions. This was despite United Brands' argument that they imposed this requirement to ensure that the consumer obtained a better product. Some of the prices charged by United Brands differed by up to 100% in different Member States, such was their power to impose discriminatory pricing. Finally, United Brands refused to supply one of its main customers who had invested heavily in the appropriate plant and buildings, because it had taken part in an advertising campaign for a competitor. Such is the power of the undertaking in a dominant position.

Anti-competitive abuses are less easy to prove than exploitative abuses. They are not usually so harsh, but they have the same effect, in that they reduce or eliminate competition, for example, the tying-in agreement which came before the Court in *Hoffman-La Roche* (1977). This undertaking had a dominant position in seven separate vitamin markets. Customers undertook to buy all or most of their requirements from La Roche as part of tying-in agreements. As a 'reward', such companies received fidelity rebates in the form of discounts. The agreements also included 'English' clauses, which allowed a customer who found suppliers offering similar products elsewhere to ask La Roche to match these prices. If La Roche failed to do so, the company was free to purchase the products elsewhere. Although not oppressive for the companies concerned, the Commission found that these tying-in agreements limited their customers' freedom to buy from alternative suppliers. Once the alternative suppliers had been identified, La Roche was of a size to be able to take pre-emptive action to remove its competitor. Both the Commission and the Court found these practices to be abusive.

The kind of predatory pricing used by La Roche is another example of anti-competitive abuse. In *AKZO Chemie BV* (1986), a firm in a dominant position in the production of organic peroxides used this strategy where prices are reduced below cost in order to drive potential competitors out of the market. Other examples of anti-competitive abuse include refusal to supply, exclusive reservation of activities and import and export bans. In *Continental Can*, the Commission applied **Art 102 TFEU** (then **Art 86**) in the context of a proposed merger or takeover. The Commission's decision said that the proposed takeover constituted an abuse of their dominant position within the common market, that is, in Germany. Such a case is unlikely to happen now under **Art 102 TFEU** as there is now **Regulation 139/2004**, a special measure to deal with mergers and acquisitions.

QUESTION 31

Analyse TWO of the following cases that came before the ECJ, and explain their importance in the development of Community law:

(a)   *Consten and Grundig v Commission* – Cases 56 and 58/64;

(b)   *ICI (Dyestuff)* – Case 48/69;

(c)   *United Brands* – Case 27/76.

How to Answer this Question

When approaching a question like this, the temptation is to produce too descriptive an answer. The facts are important, but are only one element of the answer. You should deal with the following:

❖   the facts, the legal points raised and the decision of the Court;

❖   the kind of case it was – whether a preliminary reference or a direct action and which Article of the Treaty it was based upon;

❖   the cases chosen for this type of question have usually played their part in developing or reinforcing European Court judgments – what part has this case played?

Answer Structure

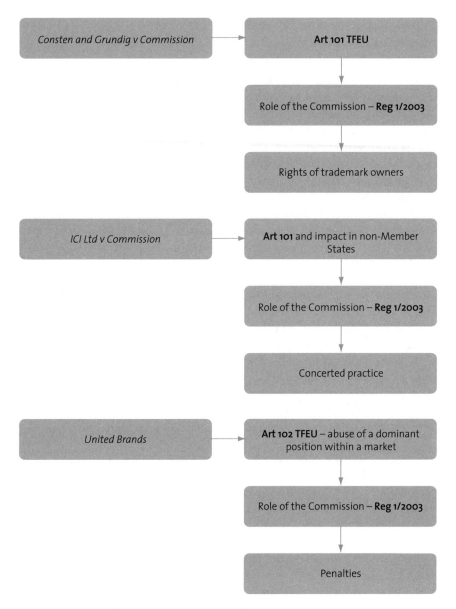

This diagram shows the key points to be discussed.

ANSWER

(A) *CONSTEN AND GRUNDIG v COMMISSION –* CASES 56 AND 58/64

This case concerned attempts by private traders to carve up the internal market in the face of one of the fundamental objectives of the Community: the removal of national barriers to trade. Consten was a French firm of wholesalers for electrical products. Grundig was a German firm which manufactured radios, television sets and similar products in Germany. The reason the two cases are joined is because they both arose from the exclusive distribution contract made between the two businesses in 1957. Under this contract, Grundig promised not to deliver to any other French distributor and to include in any contract they entered into with other firms .elsewhere a clause preventing their goods from being transferred to France. Consten promised in return to buy Grundig's products, and not from any other competitors, and not to deliver outside France. One final fact was that the products subject to the contract all carried the trade mark GINT, that is, Grundig International. Consten registered this mark in France with Grundig's consent.

Two important events happened subsequent to this contract in 1957. First, in 1958, the Treaty of Rome, setting up the European Community, came into force and with it the Articles dealing with anti-competitive activity. In 1962, Regulation 17 was adopted (now replaced by Regulation 1/2003), which provided the machinery for the Commission to deal with any anti-competitive behaviour. Under this regulation, agreements like the one between Grundig and Consten had to be registered. This was done by Grundig. Second, also at this time, French competitors were getting Grundig products into France and selling them at lower prices. Consten had sued a number of these businesses in the French courts for unfair competition and infringement of their trade mark.

Acting under Regulation 17, the Commission, in 1964, took a decision addressed to Grundig and Consten stating that their contract was in breach of Art 101 (then Art 85(1)). They were forbidden to hinder the acquisition by competitors of the goods covered by the contract for resale in France. The firms wished to challenge these decisions, which they did under Art 263 TFEU (then Art 173) in an action for annulment. Article 101 TFEU prohibits agreements which may affect trade between Member States and which have as their object or effect the prevention, restriction or distortion of competition within the common market. Grundig and Consten claimed that they were not competitors and so there was never any question of them promising not to compete with each other. Supported by the Italian Government, they argued that the word 'agreement' in Art 101 (then Art 85) only applied to contracts between competitors at the same level – horizontal agreements. However, the Court held that Art 101 TFEU refers in a general way to all agreements which distort competition within the common market. Therefore, as the Treaty does not make a distinction between the level at which the firms operate or whether they are competitors or not, such a distinction cannot be implied into the Treaty.

Competition can be distorted within the meaning of Art 101 by agreements which prevent or restrict competition between one of them and third parties. The contract created an unjustified advantage at the expense of the consumer, contrary to the aims of Art 101 TFEU.

The firms also argued that the Art 101 reference to 'affect' meant affect in a detrimental way, ie, for the worse. The contract, they argued, strengthened Grundig and allowed for greater competition between them and their rival manufacturers. The Court held that what is important is whether the agreement is capable of constituting a threat, either direct or indirect, actual or potential, to freedom of trade between Member States in a manner which might harm the attainment of the objectives of a single market between States. Thus, the fact that the agreement encouraged an increase in the volume of trade between States is not sufficient to exclude the possibility that the agreement may 'affect' such trade, especially as Consten was prohibited from re-exporting to other Member States.

The final argument put forward against the Commission's decision was that Consten owned the trade mark in France. Under Art 345 TFEU (then Art 222), it is stated that the Treaty does not prejudice the rules in Member States governing the system of property ownership. Yet, the Commission's decision had stopped Consten's use of its trade mark protection to prevent parallel imports of Grundig products. The Court's view was that the GINT trade mark was intended to place an obstacle in the way of parallel imports. As the agreement was void under Art 101 (then Art 85(2)), this would be ineffective if the trade mark could still be used by Consten to achieve the same objective. There is a distinction between the rights inherent in a trade mark, which are recognised by Art 345, and the exercise of those rights. The rights of the owner of a trade mark are limited, to the extent that the exercise of those rights may infringe Art 101.

(B) *ICI LTD v EC COMMISSION* – CASE 48/69

This case, which is often called the *Dyestuff* case, involves the competition policy of the European Community and, in particular, Art 101 TFEU. This Article is concerned with restrictive practices arising from agreements and concerted practices which affect trade between Member States. However, what amounts to a concerted practice was one of the key questions in this case.

ICI was among the undertakings producing aniline dyestuffs which together accounted for 85% of the market. There had been three uniform price increases introduced almost simultaneously in 1964, 1965 and 1967. The increases covered the same product. In January 1964, there was a 10% increase, followed in autumn 1964 by a 10–15% increase which was to come into effect in January 1965. At a meeting in Basle in August 1967, one of the producers announced an 8% increase and two other producers subsequently announced a similar increase. The Commission concluded that there had been a concerted practice between the undertakings, and using its powers to enforce the

Community's competition policy it imposed fines on all the undertakings involved. The undertakings challenged the Commission's decision by a direct action before the European Court under Art 263 TFEU (then Art 173). They claimed that the price increases merely reflected parallel behaviour associated with an oligopolistic market, where each producer followed the price leader.

The Court upheld the Commission's decision. In its judgment, the Court stated that the inclusion of concerted practices in addition to agreements between undertakings in Art 101 (then Art 85) was for a specific purpose. The object is to bring within the prohibition of the Article a form of co-ordination between undertakings which, without having reached the stage where an agreement properly so called has been concluded, knowingly substitutes practical co-operation between them for the risks of competition. The behaviour of the participants is therefore important, because it is that which is identified as the concerted practice. However, the Court recognised that this behaviour could not be conclusive, but it was strong evidence to suggest that the market was not 'operating normally', having regard to the nature of the products, the size and number of undertakings involved and the market volume they controlled. This idea of the 'normal conditions' of the market has been criticised, as it does not take into account the type of activity which occurs in oligopolistic markets, although on the facts of the case it is very difficult to find any support for the dyestuff producers.

The identification of a concerted practice requires the evidence provided by the Commission to be considered as a whole, taking into account the parties involved and the specific features of the market for the product in question, that is, the freedom of the consumers to choose their supplier. In this instance, the general and uniform increase in prices can only be explained by a common intention on the part of the undertakings. This intention was to adjust the price level and to avoid the risk which could accompany such price increases of changing the conditions of competition.

(C) *UNITED BRANDS* – CASE 27/76

United Brands Co is a conglomerate owned by a company based in the USA. It is the world's largest seller of bananas. In the opinion of the European Commission, United Brands holds a dominant position in the banana market in a substantial part of the European Community. This is based upon the fact that it handles 40% of the trade in bananas in the EU and has overwhelming economic power based upon the vertical integration of its banana business. United Brands owns numerous plantations in tropical banana-growing countries and a fleet of refrigerated banana boats. In addition, it controls banana ripening in consumer countries and takes direct charge of the advertising campaigns and sales promotion activities related to its brand, Chiquita. It is the only firm to have all these advantages in the banana market, and is thus in a position to use them to place major obstacles in the way of effective competition in the banana market.

The European Commission reached the decision that United Brands was abusing its dominant position, contrary to Art 102 TFEU (then Art 86). This was based upon a number of points, including:

(a) United Brands prohibited its distributors and ripeners from selling green bananas, which meant there was market fragmentation;

(b) it charged its customers prices which differed according to the Member State in which they were located. Such differences could amount to 100%, although there were no objective reasons for this discrimination;

(c) it charged unfair prices for sales to its customers in Germany, Denmark and the Benelux countries; and

(d) finally, for no objectively valid reason, it refused, for nearly two years, to supply one of its main Danish customers.

The Commission considered these to be serious violations of Art 102 TFEU (then Art 86) and imposed a heavy fine of €1m and ordered United Brands to put an end to its infringements. The importance of this case lies in the fact that the Commission investigated United Brands' entire marketing policy in the light of Art 102, perhaps because of the problems it had experienced in *Continental Can* (1972). They were not attacking the commercial dynamism of United Brands, which is not contrary to Art 102, but because a dominant firm has an obligation not to indulge in business practices which are at variance with the goals of the Community's competition policy. It is not being in a dominant position which is contrary to Art 102, but the abuse of that position.

United Brands appealed to the European Court against the decision of the Commission, seeking its annulment under Art 263 (then Art 173). They claimed that the 'relevant market' identified by the Commission was too narrow and should have been the fresh fruit, rather than the banana market. The Court upheld the Commission's choice of bananas as the relevant market. However, it quashed the Commission's decision that United Brands' prices were excessive, because the Commission should at least have asked United Brands about its costs. Overall, the Court upheld the Commission's decision, including its condemnation of United Brands' refusal to supply, although the fine was reduced to €850,000. The definition of a dominant position given in the Court's judgment has been followed very closely in subsequent cases involving infringements of Art 102. The definition is that a dominant position involves economic strength, which enables an undertaking to prevent effective competition and to act independently of its competitors, customers and ultimately of consumers.

QUESTION 32

Critically review the Commission's application of the Merger Regulation.

How to Answer this Question

It is quite rare to have a problem question set on mergers, although this may change as the case law on the Merger Regulation develops. Where questions are set they are generally this type of essay. The main points which should be covered in your answer are:

❖ the role of Arts 101 and 102 TFEU (formerly Arts 85 and 86 EC) in merger policy;
❖ the need for a specific merger policy;
❖ the Merger Regulation 139/2004;
❖ the requirements of the regulation;
❖ the benefits of the regulation;
❖ the case law of the General Court with regard to the Merger Regulation.

Answer Structure

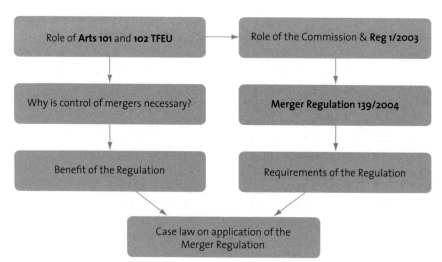

This diagram shows the key points to be discussed.

ANSWER

Although the competition policy of the EU has a strong emphasis against restrictive practices or the abuse of a dominant position, these are not the only activities that EU law seeks to control. There are also activities of Member States or mergers of public companies that can be seen to be anti-competitive. EU law seeks to control or limit these in so far as they impact on the Community. The competence to deal with mergers is given to the Commission under Regulation 139/2004. This regulation replaced the previous regulations to facilitate greater procedural harmony in the assessment of different types of concentrations. If a proposed merger qualifies as a concentration, the next question is whether it has a 'Community dimension'. The test for this is one of sales or turnover. Art 1(3) provides that those mergers involving a worldwide turnover of €2,500 million where the aggregate Community turnover is more than €100 million will be subject to examination by the European Commission. Such mergers must be notified to the Commission and so this has increased the supervision role of that institution.

Mergers can be categorised into horizontal, vertical and conglomerate mergers. Horizontal mergers arise where companies make the same products and operate in the same level of the market. Vertical mergers are those where the undertakings operate at different levels but in the same product market. Lastly, conglomerate mergers are where there is no connection between the businesses in any product market. With regard to the impact on competition, it is horizontal mergers that have the most damaging potential.

It is the European Commission that has the responsibility to police the competition policy of the European Community, including that relating to mergers. Within the Competition Directorate DG IV, there is the Merger Task Force (MTF), which oversees merger control within the EU. For the policy to be effective there has to be notification by the companies concerned. Article 4 of Regulation 139/2004 requires such notification to the MTF and failure to do so can lead to fines being imposed under Art 14(1)(a). Where the MTF considers that the notification falls within the ambit of the Merger Regulation, it must publish that notification. The MTF can instigate an investigation into the proposed merger or concentration, during which time the merger should be suspended. Failure to do so can lead to a heavy fine being imposed by the Commission (Art 14(2)).

The investigation by the MTF is conducted in two stages. In the first stage the MTF can decide under Art 6(1) whether the concentration is outside the regulation. The second stage arises where the Commission has serious doubts about the compatibility of the merger or concentration with the common market. Article 8 of the regulation provides a number of options for the Commission, including finding that the merger or concentration does not in fact breach the criteria by which such matters are judged. The regulation states that the Commission has four months from the initiation of the proceedings to make its decision. If it fails to do so, the merger will be deemed to be compatible with the common market. However, if the Commission determines within the time limit that it is incompatible with the common market because competition will be significantly impeded, the Commission can issue a decision to that effect. This may stop the merger going ahead or demand the reversal of a merger that has already taken place.

The Commission has made it clear that the determination of whether or not a concentration exists will be based on issues of law and fact. However, the Commission has been criticised for some of its decisions, such as where it blocked the merger between Aerospatiale-Alenia and de Havilland. The criticism of the decision centred on the Commission's definition of the relevant product market. Those who supported the merger claimed that the Commission had taken too narrow a definition of the market as 20- to 70-seater aircraft. However, the Commission has resisted all attempts to re-open the case. This case can be seen as an exception in that the majority of notifications do not lead to the Commission blocking the merger. This is helped by the fact that the

Commission can, where it has some concerns, impose conditions before clearing a merger, such as in the merger between Nestlé SA and Perrier SA in 1993.

However, the most recent difficulty that has arisen for the Commission relates to collective dominance. The Commission has taken the view that the Merger Regulation applies to collective dominance, where a merger creates or strengthens a dominant position between the parties and others in the market for particular goods or services. In *Gencor Ltd v Commission* there was a proposed concentration between two firms in the platinum market, which the Commission thought could lead to a dominant position between these two undertakings and another business. On appeal to the General Court, the Court confirmed that this type of collective dominance was covered by the Merger Regulation and issued guidance for its application. Following on from the tests established by the ECJ in the *Woodpulp* case, the Court of First Instance said that the extra-territoriality of the regulation was satisfied because the platinum was to be sold in the EU although it was produced in South Africa. The Court thought that under public international law it was foreseeable that the proposed concentration would have an immediate and substantial effect in the EU.

The wide interpretation given by the General Court to the regulation with regard to collective dominance has caused some problems for the Commission when it comes to proving the *existence* of collective dominance. In *Airtours plc v Commission*, the CFI held that the Commission had made errors of assessment in its analysis of competition in the 'relevant market'. In the UK the tour operator market is dominated by a small number of large operators. The operators were Thomson's with 27% of sales, Airtours with 21%, Thomas Cook with 20% and First Choice with 11%. If Airtours combined with First Choice they would have a larger share of the market, but more importantly there was the opportunity for the remaining three large operators to have a dominant position on the market as no other operator had more than 5% of sales. The Commission had not supported its assessment of the foreseeable reaction to the purchase by Airtours of First Choice plc, one of its main competitors. Therefore, the Commission's decision blocking the concentration was annulled. The outcome of this case has emphasised the role of the transparency test in deciding whether there is collective dominance. But, as with the tests for dominance under Art 102, this is difficult to prove. In the case of *Schneider Electric SA v Commission*, a merger by Schneider with another French producer of low-voltage electrical equipment blocked by the Commission was annulled. The economic analysis by the Commission, in the view of the CFI, was flawed. This was followed soon after by the case of *Tetra Laval BV v Commission*, where the CFI was very critical of the Commission's analysis. The Commission overestimated the anti-competitive effects of the merger and the evidence produced by the Commission was insufficient to support its conclusion.

The Commission's powers with regard to mergers are no longer dependent on trying to use Art 102 TFEU as it did in *Continental Can* (1973) or Art 101 in *Philip Morris* (1987). The demands of business and the EC have led to the present Regulation 139/2004 to provide a 'one-stop procedure' and this is now under review. This provided businesses with a clear reporting requirement showing the distinctive involvement of the Commission as against the various merger bodies within the Member States. The Commission has strong powers of investigation and the ability to impose fines. However, one large problem has been the tight time limits within which it has to act. Although it can be understood in the modern global economy that decisions have to be made swiftly, it does impose burdens and constraints on the Commission. The cases above of *Tetra Laval* and *Schneider* illustrate that to investigate the market and the likely impact of the proposed merger or concentration within the time scale of the regulation creates problems. It is likely that the Commission will be seeking the views of the Member States and the business community on reforming the application of the Merger Regulation. Following previous reviews by the Commission a new Regulation 139/2004 was introduced, coming into effect in May 2004. This new regulation simplified the notification proceedings to speed up the decision making on 'compatibility with the common market' for any proposed 'concentration'. Although the system has been criticised by some corporations and national bodies, the Commission did manage to act timely in the financial crisis of 2008. At that time the Commission approved the acquisition by Lloyds Bank of HBOS.

The Free Movement of Workers

8

INTRODUCTION

This is perhaps the most developed area of mobility within the Community, apart from the free movement of goods. Very often, there are problem questions associated with the rights of workers and their dependants to move around the Community in order to search for work or take up offers of employment. The starting point on this topic should be Art 45 TFEU, the directives and regulations adopted to provide the detail for this Community freedom and the judgments of the ECJ which have developed the principles of interpretation and application of Community law.

Checklist ✔

You need to put this free movement policy for workers within the context of the development of a 'common market for labour' as a necessary factor of production. In particular, you should understand:

- the right given to workers under **Art 45** to enter and remain in a Member State;
- the possible derogation by Member States under **Art 45** and **Directive 492/2011**
- the possible reservation of 'public service' jobs under **Art 45**
- **Directive 2004/38** on the rights of entry and the right to remain; and
- **Directive 2004/38** and the right to remain after employment.

QUESTION 33

Maria is a Spanish single parent living in Madrid with her young daughter and mother. She has recently lost her job due to redundancy. While she was a student, Maria had spent some time in England on an exchange programme. Remembering the vacancies she had seen advertised in the newspapers, she decides to travel to London to seek employment.

Unfortunately, she finds it hard to find employment and is considering seeking help from social security. She is informed at the social security office that her child and mother must return to Spain immediately if she cannot support them. If she cannot find a job within three months, she will have to return to Spain herself.

▶   Advise Maria.

How to Answer this Question

This question requires you to apply the principles of free movement of workers to a problem involving Maria. What are we going to do about Maria? It is necessary to state the laws affecting her, her daughter and her mother and then apply them to the specific information in the problem. Obviously, the bulk of the answer will centre on Maria, because generally the rights of the daughter and mother are derived from hers. You should cover the following points:

❖   Art 45 and the right to accept offers of work;
❖   Directive 2004/38 and the case of *Procureur du Roi v Royer* (1976) on searching for work;
❖   time limitation on searching for work and the factor of social security; and
❖   Regulation 492/2011 and Directive 2004/38 on dependants.

Answer Structure

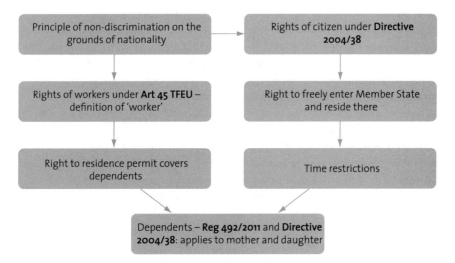

This diagram shows how to apply the law under *Art 45 TFEU* for Marie.

ANSWER

Maria only needed a valid passport or identity card to enter the UK. No visa or equivalent documentation could have been demanded from her or her family. However, if she wishes to remain in the UK to look for work, she will have to meet certain requirements. As there is no indication in the problem that Maria is contemplating setting up her own business or wishes to practise a profession, it is assumed that she comes within the category of 'worker' as far as the European Community is concerned. Article 49 or 56 TFEU will not be considered, as they refer to the right of establishment and the right to provide services on a temporary basis.

Article 45 TFEU gives an individual who is a worker in one Member State the freedom to move to another Member State to accept offers of employment actually made. There is no definition of worker in the Treaty, but subsequent secondary legislation and case law have provided such a definition. In *Lawrie-Blum* (1987), the ECJ suggested that the essential characteristics of a worker are of someone who performs services for another during a certain period of time and under the direction of another in return for remuneration. Unfortunately, Maria has not received such an offer of employment before coming to the UK and, therefore, does not come within the definition of either Art 45 TFEU or of a worker. However, does she have any rights as an individual who is seeking employment as a worker?

Since 1968 Directives have been used to abolish restrictions on the movement and residence of workers and their families. These were generously interpreted by the ECJ in oder to facilitate a wide range of activities, including the right to esarch for employment. In the case of *Procureur du Roi v Royer* (1976), the Court held that that Directive 68/360 (now repealed) included the right to enter a Member State to search for work. When that Directive was being adopted, it had been minuted that individuals who moved to another Member State without a specific job offer should be allowed to enter that Member State in order to look for work. This had been pointed out in *Levin* (1982). However, this right was to be for a limited period of three months on the proviso that the individual could support him or herself without recourse to public assistance. Although this minute had no legal effect, the Court held, in *Antonissen* (1991), that Community law gives immigrants seeking employment the right to enter another Member State and stay there for a sufficient period of time to find out about the job market opportunities and, if appropriate, to find employment. Now this is covered by Directive 2004/38 which deals specifically with the citizens' right of free movement and residence.

This case law was given a new dimension in 1992 when the Maastricht Treaty created the persona of the EU citizen, which applies to all nationals of the Member States. Article 20 TFEU is now the source of the rights arising from being such an EU citizen and these are given more detail in the Citizens' Right of Free Movement and Residence Directive 2004/38. Under Art 6 of the Directive Maria does have the right to enter the UK for the purpose of seeking work and this is for a period of 3 months. Why 3 months? This was perhaps due to the reference, in the EU legislation on social security in Regulation 1408/71, to the fact that payment of unemployment benefit for up to three months could be made in another Member State while the claimant is looking for work. In fact, under UK law, the period is stated to be six months. However, in the *Antonissen* case mentioned above, the Court went on to say that if, after this period, the immigrant provides evidence that he or she has a genuine chance of obtaining employment, he or she should not be subject to immediate deportation. The corollary of this is that if he or she has not found employment and cannot satisfy the authorities he or she has any genuine job opportunity; he or she can be deported. Article 7(1)(b) of Directive 2004/38 states that if she has sufficient resources for herself and her family members so that they do not become a burden on the social assistance system and they have comprehensive sickness insurance cover they can remain for longer than this initial period. Regulation 492/2011, which codified the often amended Regulation 1612/68 which it replaced, deals specifically with the freedom of movement for workers within the EU. This regulation gives added protection to Maria so that she is not discriminated against on the grounds of her nationality and that she should receive help and support available to any national of the UK when seeking employment.

It would appear that Maria does have a period in which she can seek employment in the UK, but what of her mother and daughter? Obviously, the daughter does not come within the category of someone seeking to exercise her rights as a worker within the EU. The mother may be of such an age that she too could claim the same right as Maria, that is, to remain for six months whilst she is seeking employment. However, if we assume that she is dependent on Maria, what are her rights? The situation seems to be a little complicated, in that the rights of members of a worker's family and dependants are dependent upon the status of worker being granted to an individual, such as Maria. Those who may be identified as having the right to install themselves with the worker are defined in Art 2(2) of Directive 2004/38. They include the worker's spouse, descendants who are under the age of 21 and dependent direct relatives. There is no difficulty in concluding that the mother and daughter come within this definition in relation to Maria. However, as indicated above, Maria is not yet a worker within the Community definition. The concern that those who are seeking employment and their dependants should not become a burden on another Member State would indicate that the rights of people seeking employment could be terminated if they become such a burden. Therefore, if this is what is happening, the case of Maria and her family's rights are terminated and they could be deported. The recent Supreme Court judgment in *Patmalniece v Secretary State for Work & Pensions* (2011) stated that the claimant using Regulation 1408/71 to request a UK retirement pension could be denied. She was not being discrimnated against on the basis of her nationality (Latvian), which would have been contrary to the Lisbon Treaty. The UK's refusal was a proportionate response to the legitimate aim of protecting the UK public purse!

The only way that Maria and her family can remain in the UK is if she can find employment. It is worth it for Maria or even her mother to consider part-time employment if full-time employment is not available. However, if her mother obtained employment, it may not be so easy to prove that Maria and her daughter are dependent upon her. This is because it was held in the *Levin* case, mentioned above, that the term worker and its associated rights applied to those who only worked part time provided the work was 'real' work and not nominal or minimal. In *Kempf* (1986), a part-time music teacher from Germany was working in the Netherlands and receiving supplementary benefits from the Dutch Government due to her low income from teaching. When she claimed a residence permit as a worker it was refused, even though such a permit is a recognition of the worker's rights under the Treaty and not a prerequisite for finding employment.

However, the Court held that a person who pursued a genuine and effective activity as an employed person, even on a part-time basis, could have the status of a worker. In *Raulin* (1989), the ECJ said that the national court should take account of all the services actually performed, and the duration of the activities, when considering whether the work is genuine and effective. Although it concerned someone given accommodation and 'pocket money' by the Salvation Army, the judgment in *Trojani* (C-456/02) 2004 does provide some guidance to national authorities making such decisions. If Maria can gain this status, she will be granted a residence permit for at least five years and this will be automatically renewable. The rights and benefits associated with such a status, such as not to be discriminated against on the grounds of nationality with regard to education, social advantage, access to employment and training and housing, will also apply to her mother and daughter as long as she remains as a 'worker'. This is because their rights depend upon the national of one Member State pursuing an activity as an employed or self-employed person in the territory of another Member State. In *Ninni-Orasche* (2003) the ECJ stated that ultimately whether a person is a 'worker' was a question for the national court to decide.

QUESTION 34
Who is an EU citizen and what rights are associated with that status?

How to Answer this Question
This essay type question allows you to demonstrate your knowledge and understanding of the important rights of the EU citizen which applies to those who wish to enter and reside in a member State as workers or to exercise the right of establishment and the right to provide services discussed in the following chapter. It also applies to those who are not economically active, for example are retired or students and who are not claiming on the host country's social security. As you can see there is therefore a wide scope to develop your discussion in your answer.

The main points you should cover are:

❖   Art 18 TFEU – prohibiting discrimination on the grounds of nationality;
❖   Art 20 TFEU – establishing citizenship in the EU;
❖   Art 21 TFEU – right to move and reside in another Member State;
❖   Art 22 TFEU – voting rights;
❖   Rights itemised in Directive 2004/38; and
❖   Rights of the family or dependants of the EU citizen.

Answer Structure

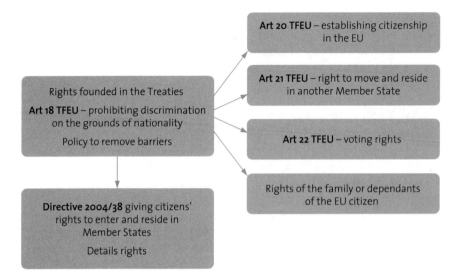

This diagram shows the key points to be discussed.

ANSWER

The idea of the EU citizen was introduced in the Maastricht Treaty in 1992 in order to demonstrate that the European Union was wider than the business community ethos of the Single European Act. It is now to be found in Arts 20–24 TFEU and the subordinate legislation, notably Directive 2004/38 which deals with the right to move and reside freely within the territories of the member States. EU citizenship applies under Art 20(10) TFEU to all the nationals of the 27 Member States and is in addition to their national citizenship. Other benefits relate to voting, travelling to third countries, petitioning and applying to the Ombudsman (Art 24 TFEU). She may also write to any of the EU institutions in one of the 22 official languages listed in Art 55(1) TEU plus Irish and have an answer in the same language.

Any EU citizen may stand for EP and municipal elections of the Member State where they reside on the same basis as nationals of that State. In addition under Art 20(2)(b) they have the right to vote in such elections. This seeks to ensure that any EU citizen who moves to another Member State for employment, professional or other purpose can still play a full part in electing those who become MEPs. This is especially important now that under the Lisbon Treaty the European Parliament shares equally so many powers with the Council. Article 23 TFEU is designed to ensure that when an EU citizen is travelling in a third country they will have recourse to assistance from the diplomatic or consular services of another Member States if their own country is not represented. This needs to be seen in the context that EU assistance maybe available. Article 27 TEU specifies the appointment of a High Representative of the Union for Foreign Affairs and Security Policy. The present High Representative is Baroness Catherine Ashton. Since October 2009 she has been involved with establishing the European External Action Service (EEAS), which may complement this support for the EU citizen in the future.

However, the most significant right given to the EU citizen is the right to move and reside freely within the Member States (Art 21 TFEU). This is not a new right as it is one that has been incrementally developed since the 1960's but importantly has now been codified in Directive 2004/38 so that the citizen has a clear statement of her rights and those of her family. Workers were the first to be the focus of EU law on free movement with Regulation 1612/68 but this has been added to by a number of directives including Directive 73/148 dealing with the provision of services and others dealing with non-economic active citizens and students. It is clear that the right of residence in another Member State is conferred directly on Union citizens and is not dependent on any administrative process being completed. This does not mean that there are no controls or derogations but these must be exercised by the Member State in such a way that the fundamental right is not unproportionally restricted. The case law developed by these early directives and regulation and the current Directive 2004/38 provide a clear indication of the rights of the EU citizen.

There are restrictions on the EU citizen with regard to the right to move and reside in another Member State. Article 21(1) TFEU makes it clear that there are qualifications and exceptions. A fundamental principle is non-discrimination on the grounds of nationality (Art 18 TFEU). The case of *Grzelczyk* (C-184/99) 2001, involving a French national studying at a Belgian university who was refused social security because he was not a worker within Regulation 1612/68 is an example of this. If he had been a Belgian student he would have been entitled to the benefit even if he was not a worker so there was discrimination on the grounds of nationality. This is not the only case to arise concerning social security provisions for nationals and EU citizens.

The rights of EU citizenship can also bring benefits to non-EU nationals. In the *Zhu and Chen* case (C-200/02) in 2004 a Chinese nationals who was the mother of a child born in Northern Ireland and therefore automatically an Irish citizen relied on Art 21 TFEU to reside in the UK. The child was an EU citizen by being an Irish citizen and therefore had the full rights guaranteed by the Treaties. In the *Zambrano* case (C-34/09) in 2011 the ECJ said that the status of a child who was an EU citizen meant that the parents, who were third country nationals, were allowed to reside and work in that Member State as to do otherwise would deprive the child of their rights. The key point from these cases was that there should not be direct discrimination. It is possible for there to be indirect discrimination against an EU citizen if it is based on objective considerations independent of the nationality of the person and is proportionate to a legitimate aim. In *Bressol* (C-73/08) in 2010 a Belgian law had set down eligibility criteria to study in Belgium as the French speaking community wished to restrict the number of non-residents enrolling on specific courses due to fears of excessive financial burden and a risk to the public health system. The ECJ rejected the argument about excessive burden but said that it was for the national court to interpret the national law and the facts. However, the guidance provided by the Court was that the Belgian Constitutional Court should ensure that the restrictions can be objectively justified and are proportionate. Recently the UK Supreme Court applied that decision in the case of *Patmalniece (FC) v Secretary of State for Work & Pensions* (2011). It held that the refusal of a pension credit to the claimant, who was Latvian, was a proportionate response to the legitimate aim of protecting the public purse.

The European Union citizenship arrives at birth and provides many rights immediately to that person and their dependants or parents irrespective of their nationality and depending upon their status. The right to freely enter and reside in a member State is a very important right although as was shown above there maybe some restrictions on the exercise of that right. Most importantly such a citizen should not become an unreasonable burden of the social security system of the host Member State. There are time scales associated with these rights in the sense that it is initially for 3 months with no travel documents are required but they may have to report their presence within a reasonable time (Art 6 Directive 2004/38). Under Art 7 they subsequently have the right of residence if they are workers or self-employed or have sufficient means not to become a burden on the social security system or enrol as students in the same circumstances. If the Union citizen satisfies one of these criteria then all the family members accompanying her also have right of residence regardless of their nationality (Art 2). This right coupled with the right not to be discriminated against on the basis of nationality in Art 18 TEU provides the European citizen with the same opportunities as a national of that Member State.

Aim Higher ★

It is important to demonstrate your knowledge of the links between the right of the EU citizen and the free movement of workers, the right of establishment and the provision of services. Although the latter has become more important in recent years it has benefited from the case law developed by the others. The impact of social security provision should also be made clear.

QUESTION 35

Alfonse is a German national who qualified as an accountant and who has been working in Germany, where he was trained. He recently applied for a job with the Wessex local authority in England, which had advertised for accountants. Although it had already filled the post, Wessex offered him an associate contract which amounted to two-thirds of a full-time post. Alfonse wishes to accept this offer of employment, but he has been informed by the British immigration authorities that he cannot take up this post because:

(a) UK legislation requires that posts with local authorities must be filled by UK nationals only; and

(b) as the post is not full time, it does not come within EC legislation and has to be based on UK law alone.

▶ Advise Alfonse.

How to Answer this Question

As Alfonse is an accountant, this question could have been worded differently so that it came within the context of the right of establishment dealt with in Chapter 9. This illustrates the need to read any question, especially a problem question like this one, very carefully. The main points to cover in this question are:

❖ Art 45 TFEU and Regulation 492/2011 on the rights of workers and Directive 2004/38 on the rights of EU citizens;

❖ What is a worker? – *Levin* (1982) and *Lawrie-Blum* (1987); and

❖ restrictions under Art 45 TFEU and the case of *Belgium* (1981).

Common Pitfalls ✗

This kind of question looks very simplistic but students generally lose marks because their answer is too descriptive. Remember that your answer has to reflect that you are studying on an undergraduate course.

Answer Structure

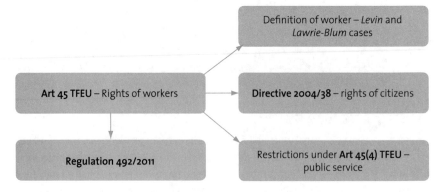

This diagram shows how to apply the law under Art 45 TFEU for Alfonse.

ANSWER

Under EU law, there is a freedom of movement for workers to move around the Community to take up offers of employment. This is based upon Art 45 TFEU and the associated secondary legislation which has been issued to provide the detail necessary to identify the specific rights of the Community worker. The main question in this problem is whether Alfonse comes within this category of worker, and whether there are any specific characteristics of the post which could deprive him of the ability to exercise his rights. However, if he is not 'a worker' he may utilise Directive 2004/38 as an EU citizen in order to come to the UK to resolve this issue.

Article 45 TFEU is quite clear in providing the right for workers who are EU nationals to accept offers of employment actually made. This is confirmed by Art 1 of Regulation 492/2011 that replaced Regulation 1612/68 on freedom of movement of workers within the Community. Article 1 of the Directive refers to the right to 'take up an activity as an employed person'. Unfortunately, neither gives a definition of worker, but the ECJ has decided that the words should be given their ordinary meaning and should not be interpreted restrictively. However, the concept only covers pursuit of effective and genuine activities. In *Levin* (1982), the Court held that the concept of 'worker' is a Community concept and is not dependent for its meaning on the laws of the Member State. How does the Court decide if someone comes within the Community concept of worker? In *Lawrie-Blum* (1987), the Court suggested that the essential characteristics which should be identified in a 'worker' are that he performs services in a particular time period for and under the direction of another in return for remuneration. Obviously, Alfonse satisfies the basic requirement under Community law in that he is a national of a Member State, but does he come within the definition in *Lawrie-Blum*? From the facts given in the problem, it would seem that he is going to perform the service of an accountant for Wessex local authority, in return for which it is going to pay him a salary as remuneration. Does the fact that he is only employed on a two-thirds contract affect his position? In the *Levin* case mentioned above, the Court held that the term 'worker' applied even to those who worked to a limited extent, that is, part-time, provided that the work was real. There has to be some economic activity on the part of the person who claims to be a worker. This was confirmed in *Kempf* (1986), where a music teacher was working part-time in the Netherlands and applied for a residence permit. In normal circumstances all those who are workers exercising their rights under Art 45 have a right to such a residence permit, which must be valid for at least five years and automatically renewable. This permit is proof of the right granted by the Treaty itself and which exists independently of the document.

The definition of 'worker' in the Community sense rarely causes difficulty in practice, because if an economically active claimant under Art 45 TFEU, like Alfonse, is not a worker he is probably self-employed, in which case Arts 49 or 56 TFEU come into play. Article 56 TFEU deals with the right of establishment, including the right to take up and pursue activities as a self-employed person or to set up a business. Article 49 TFEU deals with the freedom to provide services. The European Court has held that Arts 45, 49 and 56 are based on the same principles as far as entry and residence and non-discrimination on the grounds of nationality are concerned. Therefore, categorisation under Art 56, as opposed to Art 49 or 45, will rarely be crucial. Directive 2004/38 specifically gives rights to EU citizens to enter and reside in another Member State.

However, even if Alfonse does have a right to enter the UK to take up his post, albeit part-time, does the second point mentioned by the immigration authorities' raise any obstacles for him? It is specifically recognised that Art 45(4) TFEU will not apply to employment in the public sector. In other words, it is possible for a Member State to discriminate in favour of its own nationals on the grounds of nationality for certain jobs. This appears to provide a wide discretion to Member States, but it has been given a very narrow interpretation by the ECJ. In *Sotgui v Deutsche Bundespost* (1974), Sotgui was employed as a postman. His employers, the German post office, paid an extra allowance to workers living apart from their families in Germany, but refused it to Sotgui, an Italian national working in Germany. The Court held that the exemption provided by Art 45(4) TFEU (then Art 48(4)) did not apply to all employment in the public service, as this was too wide a definition. Rather, it applied to those activities in the public service which were connected with the exercise of discretion or official authority involving the national interest. On the specific point of discrimination raised by *Sotgui*, the Court went on to say that Art 45 (then Art 48(4)) only applied to access to employment and did not permit discrimination once a person had been employed in that occupation.

In another case, *Commission v Belgium* (1981), which is similar to that facing Alfonse, the Court held that a Belgian law which stated that posts in the public service could be limited to Belgian nationals was declared to be contrary to Art 45 TFEU (then Art 48). As with the term 'worker', the concept of 'public service' is a Community concept and is not to be interpreted only on national terms. It should apply only to those exercising official authority, as it was intended to apply only to employees safeguarding the general interests of the State. In *Anker* (C-47/02) 2004 the ECJ said that Art 45(4) allows Member States to restrict such employment to their own nationals only where such authority is being exercised on a regular basis and are not a minor part of their activities. Does this mean that Alfonse can take up his post? It would appear that he will not be in a position to exercise official authority. He will not have the status of a civil servant, although this was held by the Court, in *Lawrie-Blum*, not to mean that Art 45 (then Art 48(4)) applies.

To enter the UK to take up this offer of employment all Alfonse needs is a valid passport or identity card to exercise his rights as an EU citizen using Directive 2004/38. This will provide him with a period to find employment but as he has already been offered employment by Wessex he has Art 1(2) of Regulation 492/2011 on the freedom of movement for workers as well. This Article states that he will have 'the right to take up available employment in the territory of another Member State with the same priority a nationals of that State'. Unless the case law mentioned above is satisfied to deny Alfonse

the job he will be entitled to a residence permit, renewable automatically at the e
five years, and not to be discriminated against on the grounds of nationality with reg.
to conditions of employment, housing, social security, etc.

QUESTION 36

Analyse TWO of the following cases that came before the ECJ, and explain their
importance in the development of EU law:

(a) *Lawrie-Blum* – Case 66/85;
(b) *Rutili* – Case 36/75;
(c) *Bonsignore* – Case 67/74.

How to Answer this Question

When approaching a question like this, the temptation is to produce too descriptive an
answer. The facts are important, but are only one element of the answer. You should try
to deal with the following:

❖   the facts, the legal points raised and the decision of the Court;
❖   the kind of case it was – whether a preliminary reference or a direct action and
     which Article of the Treaty it was based upon;
❖   the cases chosen for this type of question have usually played their part in
     developing or reinforcing European Court judgments – what part has this case
     played?

Answer Structure

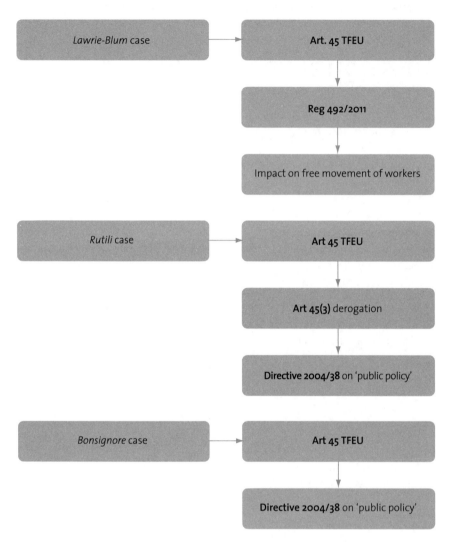

This diagram shows the key points to be discussed.

ANSWER

(A) *LAWRIE-BLUM* – CASE 66/85

Deborah Lawrie-Blum was a British national who passed the first examination at the University of Freiburg to become a teacher at a *Gymnasium*. She was refused admission to the probationary service leading to the second examination, which qualifies successful candidates for appointment as teachers. The law of the *Land* Baden-Württemberg required the possession of German nationality for admission to the probationary service. Mrs Lawrie-Blum contended that this refusal on the grounds of nationality had infringed her rights under Art 45 TFEU (then Art 48), whereas the *Land* argued that a probationary teacher is not a 'worker' within the meaning of Art 45 TFEU. During the proceedings which followed in the German court, a preliminary reference was made to the European Court under Art 267 TFEU (then Art 177).

The *Land* claimed that since a trainee teacher's activity falls under education policy, it is not an economic activity within Art 2 of the Treaty. The term 'worker' within the meaning of Art 45 (then Art 48) and Regulation 1612/68 (now Regulation 492/2011), they argued, covers only those persons whose relationship to their employer is governed by a contract subject to private law and not persons whose employment relationship is subject to public law. The period of preparatory service should be regarded as the last stage of the professional training of future teachers.

The European Commission took the view that the criterion for the application of Art 45 (then Art 48) is the existence of an employment relationship, regardless of the legal nature of that relationship and its purpose. The fact that the period of preparatory service is a compulsory stage in the professional development of a teacher, and that it is spent in the public service, is not relevant if the objective criteria for defining a 'worker' are satisfied. These criteria would include such things as the existence of a relationship of subordination *vis à vis* the employer, the actual provision of services by the employee and the payment of remuneration.

The ECJ said that the freedom of movement for workers was one of the fundamental principles of the Community. Therefore, the term 'worker' should not be left to be defined by the individual Member States, but should have a Community meaning. Given its fundamental importance, the Community concept of 'worker' must be given a broad interpretation. The essential feature of an employment relationship is that for a certain period of time a person performs services for and under the direction of another person, in return for which he receives remuneration.

Applying this concept to the facts of Mrs Lawrie-Blum's case, for the entire period of preparatory service she is under the direction and supervision of the school to which she is assigned. It is the school that determines the services to be performed by her and her working hours and it is the school's instructions that she must carry out and its rules she must observe. The amounts she receives may be considered as remuneration for the services provided and for the duties involved in completing the period of preparatory service. Consequently, the three criteria for the existence of an employment relationship are fulfilled in this case.

The argument put forward by the *Land*, that services performed in education do not fall within the scope of the Treaty because they are not of an economic nature, was rejected.

The Court said that all that is required for the application of Art 45 TFEU (then Art 48) is that the activity should be in the nature of work performed for remuneration, irrespective of the sphere in which it is carried out. The economic nature of someone's activities cannot be denied merely because their activities are governed by public law. The Court had already stated, in *Sotgui* (1974), that the nature of the legal relationship between employee and employer is immaterial as regards the application of Art 45 TFEU (then Art 48).

(B) *RUTILI* – CASE 36/75

Roland Rutili was an Italian national, although he had lived in France since birth. He had married a French woman and, until 1968, had held a privileged resident's permit. He was resident in the département of Meurthe-et-Moselle, where he worked and engaged in trade union activities. As a result of Rutili's alleged political actions during the parliamentary elections in March 1967 and the events of May and June 1968, and of his participation in a demonstration during the celebrations of 14 July 1968, the Ministry for the Interior made a deportation order against him. On 10 September 1968, an order was issued requiring Rutili to reside in the département of Puy-de-Dôme. In November 1968, the Minister for the Interior revoked the deportation and residence orders affecting Rutili, but decided to prohibit him from residing in particular départements. In January 1970, Rutili applied for a residence permit for a national of a Member State of the EC. In October 1970, following an appeal by Rutili, he was issued with a residence permit by the Prefect of Police valid for five years, but restricting his residence in line with the views of the Minister for the Interior. In December 1970, Rutili brought proceedings seeking the annulment of the decision limiting the territorial validity of his residence permit.

The *Tribunal Administratif* in Paris decided to stay the proceedings under Art 267 TFEU (then Art 177), so that questions could be put to the ECJ. The first question concerned the interpretation of 'subject to limitations justified on grounds of public policy' in Art 45(3) (then Art 48). The Court said that this concerned both those legislative provisions adopted by each Member State to limit the freedom of movement and residence within its territory, and the individual decisions taken in application of such provisions. The object of the provisions of the Treaty and secondary legislation is to regulate the situation of individuals and to ensure their protection, thus the national courts must examine whether individual decisions are compatible with Community law. The second question asked for the precise meaning of the word 'justified'. The freedom of movement of workers is one of the fundamental principles of the Treaty, and therefore any derogation must be strictly interpreted so that its scope cannot be determined unilaterally by each Member State. Therefore, the word 'justified' seeks to limit the discretionary powers of Member States and to protect the rights of those who are seeking to exercise their rights under Art 45.

Directive 2004/38 states in Art 1(c) that this Directive lays down the limits placed on the Member States to derogate on the grounds of public policy, public security or public health. This Directive replaced Directive 64/221 and specifies in some detail in Chapter VI how these restrictions are to operate. Article 27(2) of the Directive states that the principle of proportionality shall apply and that the measure adopted must be based exclusively on the personal conduct of the individuals concerned, and to refrain from adopting any measures which are not related to the requirements of public policy, or which adversely affect the exercise of trade union rights. They should immediately inform anyone against whom a restrictive measure has been adopted of the reasons on which the decision is based, so that these people can consider an appeal.

In particular, measures restricting the rights of residence which are limited to only part of the national territory may not be imposed by a Member State on nationals of another Member State who are subject to Art 45, except in the case and circumstances in which such measures may be applied to nationals of the State concerned. Therefore, the judgment in *Rutili* reinforces the non-discrimination approach of the Treaty. A Member State does not have the power to restrict the movement of nationals of other Member States within its territory unless it has the power in similar circumstances to restrict its own nationals. Rutili was therefore important in developing the EU law on the protection of the individual against the powers of the Member State in which they reside.

(C) *BONSIGNORE* – CASE 67/74

Carmelo Angelo Bonsignore was an Italian national residing in Germany. He was convicted of a firearms offence, in that he was in unlawful possession of a firearm which accidentally caused the death of his brother by his careless handling of the firearm. The local German criminal court found him guilty of possession of the firearm and imposed a fine for breach of the firearms legislation. The court also found him guilty of causing death by negligence, but imposed no penalty on this count, considering that no purpose would be served in the circumstances, notably the mental suffering caused by the death of his brother. Following this criminal conviction, the Aliens Authority ordered that he be deported. Bonsignore appealed against this decision, during which a reference was made to the European Court under Art 267 TFEU (then Art 177).

The reference was required because the German court wished to know the interpretation of Art 3(1) and (2) of Directive 64/221 (now replaced by Directive 2004/38), which dealt with the co-ordination of special measures concerning the movement and residence of foreign nationals which are justified on the grounds of public policy, public security or public health. These are the grounds available under Art 45 TFEU which allow a government of a Member State to derogate from its obligations under the Treaty.

The German court hearing the appeal was of the view that deportation was not justified because of the special circumstances of the case. There was no special preventive characteristic of Bonsignore in the case. The only reason could be to deport Bonsignore as a general preventive measure, as an example to others who may also be in illegal possession of firearms. The Directive had been introduced into German law by a special Law on the Entry and Residence of Nationals of Member States of the European Community, passed in 1969. The German court wanted to ensure that the German legislation was applied in accordance with the requirements of Community law, hence its request for interpretation.

The first question refers to whether the then Art 3(1) and (2) of the Directive are to be interpreted as excluding the deportation of a national of another Member State as a deterrent to other foreign nationals from committing criminal offences of the type committed by the person to be deported. The second question posed the alternative meaning of these Articles in the Directive, namely, that the EC national to be deported will commit further offences if he remains in the Member State.

The ECJ said that according to the then Art 3(1) and (2) of Directive 64/221, measures taken on grounds of public policy or of public security shall be based exclusively on the personal conduct of the individual concerned and that previous criminal convictions shall not in themselves constitute grounds for the taking of such measures. These Articles have to be interpreted in the light of the objectives of the Directive and the need to ensure the uniform application of Art 45 TFEU, without discrimination between nationals and non-nationals of a Member State.

Article 3 of the then Directive 64/221 provided that measures adopted on grounds of public policy and for the maintenance of public security against nationals of Member States cannot be justified on grounds outside the personal conduct of the individual involved. This has to be the situation where a government is seeking to depart from one of the fundamental principles of the Community, that is, the free movement of persons. Thus, we have the requirement that a deportation order may only be made for any breaches of the peace and public security which might be committed by the individual concerned. Therefore, the outcome for Bonsignore was that the European Court said, in answer to the Art 267 TFEU (then Art 177) reference, that Directive 64/221 prevents the deportation of a national of another Member State if the purpose is solely to deter other aliens, that is, of a preventive nature. In the recent 2005 cases of *Orfanopoulos* and *Oliveri*, the ECJ stated that the Member State should take into consideration a number of factors before making an expulsion on grounds of public policy. These included how long the individual had been in residence, his age, stated health, family and economic situation, and integration into the host Member State. Builidng upon the case law, including the *Bonsignore* case the current Directive 2004/38 that deals with the Citizens Right of Free Movement and Residence goes into great detail about the rights of the individual, the procedure to be followed and the protect given against arbitrary expulsion.

Aim Higher ★

Look out for contemporary examples of how the law applies. For example, the French government's decision concerning Romas being sent back to Romania (another Member State).

The Freedom of Establishment and the Freedom to Provide Services

INTRODUCTION

Very often, these topics are joined with the free movement of workers, and therefore a good understanding of all three aspects should be obtained. This is especially true as the Court has held that the principles of non-discrimination, etc, are the same whether it is Art 45 TFEU (the free movement of workers), Art 49 TFEU (the freedom or right of establishment for the self-employed and companies) or Art 56 TFEU (the freedom to provide services). Problem questions are very popular in this area of Community law although, on law degrees, it is not uncommon to have an essay question on the freedom of establishment for lawyers.

> ### Checklist ✔
>
> **You should be familiar with the following areas:**
>
> - **Art 49 TFEU** and the freedom of establishment;
> - **Art 56 TFEU** and the freedom to provide services;
> - **Art 57 TFEU** and what constitutes a service;
> - the right to receive services;
> - derogation under **Art 52 TFEU** and **Directive 2004/38** on the right of entry and residence;
> - **Directive 2004/38** on the right to remain after employment for the self employed and their families;
> - the special problems of 'professionals' and the **Mutual Recognition Directive 2005/36**; and
> - special measures to deal with companies operating within the Community.

QUESTION 37

Pierre is a fully qualified engineer in France. As a result of attending the 'Engineering 2012 Fair' in Paris, he applied for a two-year postgraduate course at a British university. He was accepted onto the course and arrived at Dover with Anne-Marie, his Canadian cohabitee.

His luggage was searched and found to contain pornographic videos, which were confiscated. The immigration officer checked the Home Office computer, which indicated that the French police had reported that Pierre was a member of an anarchist organisation. On the basis of this information, the immigration officer refused them permission to enter the UK, on the grounds that their exclusion would be conducive to the public good.

▶   Advise Pierre on his rights, if any, under EU law.

How to Answer this Question

This question deals with the mobility of students within the Community but the principles apply generally to EU citizens. It concentrates on the right of individuals to move to another Member State to receive services as against the provision in the Treaty which deals with the right to provide services. This provision should be discussed and applied, along with the following points:

❖   Arts 45, 49 and 56 TFEU to identify if Pierre is covered by any of these provisions;

❖   the case of *Luisi*, which identified rights of recipients of services;

❖   the meaning of vocational courses – *Gravier v City of Liège* (1984); and

❖   Directive 2004/38 Citizens' Right of Free Movement & Residence.

Answer Structure

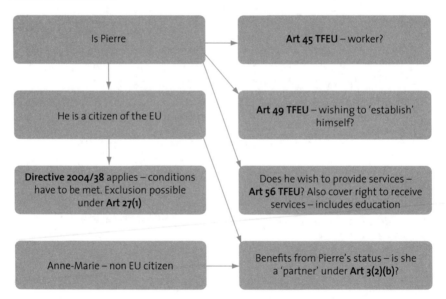

This diagram shows how to apply the law to Pierre's situation.

ANSWER

The TFEU Treaty has, as one of its basic freedoms, that of the ability of individuals to move between Member States in order to carry out certain activities. The Treaty specifies three situations, namely, the free movement of workers, the right of establishment and the freedom to provide services. As Pierre does not seek to establish a business in the UK, the Treaty provisions associated with establishment have no application to the problem. Is he a worker? The concept of worker is a Community concept and is not dependent for its meaning on the laws of any particular Member State. The essential characteristic of a worker, according to *Lawrie-Blum* (1986), is that he performs services during a particular time period for and under the direction of another in return for remuneration. This concept has been generously interpreted by the ECJ, in *Procureur du Roi v Royer* (1976), to include the right to enter another Member State in order to search for work. However, although he is a qualified engineer, Pierre is not seeking to enter the UK as a 'worker', but to take up his place on a two-year postgraduate course. Article 45 TFEU, specifying the rights of workers, does not provide any assistance to him. It is the last category associated with services which needs to be considered if the EU law is to provide any assistance to Pierre and Anne-Marie. There is also Directive 2004/38 that may provide some possible assistance.

Articles 56 and 57 TFEU provide for the removal of restrictions on the freedom to provide services. More importantly for Pierre, they have been interpreted by the ECJ to embrace the freedom to receive services. This would include the postgraduate course which he wishes to take. It was stated by the Court, in *Luisi v Ministero del Tesoro* (1983), following the Commission's view in *Watson and Belman* (1976), that there was a freedom for the recipient of services to go to another Member State, without restriction, in order to receive a service there. Although the case involved the transfer of money out of Italy in breach of Italian currency law for the purpose of tourism and medical treatment, the principle in the judgment included persons travelling for the purpose of education. The right of residence exists during the period for which the service is provided, which, in Pierre's case, would be the two years' duration of the course. Any breach of this freedom would be *prima facie* a breach of Arts 56 and 57 TFEU.

Would Pierre's course qualify under this right to receive services? As an economic-orientated Treaty, the main concern would seem to be education or training of a vocational kind. However, the Court has given a wide definition to the meaning of vocational education. In *Gravier v City of Liège* (1984), it was held to include all forms of teaching which prepares for and leads directly to a particular profession, or which provides the necessary skills for such a profession. Although Pierre is already a qualified engineer, the postgraduate course he has applied for would seem to satisfy this definition, in that it deals with a specialist area of engineering skills. Thus, he may claim equal access, and on the same basis as nationals of the Member State, that is, UK nationals. This was confirmed in *Blaizot v University of Liège* (1987), which involved a university veterinary studies course. However, as with all the freedoms arising from the Treaty, there are exceptions where the Member State may derogate from their obligation under the Treaty. These are specifically those in Arts 52 and 62 TFEU, which allow for derogation on the grounds of public policy, public security and public health. As there is no indication that Pierre offers any threat with regard to public health, it is public policy or public security which may be used by the UK Government to justify its actions. The public policy provision has been interpreted strictly by the European Court to ensure, as it stated in *Van Duyn v Home Office* (1975), that its scope is not unilaterally determined by the Member State without control by the European Community institutions. In *Rutili v Ministre de l'Intérieur* (1976), the Court held that restrictions on the movement of an EU national on the grounds of public policy could only be accepted where the behaviour of the individual constitutes a genuine and sufficiently serious threat to public policy.

Article 27(1) of Directive 2004/38 states that any exclusion on the grounds of public policy or public security must be based exclusively on the personal conduct of the individual. Is Pierre's membership of an anarchist association sufficient personal conduct to exclude him? In *Van Duyn*, a Dutch national was refused entry to the UK to take up employment with the Church of Scientology because the UK regarded the activities of the Church as objectionable and socially harmful. The Court held that, although past association with an organisation does not count as personal conduct, present association does, and the activities in question must constitute a genuine and sufficiently serious threat to public policy affecting one of the fundamental interests of society. Do French anarchists pose such a threat, given that there are probably British anarchists? In *Van Duyn*, mentioned above, the Court allowed the UK to apply a stricter standard on an EU national than the one it applied to its own nationals, because the UK deemed that it was necessary. It would appear that, if Pierre is a member of such an organisation and the UK Government does believe that he constitutes a genuine and sufficiently serious threat to society, it can exclude him. If they do, it must be on the membership of the anarchist association, because the pornographic videos would not, in themselves, amount to a reason to exclude him. In *Bonsignore* (1975), it was accepted that the concept of personal conduct expresses the requirement that a deportation order may only be made for breaches of the peace and public security which might be committed by the individual concerned.

Under Art 30 of Directive 2004/38, Pierre is entitled to know on which ground, that is, public policy or public security, the decision is based, unless this information contravenes State security. This allows the individual to prepare his defence. If the UK fails to comply with Art 30, it may lead to the quashing of a deportation order, as happened in *R v Secretary of State for the Home Office ex p Dannenberg* (1984). Under Art 31, Pierre is entitled to the same legal remedies in relation to a decision on entry. In the UK, an immigrant normally has a right of appeal against immigration decisions to a person called an adjudicator and then to the Immigration Appeal Tribunal. Such appeals cover issues of fact, law and the exercise of discretion, so the merits of the decision would be fully reviewed.

In June 1992, a directive specifically issued to cover the situation of students came into force but it has since been repealed by the important Directive 2004/38. This Directive gives the EU citizen the right to freely enter and reside in another Member State. Article 7(c) of the Directive is specifically designed for students who wish to attend 'a course of study, including vocational training. Therefore as an EU citizen Pierre can enter the UK to enrol on his course if he has sufficient means not to become a burden on the social security and has comprehensive sickness insurance cover. What about Anne-Marie? She is a Canadian national and, as such, does not receive the benefits associated with the European Union, which are for EU nationals only. However, does her relationship with Pierre provide her with any rights of entry? If Pierre was allowed entry to take up his place on the postgraduate course, would she be able to enter with him? If Anne-Marie was married to Pierre, there would be no problem, in that the nationality of the spouse does not need to be that of one of the Member States. However, she is his cohabitee. In *Netherlands State v Reed* (1986), the Court held that the term 'spouse' included cohabitee. Although this case was concerned with the mobility of workers, it will not help Anne-Marie even if the Court applied its principles of interpretation across the mobility categories. The decision was on the basis of non-discrimination, in that the Dutch authorities were required to give Reed the right of residence, as they recognised the rights of a cohabitee under Dutch law. Therefore, the judgment will not assist migrants in a similar situation unless the State they wish to enter has the same rule as the Dutch. Article 2(2) of Directive 2004/38 deals with 'family members' and these include in Art 2(2)(b) the partner with whom the Union citizen has contracted a registered partnership, on the basis of the legislation of the host Member State if it treats such partnerships as equivalent to marriage. UK law has civil partnerships but these are not available to heterosexual relationships and so are not available for Pierre and Anne-Marie. Article 3(2)(b) refers to 'the partner with whom the Union citizen has a durable relationship, duly attested'. It is for the host Member State, ie the UK, to undertake an extensive examination of the personal circumstances and on the basis of this evidence deny entrance or residence.

It would seem that if the Court is satisfied that there are grounds for the UK Government to derogate from the Treaty, they will uphold the refusal to allow Pierre to enter the UK to take up his postgraduate course. If they are not satisfied, and Pierre is allowed to enter the UK as a student, he must be given a residence permit for the duration of the course. However, whatever happens to Pierre, it can be seen from the Reed case, above, that Anne-Marie will not be allowed to benefit from the rights given to him unless Art 3(2)(b) operates and they can show that they have a 'durable relationship'. Given that the pressure would be on the UK to undertake the extensive examination if they wished to refuse entry and residence it is likely that she will be able to benefit from Pierre being an EU citizen and receive the full rights of Directive 2004/38.

QUESTION 38

Critically discuss the development of EU law with regard to the right of a lawyer to practise in another Member State.

How to Answer this Question

This essay question requires a discussion of the development of Community law on the right of establishment and the provision of services as they apply to lawyers. In particular, the following points should be raised:

- ❖ freedom of establishment under Arts 49–54;
- ❖ Directive 77/256 and the right to provide services;
- ❖ problems of lawyers and other professionals;
- ❖ the impact of the Mutual Recognition Directive 2005/36.

Answer Structure

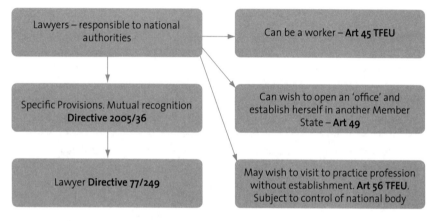

This diagram shows the key points to be discussed.

ANSWER

A lawyer could be a 'worker', in the sense that he or she is employed within an organisation to manage its legal affairs, in which case, the normal rules associated with the free movement of workers would apply. However, generally speaking, the ability to practise as a lawyer, as a professional, is more complicated and involves issues about the right to provide services and the right of establishment. The Community principle of equal treatment is not always sufficient to ensure that the immigrant is able to practise a profession in another Member State. In the case of lawyers, it is obvious that recognition of their professional qualifications and admission to the appropriate professional organisation is also required and can cause problems. Generally, each Member State has remained free to regulate the exercise of the legal profession in its territory. The ECJ said that Member States are required to recognise a legal diploma obtained in another Member State to register the holder for pre-qualifying practical training, although in the case of *Morgenbesser* (2004) the ECJ said that this was not automatic. There was the possibility that some Member States may review the individuals' qualifications with regard to the possible exceptions to mutual recognition provided by Directive 2005/36.

There is no directly applicable provision in the Treaty requiring Member States to recognise qualifications acquired in another Member State or obliging them to allow immigrants to practise a profession without the appropriate qualifications (*Auer (No 1)* (1979)). This seems reasonable, given that the services on such professionals have a big impact on those who seek their advice and services. However, Art 53 TFEU requires the Council to adopt directives on the mutual recognition of diplomas, certificates and other evidence of formal qualifications. Without a relevant directive, the migrant is likely to find that Community law is of limited assistance. The Commission had attempted to remedy the situation by promoting separate directives for each profession, such as medicine, dentistry, veterinary medicine and midwifery. The objective of these directives has been to make it easier for a person practising a profession in one Member State to practise that profession in another Member State. However, the important difference between these professions and lawyers is that, although the principles of medicine or dentistry are much the same in every Member State, those of law differ. It is therefore hardly surprising that the progress on facilitating the free movement of lawyers has been very slow. Directive 77/249 was specifically aimed at lawyers, but it is only concerned with the provision of services and not the right of establishment. It makes provision for lawyers to carry out their profession in another Member State on a temporary basis. 'Lawyer' under this Directive is defined by a list of terms to reflect the diversity in the European Union. The function of the list is to indicate those practitioners who are able to benefit from the rights conferred by the Directive and the activities to which it applies. Thus, anyone who is recognised as a 'lawyer' for the purpose of the Directive can perform the work of a lawyer in another Member State, but only on a temporary basis. While performing this work, he or she must use the title of the home country, as it would appear in that country. Thus, a French lawyer must call himself 'avocat', even when he is working in the UK or Germany. This avoids any misunderstanding and indicates the specialism of the lawyer in the law of the appropriate Member State. In this capacity, the foreign lawyer can do all the work of a local lawyer, unless the national law of the Member State reserves certain activities for its national lawyers and on the proviso that he represents a client in court work in conjunction with a local lawyer. This has meant in the UK that such foreign lawyers cannot undertake probate or conveyancing work, which is reserved for UK lawyers.

It could be expected that, in time, the European Commission would issue a directive which would widen the scope of recognition for lawyers of one Member State to establish themselves and practise in another. However, recognising the time involved in such a process as producing specific directives, the Commission changed its strategy and concentrated on producing a general directive that would apply to all professions. This Directive applies to the legal profession and is the Mutual Recognition Directive 89/48 (now replaced by Directive 2005/36). Like all directives on establishment, this early Directive benefits Community citizens with regard to qualifications awarded in a Member State. Under the then Directive recognition is to be given to diplomas as defined by Art 1(a). There must be three essential characteristics for such 'diplomas'; it must be awarded by a competent authority in a Member State following the successful completion of a course lasting at least three years at a university or equivalent institution, plus professional training. Finally, such a 'diploma' must qualify the holder for the pursuit of a regulated profession in a Member State. The profession of a lawyer is in the list of regulated professions. Article 3 of the Directive provides the basic rule that if a Member State requires a 'diploma' as a condition for exercising a regulated profession, it must accept a 'diploma' obtained in another Member State. Directive 2005/36 replced this earlier Directive but retained the essential content. In contrast to the situation where a lawyer is providing a 'service' of a temporary nature, when he or she is exercising the right of establishment, the lawyer is entitled to use the professional designation of the Member State in which he or she practises. Thus, a French *avocat* who establishes himself and practises in the UK can call himself a solicitor. Negotiations began within the EU legal organisations with regard to the Rights of Establishment Directive or the 'Lawyers Directive' 98/5, which is designed to facilitate the practice of a lawyer on a permanent basis in a Member State other than the one he or she obtained his or her qualification in. Having proved that he or she is already registered as a lawyer in another Member State, after three years as a lawyer in that Member State, he or she will have the right to gain admission to the legal profession of the host country and use the appropriate professional title. Thus, if he or she was an *avocat*, he or she could become a solicitor after that period elapsed.

This would seem to make it straightforward for a lawyer qualified in one Member State to practise in another. However, the Directive does recognise that professional training varies between Member States and allows the Member State where the individual wishes to practise to set certain conditions. This may involve an adaptation period during which supervision by a qualified practitioner is required of the foreign national or an aptitude test of professional knowledge. In England, the test for foreign lawyers wishing to practise as solicitors is called the Qualified Lawyers Transfer Test. Having successfully completed this test, the normal rules concerning registration and admission to the appropriate professional body will apply. However, such registration or admission cannot be refused on any grounds contrary to Community law. As with any member of the legal profession, once registered or admitted, migrant lawyers must obey the rules of professional conduct laid down by the Member State in which they practise. Should these rules be incompatible with the Treaty's freedom of movement principles, they will not be applied. For example, a French rule requiring migrant doctors to give up their registration in their country of origin before being allowed to register in France was contrary to the Treaty. Although it happened before this general directive came into effect, the case of *Ordre des Avocats v Klopp* (1984) illustrates this point with regard to the legal profession. This case involved a French rule that an *avocat* cannot establish chambers in more than one place. Klopp was a German who qualified as a lawyer in Germany and opened an office there. He then re-qualified in France and applied for admission as an *avocat*, but his application was refused because he was not prepared to give up his office in Germany. The Court held that such a requirement was contrary to the Treaty. Also in the case of

Wilson v Ordre des avocats dur barreau du Luxembourg (C-506/04) in 2006 where Wilson, who was a member of the Enlgish Bar and had practiced in Luxembourg since 1994, refused to attend a Bar Council hearing to assess his linguistic knowledge. The ECJ stated that the Directive was to facilitate the exercise by lawyers of the freedom of establishment and it precluded a prior test of linguistic knowledge. Only a certificate attesting to registration with the competent authority of the home Member State was necessary in order to register with the Bar in the host Member State.

Aim Higher ★

This may seem a straightforward question but to gain extra marks look to put it into the context of the free movement of professionals, the right to provide services and the Commission's quest for a common framework across all the Member States.

QUESTION 39

'Company law is one of the most important and active areas in the harmonisation of the national laws of the Member States. The European Community's objective is to create a uniform system of company law.'

▶ Discuss.

How to Answer this Question

Although it is not very common to get examination questions on European Community policy towards company law, it does form part of the syllabus of most European law courses as part of the freedom of establishment. Where questions do arise, they are generally in the form of an essay question like this one. The best way to approach these questions is on the basis of freedom of establishment and the right to provide services, and the implications these have for the recognition of companies in the various Member States. The answer will use authorities based on the Treaty, as there are very few cases on these aspects of company law. The main points to cover are:

- ❖ Art 49 TFEU and the right of establishment;
- ❖ Art 54 TFEU and the meaning of company;
- ❖ Art 54 TFEU and the need for safeguards;
- ❖ Arts 56 and 57 TFEU and the provision of services by companies;
- ❖ directives adopted for harmonisation, with examples;
- ❖ European Economic Interest Groupings; and
- ❖ the European Company.

Answer Structure

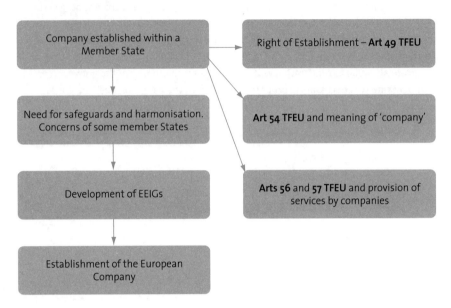

This diagram shows the key points to be discussed.

ANSWER

Although there are many developments associated with the rights of workers and the self-employed within the European Community, it must be remembered that companies play the predominant part in any modern economy. It is to be expected, therefore, that provision should be made for companies to move around the Community to take part in economic activities. The main provisions of the original **EC Treaty** concerned with the right of establishment and the freedom to provide services apply to companies. However, one of the main problems encountered is that whereas individuals, whether as workers or self-employed, are uniform in their identity across the Community, this does not apply to companies. Member States have different requirements with regard to such matters as incorporation, registration and liability. If there is to be true mobility for companies, action has to be taken to make sure that these differences are not used to create barriers to the mobility of companies. This was reinforced in the build-up to the completion of the single market policy in 1992, when the European Commission said that such an internal market cannot exist unless companies incorporated in one Member State are permitted to do business in another. The case of *Centros Ltd* (1999) confirmed this principle by requiring the Danish Trade and Companies Board to register a company set up, but not trading, in England.

The **TFEU Treaty** identifies two rights for companies, namely, establishment and provision of services. Under **Art 49**, companies have the right to establish themselves in another Member State by setting up agencies, branches or subsidiaries. Having so established themselves, the companies have the right not to be discriminated against and must be treated under the same conditions as those laid down by the Member State for its own nationals. What companies can benefit from this freedom? The same rule applies to companies as it does to individuals, who must be nationals of a Member State if they are to benefit from the freedom specified in the Treaty. Article 54 specifies that, as far as companies are concerned, they must be formed in accordance with the law of a Member State and have their registered office, central administration or principal place of business within the Community. The ECJ held, in *Segers* (1986), that to allow a Member State in which a company carried on its business to treat that company in a different manner solely because its registered office was in another Member State would render Art 54 TFEU valueless. Just as there is a requirement that workers and the self-employed should receive remuneration in order to satisfy the Treaty, so companies which are non-profit making do not come within the definition of Art 54. The remuneration requirement is repeated in Art 56 TFEU, dealing with the right to provide services. This provision deals with a company established in one Member State providing services of an industrial, commercial or professional nature in another Member State. The main difference with services is that, in contrast to establishment, the company is entering another Member State only temporarily to pursue this activity.

As indicated above, companies should be able to establish themselves or provide services on the basis of non-discrimination on the grounds of nationality. They should also not be subject to any more burdensome rules in the host Member State than are absolutely necessary. The European Community has attempted to deal with this last point by seeking uniformity in the whole Community, or at least on the basis of 'equivalents'. The now-repealed Article 293 required the Member States to negotiate conventions with each other in order to secure uniformity of recognition of business practices across the Community. That Article specifically mentioned the mutual recognition of companies within the meaning of Art 54 TFEU. As a result of this requirement, a Convention on the Mutual Recognition of Companies and Bodies Corporate was signed in 1968 by the six founder members of the EC. However, it is not in force as it was not ratified by the Member States. Given this failure, but recognising the importance of company law, the policy of the EC has been to move forward on the basis of directives dealing with specific matters.

The company law of each Member State has developed through its own legal and political traditions, and hence there are wide variations, not only in terms, but also in concepts. It was thought necessary, if the freedom of establishment was to be a reality, that there should be a minimum safeguard to protect the shareholders or members of companies and others who enter into transactions with the company. This is specifically mentioned in Art 50 TFEU where action is to be taken by means of directives. If companies in the EC are to deal across national boundaries, it is important that investors, customers and creditors are able to deal with confidence with enterprises from other

Member States, whether directly or through their subsidiaries or agencies. The fact that over 13 directives have been proposed reflects the extensive programme of harmonisation of company law embarked upon by the European Community. Although not all of these directives have been adopted, those which have cover such technical matters as company capital, company accounts, appointment of auditors and disclosure of information. These are important because companies established or providing services in different Member States facing the need to adjust to different regulatory regimes may lead to duplication of accounting, licensing and other requirements. This would act as a disincentive to penetrating other national markets. It may also reduce the opportunities for benefiting from economies of scale.

Another way of seeking to reduce the problems for companies operating in more than one Member State is to establish EC corporate structures. The first step was taken in this development with the establishment of European Economic Interest Groupings (EEIGs) by Regulation 2173/85. These EEIGs permit companies and others to co-operate within the Community on a cross-border basis, and thus provide a vehicle for joint ventures. EEIGs have the mixed characteristics of companies and partnership. They are not separate, in the sense that the companies are still liable for the debts of the EEIG, but they do have a separate legal capacity. Such groupings have to be registered, which in the UK is a requirement to register with the Registrar of Companies. An EEIG cannot have more than 500 employees, or offer any share participation to the public. Obviously, there are certain limitations with EEIGs, but they do provide a flexible vehicle for economic activity.

The ultimate aim of the Community is to have a new company formation which will have legal capacity throughout the Community. This is to be the European Company, or *Societas Europaea* (SE), which will be established by registration with the European Court in Luxembourg under a distinctive European Community company statute. Even though registration would be with the Court, the SE would be domiciled in a particular Member State. The intended role of the SE is to facilitate cross-border co-operation by means of large-scale mergers and associations. It can be seen that this is perhaps the natural extension from the EEIG, which facilitates such ventures but on a smaller scale. There have been some criticisms of the establishment of the SE, which has led to delay in the adoption of the necessary Community legislation. However, the Nice IGC in December 2000 reached a political agreement on the social aspects of the SE and in October 2001 the Council finally adopted the regulation and directive on the SE, which entered into force in October 2004.

It can be seen from the points discussed above that the Treaty clearly identified the need to harmonise areas of company law if companies were to exercise the rights of establishment and provision of services. However, Community legislation has progressed slowly as the national requirements of the Member States varied widely. The directives that have already been adopted have helped companies involved in cross-border activities, but the ultimate establishment of the European Company has not been achieved. The regulation allowing for EEIGs was a major advance, but is aimed at smaller joint ventures. The objective of the Community is to ensure that company law across the Community does not act as a barrier to economic activity by companies and provides safeguards for those who are doing business with them. To this end, the Community seeks to provide a minimum standard of uniformity in company law across the Member States. A challenge that is being encountered in the present economic situation is the way that various Member States deal with the situation when companies become insolvent and need to wound-up.

QUESTION 40

Analyse TWO of the following cases that came before the ECJ, and explain their importance in the development of Community law:

(a) *Reyners* – Case 2/74;
(b) *Van Binsbergen* – Case 33/74;
(c) *Walgrave and Koch* – Case 36/74.

How to Answer this Question

When approaching a question like this, the temptation is to produce too descriptive an answer. The facts are important, but are only one element of the answer. You should deal with the following points:

* the facts, the legal points raised and the decision of the Court;
* the kind of case it was – whether a preliminary reference or a direct action and which Article of the Treaty it was based upon;
* the cases chosen for this type of question have usually played their part in developing or reinforcing European Court judgments – what part has this case played?

Answer Structure

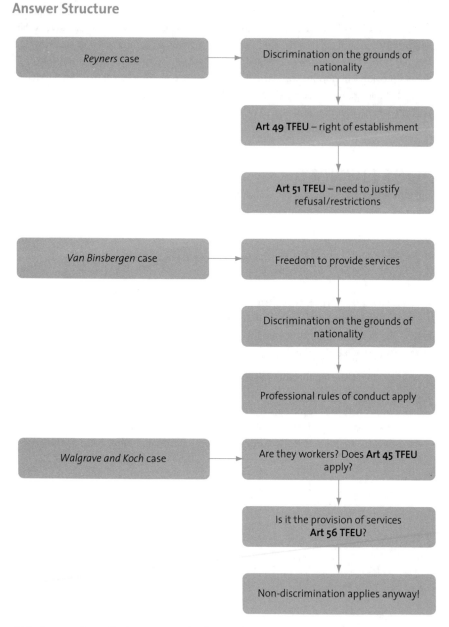

This diagram shows the key points to be discussed.

ANSWER

(A) *REYNERS* – CASE 2/74

Although born in Belgium, Jean Reyners was of Dutch nationality. Although resident in Belgium, where he had been educated and been made *docteur en droit belge*, it had not been possible for him to be admitted to the practice of the profession of *avocat* in Belgium. The reason for this is that the Belgian *Code Judiciaire* provides that no one may hold the title of *avocat* or practise that profession unless he is a Belgian and holds the *docteur en droit*. Having previously obtained this qualification, it was the nationality requirement which was impeding Reyners. It was possible to obtain dispensation from the condition of nationality in cases determined by the King, on the advice of the General Council of the *Ordre des Avocats*. This was provided for in a decree of 1970, but was limited to the nationals of countries which themselves admitted Belgians to the profession. Unfortunately, the Netherlands Bar was only open to the Dutch.

Reyners had made a number of applications for dispensation from the nationality requirement, but they had all been refused. He finally applied to the Conseil d'Etat of Belgium, the highest public law court, to have this provision of the decree quashed on the grounds of its incompatibility with the EC Treaty. To enable it to decide the case, the court stayed the proceedings and a reference was made for a preliminary ruling under Art 267 TFEU (then Art 177). The main questions under the Art 267 procedure were whether Art 49 TFEU (then Art 52) on the right of establishment became directly applicable at the end of the transitional period and whether the 'official authority' exception in Art 51 TFEU (then Art 55) applied to *avocats*.

The governments of Member States were divided on the direct effect of Art 49 TFEU (then Art 52). Although the German Government supported the possibility of direct effect in its intervention, the governments of Belgium, Ireland, Luxembourg and the UK disagreed. They based their views on the fact that Art 49 TFEU (then Art 52) was wider and vaguer than the prohibition of non-discrimination on the grounds of nationality and the fact that it was to be enforced by directives left discretion to Member States. The view of the German Government was that the provisions which impose on Member States an obligation which they have to fulfil within a particular period become directly applicable when, on the expiration of this period, the obligation has not been fulfilled.

The Court held that the rule on equal treatment with nationals is one of the fundamental legal provisions of the Community. Therefore, if there is a set of legislative provisions effectively applied by the country of establishment to its own nationals, these are capable of being directly invoked by nationals of all the other Member States. The fact that the freedom of establishment should have been attained at the end of the transitional period is made easier by, but is not dependent on, the implementation of a programme of measures. The fact that the progression has not been made leaves the obligation itself intact beyond the end of the period provided for its fulfilment. After the expiry of the transitional period, the right of establishment is sanctioned by the Treaty itself with direct effect.

Article 51 TFEU provides for a derogation from the right of establishment when the activities which are involved in that State are connected, even occasionally, with the exercise of official authority. Given that the freedom of establishment and the rule on equal treatment are fundamental to the Community, the Court stated that Art 51 (then Art 55) cannot be interpreted so as to defeat the objective of the Treaty. It wanted to avoid the effectiveness of the Treaty being defeated by unilateral provisions of Member States. Although each Member State must be looked at individually, the professional activities of *avocats* do not constitute, as such, the exercise of official authority. For Art 51 to apply, there has to be a direct and specific connection with the exercise of official authority.

This decision does not mean that any citizen can simply move to another Member State and set up in business or a profession. Each Member State has its own rules which apply to its own nationals covering such matters as qualifications. However, if the professional or other qualification is already recognised in the host country as being equivalent, Art 49 TFEU forbids the refusal of permission on the grounds of nationality (*Patrick* (1978)) or a requirement that the arrival obtain the national qualification (*Thieffry* (1977)).

(B) *VAN BINSBERGEN* – CASE 33/74

Van Binsbergen was a Dutch national who wished to challenge a social security decision against him. He had authorised Kortman, a Dutch national established in the Netherlands, to act on his behalf and bring an appeal against the decision. Kortman was an experienced legal adviser and representative in social security matters. However, during the case, Kortman moved his home to Belgium, and it was from there that he corresponded with the Dutch court. The court concluded that Kortman was now practising from Belgium. Under a Dutch statute on procedure in social security cases, legal representation could only be provided by persons established in the Netherlands. They therefore said that he could no longer act for Van Binsbergen.

Kortman invoked Arts 56 and 57 TFEU (then Arts 59 and 60) providing for the progressive abolition, during the transitional period, of restrictions on freedom to provide services within the Community. The Dutch court made a preliminary reference to the European Court under Art 267 TFEU (then Art 177). There are some similarities with *Reyners* (1974), only here it is a question of services rather than establishment. In fact, after *Reyners*, it should be quite straightforward to hold Arts 56 and 57 TFEU (then Arts 59 and 60) to have become directly effective at the end of the transitional period, at least as regards discrimination on the grounds of nationality.

The problem was to identify the discrimination involved in the case. Kortman, Van Binsbergen, the social security court and the domestic law in question were all Dutch.

However, the fact that the Dutch law did disqualify any legal adviser of any country who was not established in the Netherlands was relevant. The establishment requirement is a restriction within Art 56 TFEU, but does the Article have direct effect in the sense of providing a right which the national courts must enforce?

The European Court said that the restrictions to be abolished under Arts 56 and 57 TFEU (then Arts 59 and 60) included any requirements imposed upon the person providing the service on the basis of nationality or residence which do not apply to persons established within the Member State. This latter requirement of habitual residence could have the result of depriving Art 56 of all useful effect, as its object is to abolish such restrictions.

However, this has to be balanced against the possibility of the person providing the service taking advantage of his right to avoid professional rules of conduct which would be applied if he was established in that State. Therefore, a residence requirement could be imposed if the desired ends could not be achieved by less restrictive means. Such rules must be considered objectively and would be permissible provided they satisfied certain criteria.

These are that they are non-discriminatory, objectively justified and not disproportionate.

Following the principles in *Reyners*, the Court held that Arts 56 and 57 TFEU (then Arts 59 and 60) did have direct effect. However, the importance of *Van Binsbergen* is that it shows that the ECJ were careful to limit the area in which Art 56 TFEU (then Art 59) works directly, namely, with restrictions based on nationality and residence.

(C) *WALGRAVE AND KOCH* – CASE 36/74

Bruno Walgrave and Norbert Koch were both Dutch nationals who offered their services for remuneration to act as pacemakers on motorcycles in medium distance cycle races. They provided these services under agreement with the 'stayers', who cycle in the lee of the motorcycle, or the cycling associations or with sponsors. Competitions in which their services were requested included the world championships. The rules for the world championships to apply after 1973 stipulated that the pacemaker must be of the same nationality as the stayer. Walgrave and Koch considered that this rule was incompatible with the then EC Treaty, as it prevented a pacemaker of one Member State from selling his services to a stayer of another Member State. They therefore brought an action against the Union Cycliste Internationale, which was the body that made the rule.

The national court made a reference to the European Court under Art 267 TFEU (then Art 177) relating to the interpretation of Arts 45 and 56 TFEU (then Arts 48, 59) and Art 7 (now repealed). Article 45 TFEU (then Art 48) provides for the free movement of workers, whereas Art 56 TFEU (then Art 59) deals with the freedom to provide services. Article 7 is one of the fundamental principles of the Community, in that it prohibits any discrimination on the grounds of nationality. However, the rules in question were not made by a government of a Member State, but by an international sporting federation, which is not subject to public law. Could the prohibition be applied to them? That was the important question raised by this case.

The practice of sport is subject to Community law only in so far as it constitutes an economic activity within Art 2. The Court stated that the activities referred to in Art 56 TFEU (then Art 59) are not to be distinguished in their nature from those in Art 45 TFEU (then Art 48) merely because of the form of the regulation covering employment. The prohibition of discrimination found in these Articles does not only apply to public authorities, but extends to rules of any other nature aimed at regulating gainful employment and the provision of services.

The abolition by Member States of obstacles to the freedom of movement for persons and the freedom to provide services are fundamental objectives of the Community contained in Art 3. This abolition would be compromised if barriers of national origin could be neutralised by obstacles resulting from autonomous associations or organisations which do not come under public law. Therefore, these Articles may be taken into account by the national court in judging the validity or the effects of a provision inserted in the rules of a sporting organisation. The case of *Bosman* (1996) would be another example where the activities of professional sportsmen had been affected.

The national court had anticipated this possible answer, so it asked whether the fact that this was an international organisation made any difference. The key point for the Court was where the relationship governed by the rules was entered into or the place where they took effect. If these were within the territory of the Community, then the Community view on non-discrimination would apply. Thus, any races, for example, which took place in a Member State could not do so under rules prohibited by the Treaty.

Freedom from Discrimination

10

INTRODUCTION

The main focus of freedom from discrimination is based on the economic aspect of employment and sex discrimination. However, you should look at Chapter 2, where the protection of fundamental rights was identified as one of the general principles of Community law. The general principle has a wider meaning than merely discrimination based upon sex. This chapter concentrates on the general principle of equal pay for equal work for men and women, laid down in Art 157 TFEU, and the directives issued to provide the detail required for the full implementation of this principle. Generally, the questions asked on this topic are of an essay type, because of the wider knowledge of national employment law normally required for problem questions. Such questions are more likely to arise in employment or industrial law papers. However, it is possible for questions to be constructed in a way that deals specifically with Community law.

Checklist ✔

Following on from the general principle of non-discrimination, you should understand the following points and the appropriate cases:

- **Art 157 TFEU** on the principle of equal pay for equal work for men and women;
- the meaning of 'pay' within **Art 157 TFEU**;
- the extent of the direct effect of **Art 157 TFEU**;
- **Directive 75/117 (now 2006/54)** on equal pay for work of equal value;
- **Directive 2006/54** dealing with the Equal Treatment Directive for men and women in employment;
- **Directive 79/7 (now 2006/54)** with regard to equal treatment in matters of social security;
- **Directive 86/378** (now 2006/54) regarding equal treatment for occupational pension schemes;
- **Directive 2010/41** regarding equal treatment in self-employment;
- **Art 19 TFEU**; and
- **Directives 2000/43, 2000/78** and **2002/73**.

QUESTION 41

'The European Union has extended the scope of sex equality to other areas of discrimination.'

▶ Discuss.

How to Answer this Question

This discussion question provides an opportunity to review the case law and recent changes in the Treaty with regard to sex equality. However, that discussion must go beyond the recital of cases such as *Defrenne* or *Marshall*. This may be the starting point but the essay should then be developed to include the following points:

- ❖ *Defrenne* judgment in 1976;
- ❖ scope of Art 157 TFEU (then Art 119) through the meaning of pay and worker;
- ❖ Equal Pay Directive 75/117 and Equal Treatment Directive 76/207 now Directive 2006/54 on the Implementation of the Principle of Equal Opportunities;
- ❖ general principle of non-discrimination;
- ❖ Art 19 TFEU of the EC Treaty;
- ❖ Directives 2000/43, 2000/78 and 2002/73.

Common Pitfalls ✗

Those students who are allowed a copy of the EU Statutes with them in the examination sometimes spend too much time copying out the relevant Articles from the Treaties, Directives, etc. Remember that the examiner knows that you have access to the text so much of this will be discounted from gaining credit for your answer.

Answer Structure

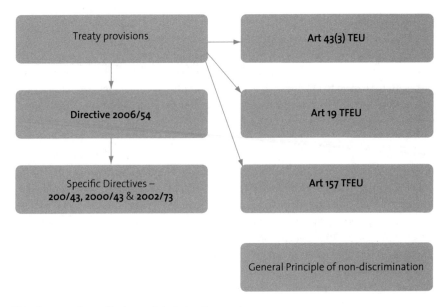

This diagram shows the key points to be discussed.

ANSWER

In Art 3(3) of the TEU Treaty, the European Union lists the main activities which it will achieve at the same time as eliminating inequalities and promoting equality between men and women. This indicates the special status given by Community law to the principle of equality. This principle has been repeated in secondary legislation, mainly directives, and the case law of the European Court. In fact, it has mainly been the judgments of the Court that have elevated the principle to its special status.

The main example given of this special status accorded to the principle of equality can be seen through the case law relating to equal treatment of men and women in terms and conditions of employment within the European Community. It is the cases associated with Art 157 TFEU which show this development clearly. Article 157 requires each Member State to ensure that men and women should receive equal pay for equal work. Equal pay, under this Article, refers not only to wage levels but also to any payment in kind in respect of remuneration for employment.

In its judgment in *Defrenne (No 2)* (1976), the Court held that Art 157 TFEU (then Art 119) has a double aim which covers both economic and social aspects of employment. It seeks to ensure that States which have implemented the equality principle do not suffer a competitive disadvantage, and to achieve social progress. In 1978, whilst delivering its third judgment associated with Madame Defrenne's case, the Court expanded the principle of equal pay into a general fundamental right of equality which required the elimination of discrimination based on sex. With regard to the application of the principle of equality in employment, it is not only Art 157 which is important, as a number of important directives have been adopted which have expanded the application of the principle. Article 157 TFEU itself refers expressly to pay but the ECJ has adopted a liberal interpretation to the question of what constitutes pay. In *Garland v BREL* (1982), the Court held that the grant of special travel facilities to former employees after retirement constituted pay, even in the absence of any contractual entitlement to such facilities.

In *Bilka-Kaufhaus v Weber von Harz* (1986), Weber was a female part-time worker who was seeking to challenge her employer's occupational pension scheme. Although the scheme was non-contributory for full-time employees, with the employer paying all the contributions, this was not the case with part-timers. The Court held that the benefit constituted consideration paid by the employer to the employee in respect of her employment and thus came within Art 157 TFEU (then Art 119). In this case, the Court seemed to draw a distinction between contractual and statutory pension schemes. However, Art 157 was held to be applicable to a statutory social security benefit in *Rinner-Kuhn v FWW Spezial Gebäudereinigung GmbH* (1989). This case also involved a part-time employee who was employed as a cleaner. She challenged the German legislation which permitted employers to exclude workers who worked less than 10 hours per week from entitlement to sick pay. Despite statements in *Defrenne and Newstead v Dept of Transport* (1986) that social security schemes were outside the scope of Art 157, the Court held that sick pay fell within the Article. Therefore the German legislation was contrary to Art 157 (then Art 119).

It is not only the case law associated with Art 157 TFEU to which the principle of equality in employment has been applied. As indicated above, a number of directives have been adopted to implement or supplement Art 157. The Equal Pay Directive 75/117, for example, required the elimination of all discrimination on the grounds of sex with regard to all aspects and conditions of remuneration. In *Jenkins v Kingsgate (Clothing Productions) Ltd* (1981), the Court held that this Directive restates the equal pay principle of Art 157 TFEU (then Art 119) without altering its scope. Guidelines were provided in the later case of *Bilka-Kaufhaus*, mentioned above, to assist in identifying what might constitute objective justification for such differences in pay. The onus is on the employer to prove that the difference in treatment corresponded to a genuine need of the enterprise, that it was a suitable way to obtain the objective pursued by the business, and that it was necessary for that purpose. This could perhaps be described as the application of a principle similar to proportionality. Directive 2006/54 has consolidated this earlier Directive and the case law that had been developed by the ECJ. It was part of a Recast process where the existing directives and the case law are brought together so it did not require any change to domestic legislation in the UK.

Another important Directive was the Equal Treatment Directive (76/207). This Directive dealt with access to employment, vocational training, working conditions and social security. In the UK, this Directive has been used in the context of different retirement ages for men and women. The most important case in this respect was *Marshall v South West Hampshire Area Health Authority* (1986), where Marshall successfully challenged her employer's decision to force her to retire at an earlier age than male employees. The important factor in the case was acceptance by the Court that this Directive had direct effect. Article 2 of the Directive allowed for derogation from the equal treatment principle on specific grounds. This was raised in *Johnston v Chief Constable of the RUC* (1986) by the police employers as a defence to their refusal to renew Johnston's contract of employment due to the special requirements of policing in Northern Ireland and the need for the police to carry firearms. The Court held that there was no general public safety exception to the equal treatment principle available under the TFEU Treaty, and that it was for national courts to decide whether the conditions specified in Art 2 were satisfied. The Directive has also been used by pregnant employees who have been discriminated against (*Dekker* (1991) and *Webb v EMO Air Cargo (UK) Ltd* (1994)), even where this is due to the fault of a Member State rather than the employer (*Alabaster v Woolwich plc* (2004)). The current legislation is in Directive 2002/73 which replaced Directive 76/207 and extended it to include sexual harassment.

Article 157(4) TFEU allows Member States to pursue a policy of positive or affirmative action in favour of the 'under-represented sex'. In *Kalanke v Bremen* (1995), the ECJ considered Art 2(4) of the original Equal Treatment Directive (now Directive 2006/54). This Article concerns measures taken to promote equal opportunity for men and women, including removing existing inequalities which affect women's opportunities. However, the judgment in Bremen was greeted with dismay in several Member States, as it construed the provision very narrowly. The Commission issued a communication suggesting that the judgment in Bremen did not affect quota systems. The ECJ clarified the situation in *Marschall* (1997), which allows women to be given priority for promotion in the event of equal suitability, competence and professional performance. The potential weakness in the area of positive or affirmative action was recognised by the insertion by the Amsterdam Treaty of Art 157(4) TFEU.

The case of *P v S* (1996) appeared to suggest a more general prohibition on discrimination embracing transsexuality; the ECJ judgment in *Grant v South-West Trains* (1998) quashed this suggestion. In the *Grant* case, the ECJ said that EU law did not currently cover discrimination on the basis of sexual orientation. The ECJ felt that it was not its function to bring about a positive change which was properly to be enacted by legislation (*D v Council* (2001)). In *KB v NHS Pensions Agency* (2004), the ECJ held that British legislation preventing post-operative transsexuals from marrying in their acquired gender could be regarded as a breach of EU sex discrimination law because it was against the jurisprudence of the ECHR. There have been occasions when the ECJ has extended individual rights not to be discriminated against as a general principle of EC law. In

Sabbatini (1971), the plaintiff used the general principle of non-discrimination against her employer, the European Parliament. Following this, the case of *Prais v Council* (1975) extended protection to discrimination based on religion. Both cases were brought against EC institutions and the principle needed wider application.

This perhaps led to the most important recent development when Art 19 TFEU was introduced into the EC Treaty by the Amsterdam Treaty. Article 19 provides that the Community may take appropriate action to combat discrimination based on sex, racial or ethnic origin, religion or belief, disability, age or sexual orientation. There has been much activity in this field since then. In 2000, two directives were adopted. Directive 2000/43 implements the principles of equal treatment between persons irrespective of racial or ethnic origin, and Directive 2000/78 establishes a general framework for equal treatment in employment and occupation. The latter Directive covers religion or belief, disability, age and sexual orientation. The Council now has the authority to take appropriate action to combat discrimination based on sex, racial or ethnic origin, religion or belief, disability, age or sexual orientation. The new Equal Treatment Directive 2002/73 amends Directive 76/207 to bring discrimination on the grounds of sex into line with other forms of discrimination. Since the 1960s, the institutions of the EU have taken a wide view of categories of discrimination and this new Directive reflected that range. Article 10 TFEU continues to provide this protection and it has been strengthened in the Charter of Fundamental Rights.

QUESTION 42

To what extent does Art 157 TFEU give workers in the Member States directly effective rights to equality, irrespective of sex?

How to Answer this Question

This question covers the narrow area of Art 157, but it must be remembered that this Article is very important in the development of equal pay and non-discrimination on the grounds of sex. Particular reference should be made to the following cases:

❖ *Defrenne* (1976);
❖ *Macarthys v Smith* (1980);
❖ *Bilka-Kaufhaus v Weber von Harz* (1986);
❖ *Rinner-Kuhn* (1989); and
❖ *Enderby v Frenchay HA* (1994).

Answer Structure

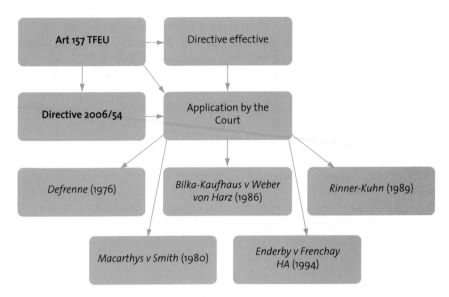

This diagram shows the key points to be discussed.

ANSWER

Article 157 TFEU requires each Member State to ensure the application of the principle that men and women should receive equal pay for equal work. Although this is an instruction to the Member States, by stating in the case of *Defrenne* (1976) that the Article has direct effect, the Court has identified a right which can be enforced by the individual employee in the courts of the Member State. Under the principle of direct effect, three conditions have to be satisfied; namely, that the provision must be clear and unambiguous, it must be unconditional and it must take effect without further action by the EU or Member States. Once these conditions are met, the individual is not dependent upon the Member State or the institutions of the Community for the right granted by the Treaty or other source of Community law.

The principle of equal pay was said by the Court in *Defrenne* (1976) to form one of the foundations of the Community. Its role was seen as a way of achieving one of the social objectives of the Community, namely, the improvement of living and working conditions for men and women. This requires a levelling up of pay for women, rather than a levelling down of that for men. As was restated in *Enderby* (1994), the purpose is to remove obstacles which disadvantage women in employment. If this was to be achieved, the Community was conscious of the need to ensure that those States which had incorporated such equality principles were not disadvantaged in a competitive sense as against those States whose undertakings were not obliged to meet such an objective.

In *Defrenne v Sabena* (1976), the ECJ had upheld the direct effect of Art 157 TFEU (then Art 119). Madame Defrenne had been employed by the Belgian airline Sabena as an air hostess. She complained of being paid a lower salary than her male colleagues, although the work they did was the same. In an Art 267 TFEU (then Art 177) reference, the Belgian court asked if Art 157 could be relied upon before national courts. In its judgment, the Court said that discrimination on the grounds of sex could be indirect and disguised discrimination or direct and overt discrimination. The latter type of discrimination was more easily identified and could be based solely upon the criteria of equal work and equal pay referred to in Art 157. In such cases, Art 157 was directly effective and gave use to individual rights which national courts must protect. It was necessary for additional measures to be taken with regard to indirect discrimination. This was achieved by the Equal Pay Directive 75/117, which supplemented Art 157 and was replaced by Directive 2006/54. Article 1 of this Directive provides for the elimination of all discrimination on the grounds of sex with regard to all aspects and conditions of remuneration. It must be remembered that Art 157 TFEU on its own is not sufficient to cover all aspects of equal pay, although this has not stopped the Court extending the scope of the Article through a number of very important judgments.

In the course of the Art 67 TFEU (then Art 177) reference in *Defrenne*, the UK Government and the European Commission submitted that Art 157 TFEU (then Art 119) would only have direct effect as between individuals employed by the State and not those employed by a private employer. In other words, they were claiming that it should only have vertical and not horizontal direct effect. The Court rejected this argument, claiming that Art 157 (then Art 119) is mandatory in nature and must extend not only to the action of public authorities, but to all contracts between individuals. This judgment cleared the way for individuals to challenge their employers directly on the basis of the TFEU Treaty in national courts, where they believed themselves to be victims of sex discrimination in matters of pay.

Article 157 states that men and women should receive equal pay for equal work. In *Macarthys Ltd v Wendy Smith* (1980), the Court held that a requirement of contemporaneity of employment is not to be read into the Article. Smith was paid £50 per week, whereas her male predecessor had received £60. Under UK legislation, the requirement was for the male and female workers to be doing the same job at the same time if a comparison was to be made. However, the ECJ held that the only issue was whether or not the work was 'equal' and it did not matter whether or not the man and woman whose work and pay were to be compared were employed at the same time in the undertaking or not.

Although it was initially thought that 'pay' in Art 157 TFEU was limited to the wages or salary received by the employee, it has been given a much wider interpretation by the European Court. For example, in *Garland v BREL* (1982), the special travel facilities granted to former employees on retirement were held to constitute pay, even if there was no contractual obligation to make such facilities available for those who had retired. Mrs Garland therefore had a right not to be discriminated against on the grounds of sex in comparison with a retired male employee.

There have been a number of cases involving pension schemes, including those where the claimant has been a part-time employee. In *Bilka-Kaufhaus v Weber von Harz* (1986), Weber claimed that the pension scheme of her employer infringed Art 157 TFEU (then Art 119). Under the scheme, part-timers had to be employed by the business for at least 15 out of the last 20 years, whereas full-time employees benefited from the non-contributory scheme without any time requirement. As the contributions paid by the employer were to supplement existing social security schemes, they amounted to consideration paid by the employer to the employee within the meaning of Art 157 (then Art 119). Perhaps the most important case in pensions is the case of *Barber v Guardian Royal Exchange* (1990). Under the employer's scheme, the normal pensionable age for women was 57, and for men, 62. The Court held that, since the worker received these benefits from his employer as a result of his employment, they constituted 'pay' within Art 157 (then Art 119). The immediate impact of the *Barber* case has been that employers have been required to harmonise pension ages for men and women in contracted-out schemes. The limitation to contracted-out schemes reflects the judgment of the Court that State pensions are not 'pay' within Art 157 (then Art 119). This was applied in *Roberts v Birds Eye Walls Ltd* (1992).

Sick pay has also been held by the Court to come within the meaning of Art 157 TFEU. In the *Rinner-Kuhn* case, a part-time office cleaner challenged the German legislation which permitted employers to exclude part-time workers from entitlement to such pay. This discretion given to employers brought the payment of sick pay to part-timers within Art 157 TFEU (then Art 119). Lastly, redundancy payments were held in the *Barber* case, mentioned above, to be pay within Art 157 (then Art 119), irrespective of whether payment is made under a contract of employment, on an *ex gratia* basis or under statute.

It can be seen from the cases above that Art 157 has been interpreted by the Court to give workers in the Member States directly effective rights to equality, irrespective of sex. Cases have been brought mainly by female workers, but males in the *Barber* case successfully used the Article to obtain equality with regard to redundancy and occupational pension payments. The direct effect of the Article has been limited by the Court, restricting it to direct discrimination, but with the support of the directives adopted on equality, notably the Equal Pay Directive, the Court has not limited the extensive application of the Article as a basic principle. This is illustrated by the way that the Court has given a wide interpretation to the meaning of 'pay' within Art 157 TFEU.

Aim Higher ★

You should use the opportunity to demonstrate parts of your knowledge about how direct effect works. This should not detract from your answer to the discrimination parts of the questions but it will show your confidence with the topic overall.

QUESTION 43

Critically review how the EU has dealt with the issue of sex discrimination in employment.

How to Answer this Question

This question deals with the general topic of discrimination but offers the opportunity to display knowledge of recent cases and new directives. In this area of law the cases are very important because they demonstrate the support given by the ECJ to the discrimination law of the EU. The following are important points:

- ❖ Art 157 TFEU;
- ❖ Equal Treatment Directive 76/207 as consolidated into Directive 2006/54 on the Equal Treatment of Men and Women in Employment and Occupation;
- ❖ *Defrenne* (1976);
- ❖ *Bilka-Kaufhaus v Weber von Harz* (1986);
- ❖ *Enderby v Frenchay Health Authority* (1994);
- ❖ *Grant v South-West Trains Ltd* (1998); and
- ❖ *KB v NHS Pensions Agency* (2004).

Answer Structure

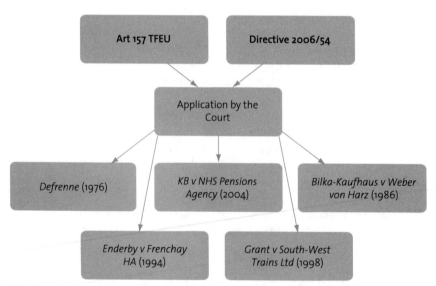

This diagram shows the key points to be discussed.

ANSWER

The Treaty requires Member States not to discriminate on the basis of nationality when dealing with citizens of the EU. This is important because the recent judgments of the

ECJ have stated that whether an individual is a 'worker' is a matter of fact for the national court (*Ninni-Orasche* (2003)). When deciding a case of discrimination, the law developed by the EU has two categories: direct and indirect discrimination. Direct discrimination is the more obvious category where a worker, normally a woman, is paid less than her male colleagues without any justification. Indirect discrimination deals with more subtle forms of discrimination between workers.

The first main area of discrimination in employment that came before the ECJ was the principle of 'equal pay for work of equal value'. This was based on the then Art 119 EC, now Article 157 TFEU. In the case of *Defrenne v Sabena* (1976), the ECJ decided that there was sufficient in Art 157 TFEU to allow Madame Defrenne to claim equal pay with male stewards working for the national Belgium airline. This was a form of direct discrimination where a worker suffers from less favourable pay or treatment and there is a causal connection between the sex of the worker and the lower pay. It is sufficient for the worker to prove an example of the equivalent work by a man being better paid than a women doing similar work. It is for the employer to then prove that the difference in pay is based on some objective criteria, not based on the sex of the worker who is claiming that he or she has been discriminated against. Direct discrimination of this type can only rarely be justified. To widen the scope of this form of direct discrimination the ECJ has given a wide definition of pay to include sick pay, contributory pension rights, bonuses and other payments such as concessionary fares.

Although the law on direct discrimination was tackled first, the European law was concerned that other forms of discrimination should be dealt with. The Equal Treatment Directive 76/207 set down a general principle for equal treatment in conditions of employment, other than pay. As part of the Recast exercise by the Commission this Directive has now been consolidated with others into Directive 2006/54. Article 2(1) of the Directive states that the application of the principle of equal treatment 'shall mean that there shall be no discrimination whatsoever on grounds of sex either directly or indirectly by reference in particular to marital or family status'. The ECJ saw a link between the narrow wording of Art 157 EC and the wider application of the Directive to indirect discrimination. Indirect discrimination is a legal concept which enables cases of unequal treatment, for which there is an objective justification but which in fact results in the woman being disadvantaged, to be included as an instance of unlawful sex discrimination. The case of *Enderby v Frenchay Health Authority* (1994) illustrates this wider context. Here Dr Enderby, a speech therapist, brought proceedings against her employer before an industrial tribunal, claiming that she was involved in work of equal value to that of a principal clinical psychologist and a grade three principal pharmacist, but her pay was substantially lower. In the *Enderby* case, her professional group was characterised as a 'purely female profession' and her counsel put forward the argument that in a purely female profession, the membership of that profession can have effects which are similar to a link with part-time work. The fact that speech therapists are almost exclusively women is also at least partly due to the connection between the social role of women and work. The opportunities of working part-time and of flexible arrangements of working are particularly attractive to women.

The Advocate General in the *Enderby* case stated that the purpose of the law was to deal with situations where women are placed at a disadvantage in their working lives. Therefore, in accordance with the teleological method of interpretation, a pragmatic approach ought to be pursued. This is a method that does not easily come to the UK judiciary. The ECJ held in the *Enderby* case that differences in pay between two different jobs assumed to be of equal value, one of which was performed almost entirely by women and the other predominantly by men, constituted *prima facie*, sex discrimination. However, the Court also accepted that the differentials could be justified by objective criteria. Thus with both direct and indirect discrimination the claimant can raise a rebuttable presumption of discrimination. In the first case with a specific comparison and in the other by a comparison of groups, which places the onus on the employer to adduce evidence in rebuttal of that presumption or to produce a justification. Article 157 TFEU (formerly 119) EC requires the employer to justify objectively the difference in pay between job A and job B.

What reasons can be put forward by an employer to justify objectively the difference in pay? In some circumstances the employer may be compelled by the labour market to offer higher remuneration for members of a particular professional group in order to attract suitable applicants. The only question then is the extent to which the objective reason can serve to justify the difference in pay. In *Nimz* (1992), the Court held that collective agreement which allows employers to maintain a distinction as regards overall pay between two categories of workers who are both performing the same type of work but on part-time and full-time bases, does constitute discrimination against female workers *vis à vis* male workers, if in fact a much lower percentage of men work on a part-time basis than women. Such an agreement must therefore in principle be regarded as contrary to Art 157 TFEU, unless the difference in treatment between the two categories of workers can be shown to be based on objectively justified factors unrelated to any discrimination on grounds of sex. In *Bilka-Kaufhaus* (1986), the employer argued that full-time employees gained experience and thus skills and abilities more quickly than part-timers working less than three-fourths of normal hours. However, the Court held that this was not sufficient to justify objectively the difference in treatment. In the case of *Danfoss* (1989), the employees' union produced statistics relating to the wages paid to 157 workers between 1982 and 1986, which showed that the average wage paid to men was 6.85% higher than that paid to women. The employers claimed that these differences were due to the application of criteria for additional payments based upon mobility, training and length of service, but the Court said that they had to be justified. If the claimant is successful, they should not be deprived of appropriate levels of damages by any national law (*Levez v Jennings* (1999)).

Clearly, EU law on discrimination in employment deals with those situations where it is based on sex or gender but the ECJ has taken the law further. The ECJ has interpreted discrimination based on sex to include transsexuals. In the case of *P v S* (1996), a male worker told his employer that he intended to undergo 'gender reassignment', which would be preceded by a period when he would dress and behave as a woman. P started his treatment to change his gender but was dismissed and he then claimed unlawful sexual discrimination. The ECJ held that discrimination arising from gender reassignment was based on the sex of the person, and therefore the EU law on discrimination applied. However, in *Grant v South-West Trains Ltd* (1998), the ECJ decided that the EU law did not cover sexual orientation discrimination, presumably on the basis that as a female homosexual, Grant was being treated the same as a male homosexual, that is, there was no discrimination on the grounds of sex. The matter was resolved when in May 1999 the new Art 13 EC, inserted by the Treaty of Amsterdam, dealing with sexual orientation (see now Arts 10 & 19TFEU), came into effect. Recently, in the case of *KB v NHS Pensions Agency* (2004), the ECJ held that British legislation preventing post-operative transsexuals from marrying in their acquired gender could be regarded as a breach of EU discrimination law. This judgment relied heavily on the case law of the European Court on Human Rights, which had held that such individuals should be allowed to marry. If they could not marry they were being treated less favourably than other relationships.

The requirements of Art 157 TFEU and the associated directives are mandatory in nature so the prohibition of discrimination on the grounds of gender between male and female workers applies to public and private organisations. The anti-discrimination law has been extended by other directives. Perhaps the most important was the Framework Directive 2000/78 which covers religion or belief, disability, age and sexual orientation. A new Equal Treatment Directive 2002/73 came into effect in October 2005. It did not repeal the Directive 76/207 but substantially amended it. It provides greater protection for workers who suffer discrimination or harassment at work and therefore brings the area of sex discrimination law into line with other discrimination law affecting employment. There has also been the extension of the law on discrimination into the areas of disability, where in C-303/06 *Coleman v Attridge Law* (2008) a mother of a disabled child relied upon Directive 2000/78 to show discrimnation even though she herself was not disabled. The Court maintained in that case that the Directive had the objective of creating a level playing field as regards employment and occupation. Such issues of discrimination are not always easy to prove but in the case on age discrimination in C-388/07 involving Age Concern in 2008 the Court stated that if there was any doubt the burden was on the Member State to prove that the national legislation reflected EU law.

QUESTION 44

Analyse TWO of the following cases that came before the ECJ, and explain their importance in the development of Community law:

(a)   *Defrenne (No 2)* – Case 43/75;
(b)   *Marshall* – Case 152/84;
(c)   *Barber* – Case 262/88.

How to Answer this Question

When approaching a question like this, the temptation is to produce too descriptive an answer. The facts are important, but are only one element of the answer. You should deal with the following:

❖   the facts, the legal points raised and the decision of the Court.
❖   the kind of case it was – whether a preliminary reference or a direct action and which Article of the Treaty it was based upon.
❖   the cases chosen for this type of question have usually played their part in developing or reinforcing European Court judgments – what part has this case played?

Answer Structure

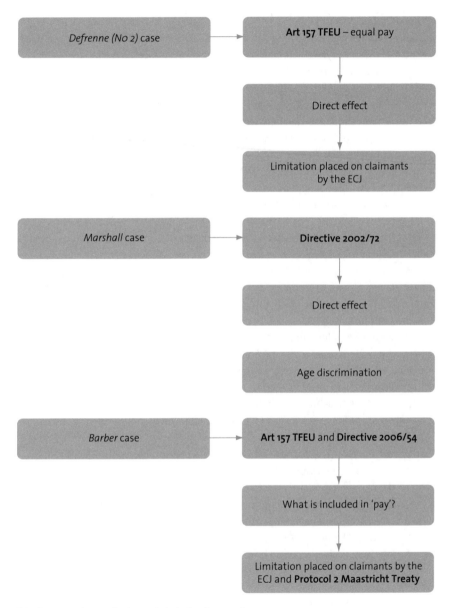

This diagram shows the key points to be discussed.

ANSWER

(A) *DEFRENNE (NO 2)* – CASE 43/75

Madame Defrenne was employed as an air hostess by Sabena, a Belgian airline company. She claimed that, in paying their male stewards more than their air hostesses, even though they were performing identical tasks, Sabena was in breach of Art 157 TFEU (then Art 119). It was conceded by the employer that Defrenne did the same job as that done by male stewards, but, until 1966, she was paid less than them under the terms of a collective agreement negotiated between Sabena and the unions. She began her action in 1968, claiming the difference between her remuneration and that of men from 1963 to 1966. Under Belgian law, there is a five-year limitation rule, so she was taking her claim as far back as she possibly could. She began her action in a Belgian labour court, which made a reference to the European Court under Art 267 TFEU (then Art 177), seeking the interpretation of Art 157 (then Art 119).

Article 157 TFEU provides that equal pay for work of equal value will be ensured during the first stage of the Community (ie, five years). This period expired at the end of 1961 without any action being taken by the Member States to implement Art 157 and the Commission had made a recommendation on the issue. As a result of this, the Member States adopted a Resolution which purported to give themselves more time, that is, extending this first stage. When this period, too, expired, the European Commission failed to use the procedure under Art 258 TFEU (then Art 169) against defaulting States, something it was criticised for by the Court. However, Madame Defrenne claimed that this failure on the part of the Member States did not affect her rights under Art 157 (then Art 119), because it had direct effect. The Member States and the Commission did not consider that the Article had, in fact, become directly effective at the end of the first stage, when the Member States had failed to fulfil their obligations under the Treaty.

The ECJ had found Articles of the Treaty to have direct effect before this case, as in *Van Gend en Loos* (1963), but, generally, this was in cases where the Articles involved a cross-border or transnational element. In the case of *Van Duyn* (1975), Art 45 TFEU (then Art 48), which deals with discrimination on the grounds of nationality, was found to have direct effect. But, that concept of discrimination is straightforward when compared with Art 157 TFEU (then Art 119) which requires 'equal pay for equal work'. However, the Court identified that discrimination could be direct or indirect. With direct or overt discrimination it was possible for an individual to make a challenge without the need for further supplementary measures to identify what the term means. With regard to such actions, the Court held that Art 157 (then Art 119) was directly effective, because the criteria set for the principle of direct effect to apply were present.

It was necessary for directives to be issued to deal with the more disguised indirect discrimination, but Madame Defrenne was successful in her action for equal pay. As part of the social policy of the Community, the Court believed that the principle of Art 157 (then Art 119) was a fundamental right of Community citizens. This 'social' right was supported by the economic fear on the part of some Member States that the failure to have equal pay would lead to variations in business overheads, and thus competition between the Member States. However, the Court recognised the financial impact of its judgment that Art 157 (then Art 119) would have direct effect in both the public and the private sector. The Court limited its ruling by stating that anyone who had not already initiated an action in their Member State would not be able to claim 'back pay' in the way that Madame Defrenne had. All future cases would not be able to claim for a period dating back to before the judgment in this case.

(B) *MARSHALL* – CASE 152/84

Miss Marshall was employed by Southampton Area Health Authority as a senior dietician until she reached the age of 62. When she reached this age, she was dismissed, even though she had expressed the wish to continue in employment until she was 65 years of age. The sole reason for her dismissal was that she was a woman who had passed the retirement age applied by the health authority to women. The authority's general policy was that its employees should retire when they reached the age at which State retirement pensions became payable. This was 60 for women and 65 for men. The authority was willing to waive its general policy for particular individuals in particular circumstances. It had done this for Miss Marshall by employing her for two more years after she reached 60. Marshall complained to an industrial tribunal against her dismissal, which she claimed was contrary to the Sex Discrimination Act 1975 and Directive 76/207 (now in Directive 2006/54), in that it unlawfully discriminated against her on the grounds of her sex.

The health authority claimed that, in laying down the retirement ages for its employees, it was merely reflecting the different retirement ages for State pensions. These differences in age were permitted by Art 1(2) of Directive 76/207 (now Directive 2006/54). In addition, they argued that an EC directive could never impose obligations on individuals and could only have direct effect against a Member State in its capacity as a public authority, and not as an employer. The case reached the Court of Appeal, where a reference was made under Art 267 TFEU (then Art 177) to the ECJ. The Court of Appeal asked two questions on the interpretation of the then Directive 76/207. The European Court's answer was that the principle of equality of treatment was one of fundamental importance, and therefore Directive 76/207 was to be strictly interpreted. Thus, the exception to the prohibition of discrimination on the grounds of sex in relation to the granting of pension and retirement ages was in this category. Article 5(1) of Directive 76/207 was to be interpreted as meaning that a general policy dismissing women when they reached the State pension retirement age constituted discrimination on the grounds of sex, contrary to the Directive.

Although the ECJ accepted the principle that a directive could not impose obligations on an individual, that is, horizontal direct effect, this was not true where the State was involved. It did not matter in what capacity the State was involved, in that it could be as an employer or as a public authority. In this case, Miss Marshall was able to invoke Directive 76/207 against her employer, the health authority, since this authority was an 'emanation of the State'. The main point was to stop a Member State taking advantage of its own failure to comply with Community law. [These Directives have now been consolidated into Directive 2006/54].

(C) *BARBER v GUARDIAN ROYAL EXCHANGE –* CASE 262/88

Barber was an employee of Guardian Royal Exchange (GRE). He was a member of a contracted-out pension scheme established and wholly financed by his employer. Under this scheme, the normal pensionable age was 62 for men and 57 for women. In the event of redundancy, the scheme provided for immediate payment of a pension to men aged 55 or women aged 50. Barber was made redundant at the age of 52, so he did not qualify immediately for a pension, but would receive a deferred pension payable when he reached the age of 62. He complained to an industrial tribunal, claiming unlawful discrimination on the grounds of sex. The tribunal dismissed his application, as did the Employment Appeal Tribunal. Barber appealed to the Court of Appeal, which made a reference to the European Court under Art 267 TFEU (then Art 177). The reference asked whether benefits paid to a redundant employee by his employer were subject to either Art 157 TFEU (then Art 119), dealing with equal pay, or the Equal Pay Directive 75/117 and the Equal Treatment Directive 76/207, both now consolidated into Directive 2006/54. The Court answered that Art 157 (then Art 119) did apply.

The previous case law of the European Court had been uncertain. In *Garland v BREL* (1982), the Court had held that certain benefits paid after retirement constituted pay. In *Worrington v Lloyds Bank Ltd* (1982), the Court rejected adjustments in gross pay designed to compensate for differential pension contributions as being incompatible with Art 157 (then Art 119). In *Bilka-Kaufhaus GmbH v Weber von Harz* (1986), it had held that a purely contractual pension paid by an employer came within Art 157 (then Art 119), whereas in *Burton v British Railways Board* (1982), the Court had held that a man denied access to a voluntary redundancy scheme on account of his age had not been a victim of a breach of Art 157 (then Art 119). In addition to this, the Community has always made it clear that State pensions are excluded from the scope of Art 157.

The reasoning of the *Barber* judgment was that the private, contracted-out occupational pension constituted consideration paid indirectly by the employer, and therefore fell within the scope of 'pay' within Art 157 (then Art 119). This also applied to any benefit paid on redundancy. Putting these two together, it meant that the pension and redundancy payments payable to Barber came within Art 157 (then Art 119). As there were different age qualifications for men and women under the pension scheme payable on redundancy, this offended against the principle of equal pay for men and women stated in Art 157 (then Art 119).

This was a very important judgment with far-reaching implications for individual workers and the administration of occupational pension schemes. Both the Commission and the UK Government had mentioned to the Court in their interventions that this case would have financial consequences for these pension schemes. They asked the Court to limit the impact of its judgment, as the Court had done earlier in *Defrenne* (1976). This is what the Court actually did. The Court ruled that the direct effect of Art 157 (then Art 119) to such occupational pension schemes would generally only apply to cases arising after the date of the judgment in this case, with one exception. This was that cases already initiated, or where claims had already been raised under national law, could proceed on the basis of direct effect of Art 157 (then Art 119).

The reason given by the Court for this limitation of the impact of its judgment in *Barber* was that the then Directive 79/7 had authorised Member States to defer from the principle of equal treatment for men and women in certain matters, including contracted-out occupational pension schemes. Thus the administrators of such schemes had been entitled to believe that they were not acting contrary to Art 157 TFEU. In the interests of legal certainty, the retroactivity of this judgment would have severe effects on the financial balance of such schemes. Protocol 2 of the Maastricht Treaty reinforced this point by stating that, although there is full and immediate acceptance of the implications of the *Barber* judgment, problems have been created for employers, pension funds, insurance companies, etc. Therefore, the Protocol confirms that equal treatment in occupational schemes must be applied in respect of employment after 17 May 1990.

External Relations

11

INTRODUCTION

The external relations of the European Community include its ability to enter into agreements with third countries and international organisations. Therefore, the key point of this topic relates to the competence of the Community to enter such agreements. Generally speaking, the questions that occur on this topic are essay type, although on very rare occasions the direct effect of a treaty provision may appear in a problem question.

Checklist ✔

Students should ensure that they understand the general point on the legal personality of the Community (Art 47 TEU) and the following points:

- the express external competence of the Community, including the common commercial policy (**Arts 206** and **207 TFEU**) and agreements with international organisations (**Art 210 TFEU**);

- the procedure laid down in the Treaty for negotiating international agreements (**Art 218 TFEU**), including the roles of the Council, Commission and the European Court;

- the implied external powers of the Community associated with the doctrine of parallelism;

- mixed agreements; and

- the direct effect of Treaty provisions.

QUESTION 45

What are the express treaty-making powers of the EU? Do individuals derive any rights from such treaties?

How to Answer this Question

This essay question, the most common form of question on external relations, requires an answer which covers the following points:

- ❖ express treaty-making powers, including the common commercial policy and association agreements;
- ❖ *Opinion 1/75 & Opinion 1/78;*
- ❖ *Opinion 1/09;*
- ❖ direct effect of Articles of treaties;
- ❖ *International Fruit Co* (1972);
- ❖ *Bresciani* (1976); and
- ❖ *Haegeman v Belgian State* (1974).

Answer Structure

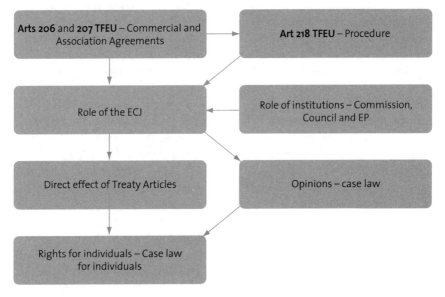

This diagram shows the key points to be discussed.

ANSWER

This question raises two issues for consideration: community competence and the ability of individuals to enforce any rights arising from these treaties. The Lisbon Treaty grants express treaty-making power in two cases: commercial agreements (Art 207 TFEU) and association agreements (Art 310 now repealed). Article 218 TFEU lays down the general rules regarding the procedure to be followed where the treaty-making power is exercised, but does not itself confer such powers on the Community. In addition, Art 220 TFEU requires the Community to co-operate with international organisations, and this is generally achieved by international agreements. The general rule is that all such international agreements are negotiated by the Commission and concluded by the Council.

The common commercial policy of the EU is a very important area of Community activity. Although it does not come within Pt 2 of the TFEU Treaty, which deals with the foundations of the Community, its appearance in Pt 3, dealing with the economic policy, reflects its importance. As the Community is based upon a customs union, it is necessary for not only a removal of internal barriers to trade, but also a common policy towards goods coming from outside the Community. This is where the common external tariff is required, as well as other measures related to the regulation of external influences of a commercial character on the internal market and its producers.

The common commercial policy is covered by Arts 206 and 207 TFEU. Article 207 gives an indication of the scope of the policy. It relates to tariff rates, trade agreements, export policy and measures to protect trade such as are necessary to deal with dumping or subsidies. The ECJ has stated that this list is not exhaustive, but merely examples of its scope. In *Opinion 1/75 (Understanding on a Local Costs Standard)*, the Court stated that the commercial policy is made up of a combination and interaction of internal and external measures. It reflects a progressive development of a body of rules which have come together to apply to the field of common commercial policy. In this Opinion, it was explicitly stated by the Court that the Community had exclusive power in this field of the common commercial policy. If this was not accepted, it would allow individual Member States to adopt positions on export credits which may differ from those of the Community and distort the institutional framework in which the common commercial policy should operate. Under Art 207 TFEU, the Commission submits proposals to the Council for implementing the common commercial policy. If negotiations are required with third countries, these are authorised by the Council but undertaken by the Commission. Any agreement is concluded by the Council on behalf of the Community.

However, in its *Opinion 1/78 on the International Agreement on Natural Rubber*, the Court did recognise that in certain circumstances the participation of the Member States in an international agreement was necessary. This Opinion concerned an international agreement designed to achieve a balanced growth between the supply and demand for natural rubber. This required a guaranteed stable export earning for exporting countries, whilst ensuring supplies for importing countries at a fair price. In order to achieve this, it was decided to establish a buffer stock to even out fluctuations in the market for natural rubber. Although the subject matter of this agreement fell within the common commercial policy of Art 207 TFEU, the financing of the buffer stock was to be provided by the Member State. If the financing had been provided by the Community, the Community would have exclusive power. Thus, as finance was to be provided directly by the Member States, they could participate in the agreement together with the Community.

If the Community enters into agreements with third countries or international organisations, can these be invoked by individuals before their national courts? The effect of treaties on individuals within the European Community varies from one Member State to another, depending upon whether it is a monist or dualist State. For example, in Belgium, France, Greece, Luxembourg and the Netherlands, treaties can usually be invoked in national courts and are normally given priority over national laws, whereas in other Member States, such as the UK and Ireland, treaties cannot be invoked at all, but are considered to be purely a matter for the executive. In such countries, the content of such treaties can only be made binding as to individuals through separate legislation.

In the second *Haegeman* case in 1974, the ECJ referred to the fact that treaties with third countries are concluded by an act of the Council and that their provisions form an integral part of Community law. The main principle which has to be considered in this respect is the direct effect of these agreements. In dealing with this question, there is no indication in the Treaty itself that such agreements may be directly effective, and the ECJ has not been wholly consistent in its approach. When deciding questions of direct effect, the Court is seeking to satisfy three requirements. These are that a measure must be clear and unambiguous; it must be unconditional; and it must take effect without further action by the EC Member State. These apply to any measure which an applicant claims is directly effective.

In the case of *International Fruit Co* (1972), the company claimed that certain EC regulations violated Art XI of the General Agreement on Tariffs and Trade (GATT). The Court had to decide whether the international agreement was capable of conferring rights on citizens of the Community which they can invoke before national courts. It was clear that the GATT agreement was binding upon the Community and thus its Member States. However, the general scheme and terms of the General Agreement were such that only the Contracting Parties or States could act if one of the other Contracting Parties acted contrary to the agreement. Therefore, the GATT agreement was not capable of conferring on citizens of the Community rights which they could invoke before national courts.

However, in the case of *Bresciani* (1976), the Court accepted that an association agreement did confer rights on Community citizens which the national courts of the Community must protect. In this case, Bresciani was importing raw cowhides from Senegal, a State which came within an association agreement under the Yaounde Convention. Under Italian law, an inspection fee was charged, covering the cost of examinations and laboratory tests. This fee amounted to a charge having an equivalent effect to a customs duty and was prohibited under the Treaty. Also, in *Haegeman v Belgian State* (1974), the ECJ accepted that the association agreement with Greece was an act of the institutions of the Community and therefore within an Art 267 TFEU (then Art 177) preliminary reference for interpretation.

Therefore, there are a number of specific subject matters where the Treaty grants express treaty-making powers to the Community, notably under the common commercial policy, the association policy and relationship agreements. This was confirmed in the 'open skies' cases concerning agreements made by some Member States and the USA (*Commission v UK* (2002)). In addition, following *ERTA* (1971), the external competence of the Community has been extended by the doctrine of parallelism, whereby an internal power may give rise to an external competence. Whatever the origins of the external power, the approach of the Court has not been consistent. The result has made the individual very dependent, on occasions, on the approach taken by the courts of the Member State towards the recognition of treaties with third countries. In Opinion 1/09 in 2011 on the proposed European and Community Patent Court the ECJ concluded that the draft was not compatible with EU law because it was taking jurisdiction away from the Court on matters that were important for the interpretation and application of EU law.

Aim Higher ★

There have been some instances where new Member States have questioned the authority of the EU in this respect and there are the continuing questions about membership of the UN for the EU. If you bring some of these points into your answer you will gain credit.

QUESTION 46

What is meant by the doctrine of parallelism? What has been its impact on the external competency of the EC?

How to Answer this Question

The doctrine of parallelism is derived from the judgment in the *ERTA* case and, therefore, the answer requires this case to be dealt with and also the following points:

- ❖   legal personality of the Community under Art 47 TEU;
- ❖   express treaty-making powers;
- ❖   *Cornelis Kramer* (1976);
- ❖   *Opinion 1/75*;
- ❖   *Opinion 1/76*;
- ❖   *Opinion 1/78*; and
- ❖   *Opinion 1/92*.

Answer Structure

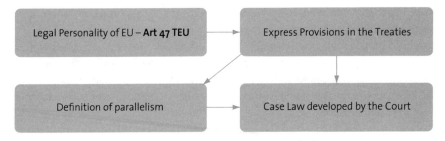

This diagram shows the key points to be discussed.

ANSWER

The doctrine of parallelism is associated with the external relations of the European Community. The Community was given its own legal personality, separate from its Member States, by Art 47 TEU. This meant that it had the power to enter into agreements with third countries or international organisations like the GATT. Having been given this authority by the Treaty, there are specific Articles of the Treaty which give express powers to enter into agreements on specific matters. For example, the Community may conclude agreements with third countries under Arts 206 and 207 TFEU on those matters which come within the common commercial policy enumerated in Art 207.

As far as the Member States were concerned, the Community only had those external powers which were expressly conferred by the Treaty. If there were no such express powers, they felt that none were to be implied. The Member States were rudely awakened when the ECJ gave its judgment in *ERTA* (1971). This case was brought before the Court because of a dispute between the Council and the Commission over the division of powers and responsibilities in exercising the external powers of the EU. This agreement provided the power to regulate the maximum driving hours for lorry drivers. The governments of the Member States claimed that, as treaty-making power had not been expressly granted to the Community, the competence for such agreements remained with them. The Commission had started proceedings under Art 263 TFEU (then Art 173) for the annulment of the Council's discussions resulting in a common position.

The Commission failed on the merits of the case because the negotiations for the European Road Transport Agreement were well advanced before the adoption of a Council Regulation on road transport. However, the ECJ laid down the general principle that the existence of Community common rules precludes Member States from undertaking obligations with third countries which affect those rules. The Member States objected to this idea, because they said that it ignored the political element of such international treaties. However, the Court had reached this conclusion based upon Art 47

TEU (then Art 210) relating to all the objectives defined in Pt 1 of the Treaty. This means that each time the Community adopts provisions laying down common rules to implement a common policy envisaged by the Treaty; the Member States no longer have the right to undertake obligations with third countries which affect those rules. This applies regardless of whether a Member State is acting individually or collectively with other Member States. They all have to operate within the framework of the Community. The result is that the Community has exclusive power in all external matters affecting the application of the Community legal system, as the internal measures are inseparable from the external aspect.

The adoption of internal rules is frequently referred to as conferring Community competence in external relations. In *Cornelis Kramer* (1976), proceedings had been instituted in the Dutch courts against fishermen accused of contravening laws limiting catches of certain fish. These laws had been adopted in accordance with a recommendation of the North East Atlantic Fisheries Commission, a body established by an international convention ratified by all EC States except for Italy and Luxembourg. The Dutch court asked, by way of an **Art 267 TFEU** (then **Art 177**) reference, whether the Community alone has authority to enter into commitments of the kind contained in the international convention. The Court held that the Community must enjoy the capacity to enter into international agreements over the whole field of Pt 1 of the Treaty. However, the Court did concede that transitional interim concurrent rights might be exercised by Member States until such time as the Community itself exercised its own functions. When this happened, the power came within the exclusive power of the Community. This case seems to apply to the *ERTA* decision.

This was discussed in the **Art 218 TFEU** (then **Art 228**) *Opinion 1/75 on Export Credits*, where the Commission argued that the conclusion of the OECD Local Costs Understanding was a matter of exclusive Community competence. However, the Member States cited *ERTA*, and argued that this could only be true if there were corresponding internal rules. In its judgment, the Court did not deal with this point, but held that the Understanding came within the Community's commercial policy under **Art 207 TFEU** (then **Arts 113 and 114**) and was thus within an exclusive Community competence. The Court spoke of the impossibility of concurrent powers being exercised at the same time in regard to the subject matter.

In *Opinion 1/76 (Laying Up Fund)*, the Court made it clear that the existence of rules was not necessarily the prerequisite for the existence of Community competence. The power to bind the Community with third countries flows from the implications of the provision of the treaties creating the internal power. Also, in *Opinion 1/76*, the Court held that the Community is entitled to co-operate with another country in setting up a public international organisation and in granting powers of decision to that organisation. However, the Court stated that the structural elements of the Community cannot be sacrificed by the competence of a new international organisation. This view was repeated in the ECJ's Opinion regarding the European Economic Area (EEA) in 1992. The Opinion of the Court (*Opinion 1/92*) was that the establishment of a joint EEA Court was incompatible with the Treaty of Rome 'and would lead to serious legal complications'. A similar view was taken by the Court in Opinion 1/09 when in 2011 when it stated that the draft agreement for a European and Community Patent Court was incompatible because it would affect the powers conferred on EU institutions, namely the Court.

Therefore, Community competence in external relations exists where there is an internal power to act, whether or not it has been exercised, and participation in an agreement is necessary. This is illustrated by the case brought by the Commission against some Member States that had entered into 'open skies' bilateral agreements with the USA (*Commission v UK* (2002)). An internal power is therefore paralleled or mirrored by an external competence. This is the basis of the doctrine of parallelism, which has greatly extended the external competence of the European Community. There have been complications on occasions where the agreement with third countries have been 'mixed' agreements. This is where there is some competence with the Community and some within the powers and responsibilities of the Member States. In *Opinion 1/78 (National Rubber)*, the ECJ accepted participation by the Community and Member States in an agreement which was clearly within the Community's commercial policy. This reflected the pragmatic view often taken by the Court. Under the 'economic' clauses of the agreement, finance was to be provided by the Member States, hence their participation. However, if the finance was provided by the Community, it would have exclusive competence and the participation by the Member States would not be accepted.

QUESTION 47

Analyse TWO of the following cases that came before the ECJ, and explain their importance in the development of Community law:

(a) *ERTA* – Case 22/70;
(b) *Cornelis Kramer* – Cases 3, 4 and 6/76;
(c) *Opinion 1/75*.

How to Answer this Question

When approaching a question like this, the temptation is to produce too descriptive an answer. The facts are important, but are only one element of the answer. You should deal with the following points:

❖   the facts, the legal points raised and the decision of the Court;
❖   the kind of case it was – whether a preliminary reference or a direct action and which Article of the Treaty it was based upon;
❖   the cases chosen for this type of question have usually played their part in developing or reinforcing European Court judgments – what part has this case played?

Answer Structure

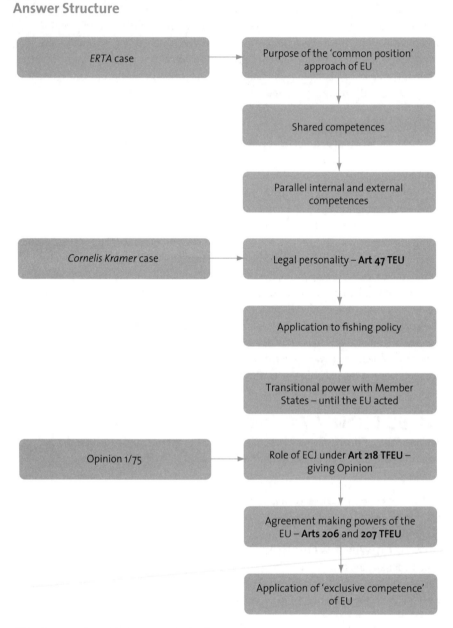

This diagram shows the key points to be discussed.

ANSWER

(A) *ERTA* – CASE 22/70

In January 1962, under the auspices of the United Nations Economic Commission for Europe, the European Agreement concerning the work of drivers of vehicles engaged in cross-border journeys (ERTA) was signed by five of the then six Member States of the Community. The Agreement never came into effect, owing to a lack of sufficient ratification. Subsequently, negotiations began again in 1967 to revise the Agreement. Meanwhile, work had been going on within the EU with regard to harmonisation of driving and rest periods for drivers of road transport vehicles, resulting in a 1969 regulation. At its meeting in 1970, the Council of Ministers discussed the attitude to be adopted towards the forthcoming ERTA negotiations. They agreed on a common position, as required by the then EC Treaty. However, the Commission disagreed with this procedure, because it felt that this was now a matter for the Community and not the individual Member States. The Commission brought this case before the European Court under Art 263 TFEU (then Art 173), seeking judicial review of the Council's common position and negotiation of the ERTA.

The main point of the case concerned the issue of who had competence with regard to external agreements on this policy area. If it was still with the Member States, then the Council of Ministers' actions would be within the Treaty. However, if it was now a Community competence, the Treaty specified how the negotiations should take place. The Council claimed that as the Community only had such powers as had been conferred on it, authority to enter into agreements with third countries cannot be assumed in the absence of an express provision of the Treaty. More specifically, Art 91 TFEU (then Art 75), which conferred upon the Community powers defined in wide terms, implementing the common transport policy, relates only to internal measures.

The ECJ, however, said that, in the absence of specific provisions of the Treaty relating to the negotiation and conclusion of international agreements in the sphere of transport policy, it is necessary to look to the general system of Community law in the sphere of relations with third countries. Article 47 TEU (then Art 210) provides the Community with legal personality to establish links with third countries over the whole field of objectives defined in Pt 1 of the Treaty. Each time the Community, with a view to implementing a common policy envisaged by the Treaty, adopts provisions laying down common rules, the Member States no longer have the right, whether acting individually or collectively, to undertake obligations with third countries which affect these rules. This applies whatever form the internal rules may take. Once this happens, the Community alone is in a position to assume and carry out contractual obligations toward third countries affecting the whole sphere of application of the Community legal system. The Member States must operate within the institutional framework of the Community, by which the Commission negotiates and the Council concludes such international agreements.

Although, on the facts, the Court found that the Council had not exceeded its powers, the judgment was to have long-term implications for the external competence of the Community. The case developed the idea of parallel internal and external Community competence.

(B) *CORNELIS KRAMER* – CASES 3, 4 AND 6/76

Criminal proceedings had been brought against certain Dutch fishermen who were accused of having infringed the Dutch rules limiting the catches of sole and plaice. These rules had been adopted on the basis of the provisions of the North East Atlantic Fisheries Convention. The Dutch court made a preliminary reference to the European Court under Art 267 TFEU (then Art 177) on the external competence of the Community. In essence, the questions asked were on whether Member States retained the power to adopt measures such as those under the Convention, whether such measures are compatible with Community law and whether the Community had exclusive competence in this policy area.

As there was an absence of a specific provision in the Treaty authorising the Community to enter into international commitments in the sphere of conservation of fish, the Court looked to the general system of Community law in the sphere of external relations of the Community. The Court recited the traditional view that Art 47 TEU (then Art 210) gave the Community legal personality, and therefore the capacity to enter into international commitments over the whole range of Community objectives. The Court said that, in this specific case, it must be recognised that authority to enter into particular international agreements may be express or implied from the provisions of the Treaty. The only way to ensure the conservation of fish, both effectively and equitably, was through a system of rules binding on all the States concerned, irrespective of whether they were members of the European Community. In these circumstances, it follows from the duties and powers which Community law has established internally that the Community has authority to enter into international commitments on fish conservation. However, having established that the Community has authority, the Court needed to look at whether the Community had assumed external responsibility.

The Community had not yet fully exercised its functions in fish conservation and therefore, when the Convention arose, the Member States had the power to assume commitments, such as the Convention. Having had the power to enter the Convention, the Member State now had the power to enforce it within the area of its jurisdiction. However, the Court pointed out quite clearly that the authority of the Member State was of only a transitional nature, until the Community had acted so as to assume exclusive competence in this policy area. This had to happen at the latest six years after accession as, by that time, the Council was required under Art 102 of the Act of Accession 1972 to introduce measures for fish conservation. Once this had happened, the Member States were under a duty to use all the political and legal means available to ensure the participation of the Community in the Convention and similar agreements.

(C) OPINION 1/75

Under Art 218 TFEU (then Art 228), the ECJ can be asked to give its opinion on the compatibility of proposed international agreements with the EC Treaty. This opinion by the Court was on a draft Understanding on a Local Cost Standard, drawn up under the auspices of the OECD. The key question was whether the Community had the power to conclude such an agreement and whether that power was exclusive.

The Treaty does include, in Arts 206 and 207 TFEU, a commercial policy which covers both internal rules and the power to conclude agreements with third countries. The field of the common commercial policy necessarily covers systems of aid for exports, and more particularly, measures concerning credits for the financing of local costs linked to export operations. These were the main provisions of this draft Treaty. The Council had already adopted directives on credit insurance in 1970 and 1971. Therefore, the Court concluded that the subject matter of the Understanding on a Local Costs Standard was within the sphere of the common commercial policy, and thus within the ambit of the Community's powers.

The Court said that a commercial policy is, in fact, made up by the combination and interaction of internal and external measures, without priority being taken by one over the others. Sometimes, agreements are concluded in execution of a policy fixed in advance, while sometimes that policy is defined by the agreements themselves. Such agreements may be outline agreements, the purpose of which is to lay down uniform principles. This was the case with the Understanding on Local Costs.

On the question of exclusive competency, the Court said that, given the Community's commercial policy, it would not be acceptable for Member States to exercise a concurrent power in either the internal or the international sphere. Article 207 TFEU (then Arts 113 and 114) shows clearly that the exercise of concurrent powers by Member States and the Community is impossible. To accept the contrary view would be to recognise that in relations with third countries, Member States may adopt positions which differ from those agreed upon by the Community through its institutions. The Court said that it was of little importance that the obligations and financial burdens inherent in the execution of the agreement envisaged by the Understanding are borne directly by the Member States.

The Member States argued before the Court that the conclusion of the Understanding was not a matter of exclusive Community competence based upon the decision in the *ERTA* case. They said that there were no corresponding internal rules, so there could not be any parallel external competence. However, the Court did not deal with this point in its judgment, but held that the Understanding fell within the Community's commercial policy. Following on from the *ERTA* case, this judgment added to the exclusive external powers of the Community.

The Internal Market and Beyond

12

INTRODUCTION

The internal market will always be topical, as the EU is based upon a customs union; therefore, the problems encountered with the reality of such an organisation will go in and out of fashion. At the moment, the main questions are on the legal implications leading up to the completion of the internal market, the important cases on the freedoms associated with the Community and the Lisbon Treaty. The Maastrict Treaty and the Treaty of Amsterdam plus the introduction of a single currency (the Euro) both played a part in the next stage in the development of the EU.

Generally, questions on this topic are essay type questions, simply because problems would usually have to be very complicated to encompass the topic. As this topic changes so rapidly, it is very important to read newspapers to follow the changing political and legal environment in which the Community operates.

Checklist ✔

You should be familiar with the following:

- the background to the **Single European Act 1986**, notably the Commission's White Paper on the completion of the internal market;
- the **Single European Act – Arts 18** and **95** on the internal market, the changes to the voting procedures in the Council of Ministers and the powers of the European Parliament;
- the **Maastricht Treaty** on Economic and Monetary Union, but more importantly on European Union; and
- the **Treaty of Nice**;
- the **Treaty of Lisbon** ;
- the **Inter-Governmental Fiscal Treaty**.

QUESTION 48

Discuss the importance of the Treaty of Nice in the development of an enlarged European Union.

How to Answer this Question

The work of the Convention on the Future of Europe received a great deal of publicity during the early 2000s as the impending enlargement of the EU approached, and it did produce discussion documents on a large number of important topics that are still part of the current debate. This type of discussion question is increasingly used to get students to discuss these current issues in the context of what the Convention recommended, the failure of the Constitutional Treaty and subsequent problems with the compromise Lisbon Treaty. You need to include the following points:

- ❖ the events leading up the Inter-Governmental Conference (IGC) at Nice in December 2000;
- ❖ the background to the enlargement to 27 Member States;
- ❖ the impact on the main institutions of the EU, namely the European Parliament, Council and Commission;
- ❖ the Laeken Declaration and the work of the Convention;
- ❖ the Convention recommendations and the Constitutional Treaty; and
- ❖ the Lisbon Treaty.

Answer Structure

This diagram shows the key points to be discussed.

ANSWER ---

As the IGC in 1996 failed to address the issues of institutional reform and enlargement of the EU, the resulting Treaty of Amsterdam in 1997 neglected these issues. The result was that these matters became more pressing for the next IGC that culminated in the Treaty of Nice, concluded in December 2000. The then EU of 15 Member States realised that with the enlargement to 25 or more States in the near future, it was imperative that the institutions were reformed, not only in their membership, but also in the way they operated. Also, if the present policies were continued in the Common Agricultural Policy or the Regional Development Funds, there would be serious financial implications following enlargement. This essay will concentrate on the institutional issues that form an important part of the Treaty of Nice and which are the bases of current EU institutional practices as consolidated in the Lisbon Treaty.

It was recognised that with the expansion of the EU from 15 to 25 Member States in 2004 and 27 in 2007, the institutions needed to be reformed. Suggestions had been made by the 'Three Wise Men' in their report in the 1970s but there had never been the political will to take the initiatives needed to deal with the Commission and the Council of Ministers. Although the European Parliament had changed – especially since 1979, when direct elections were introduced – the European Commission had been ignored. There had also been suggestions that had raised doubts as to whether the Commission in its 1990s form could work effectively to fulfil its responsibilities under Art 17 TEU.

The then Commission had 20 members; each Member State nominating one Commissioner but France, Germany, Italy, Spain and the UK nominating two. This was very convenient for the UK, as it was allowed to nominate one person from the government, Neil Kinnock, and one from the main opposition party, Chris Patten. However, if that system were to continue, we would have over 30 Commissioners following enlargement, and this at a time when some argued that it was difficult to find meaningful roles for 20. There would also be the difficulty of managing a Commission of that size, despite the power given to the President of the Commission by the Treaty of Nice, and the maintenance of the principle of collective responsibility. The agreement reached in Nice was for each Member State to be limited to one Commissioner from 2005 onwards. This postponed the difficult decision with regard to the size of the Commission because it is inclusive, in that all Member States have at least one Commissioner. This still raises the problem as to the roles or portfolios they may be given. However, from the next stage of enlargement, when there were to be 25 members, the size of the Commission was to be smaller than the number of Member States. This reduction was to be achieved by a selection process based on a rotation system with the principle of equality being paramount. This is likely to lead to challenges by disappointed Member States before the ECJ and in fact did have an impact on the referendum held in Ireland on the Lisbon Treaty in 2008. That referendum resulted in a 'no' vote and the Treaty could not be ratified. After a time for more reflection another referendum took place in 2009 which gave a 'yes' vote but only after the Irish were promised that they would not lose their Commissioner in 2014. There is still one Commissioner for each Member State in a European Union of 27! However, this is due to change in 2014 under the Treaty of Lisbon but this remains to be achieved in practice.

The European Parliament, as the main democratic institution of the Union, had to be able to accommodate elected representatives from the new Member States. The number of MEPs was increased with the unification of Germany and this amounted in total to 626 members of the European Parliament. There was also the factor that the Parliament's building had been newly refurbished at great expense and could not be increased in size without even more expense. The solution was to put a cap on the number of MEPs, irrespective of any further enlargement. The IGC wanted to ensure appropriate representation of the peoples of the Member States and stated that the number of MEPs may not exceed 732 in the 2009 elections. In the Lisbon Treaty this has been set for 751 in the 2014 elections. Therefore, as new Member States joined, the number of MEPs for existing members was to be decreased proportionately. However, importantly for the European Parliament, the Treaty of Nice extended the co-decision procedure to seven more areas of policy. This gave more authority to the European Parliament in these areas, although it does not extend to taxation or social security policies.

The Council generally takes decisions by a qualified majority, which requires a mixture of large and small Member States to agree on a particular issue. Article 205 listed the weighted votes for all Member States, with the larger countries having 29 votes and the smallest only three. Many of the new Member States had small or average size populations, and this was thought by some Member States such as Germany to act to the detriment of the larger existing Member States. Therefore, it was agreed in the Treaty of Nice to change the system of qualified majority voting. The new system is often referred to as the 'triple majority', as there are three aspects to it. Any decision must command the agreement of the majority of the overall number of Member States, it must have 255 out of the 342 weighted votes, or 73.9% and, lastly, the votes in favour must represent 62% of the total population of the EU. This last requirement only arises where a Member State so requests. There was also the issue of whether the existing rotation arrangement for the presidency of the Council every six months was workable within an enlarged Community. These details are now found in Art 16 TEU and Protocol 36.

With enlargement came an increase in the number of cases coming to the Community Courts, generally from the new Member States. Given the workload that the ECJ annually faces and the demands for a reduction in the time taken for preliminary rulings to be dealt with, reform was necessary. The Court of First Instance was therefore given an increase in powers so that it could hear direct actions and answer questions from the national courts using the Art 267 preliminary reference procedure. The time-consuming staff cases were delegated to a specialised chamber, the European Union Civil Service Tribunal.

Although the Nice Treaty was concluded in December 2000, some linguistic problems had to be resolved, so the final version is dated February 2001. The next stage was the ratification by the various Member States, which proved a problem in one country. In Ireland, a referendum required by the Irish Constitution resulted in a 'No' vote in June 2001. This was finally reversed in another referendum in October 2002, and thus removed the last barrier to the implementation of the Treaty of Nice, which came into force on 1 February 2003. However, some matters were not settled at Nice. These included the delimitation of powers between the EU and the Member States, the simplification of the treaties, the roles of the national parliaments and the legal status of the Charter of Fundamental Rights. Following the Treaty of Nice , there was the Laeken Declaration in

December 2001, which clarified these issues, but which established the Convention on the Future of Europe to take the discussion further by including representatives drawn from all the stakeholders in the debate. As a discussion forum, the Convention brought together a wide range of views on a 'Constitution for Europe' and other issues, such as a 'United States of Europe with an elected President'.

However, the proposals of the Convention were not put into law because of the rejection in referenda of both the Constitutional Treaty in 2005 and, following 'a period of reflection', the subsequent Lisbon Treaty in 2009. Originally the Treaty of Nice was seen as the first step in the preparation for an enlarged EU, but there have been no follow-up treaties so far. The importance of the Treaty of Nice is that currently it is the only reforming treaty recognised by law that was introduced for the expansion of the EU.

QUESTION 49

Why was it thought necessary to have a Constitutional Treaty? What were the consequences of its rejection?

How to Answer this Question

This question deals with a very specific topic which has raised a lot of debate since the Treaty of Nice was agreed and the European Council set the task for simplifying EU law and making it more accessible to the citizens of the Union. It is a contemporary issue that will require knowledge of EU law and the current political reality in the Union. The www.europa.eu.int website still contains the drafts of the Convention and is a good source for the latest information on the Constitutional Treaty and subsequent proposals. The following are important points:

- ❖ the Treaty of Nice and the Laeken Declaration ;
- ❖ the role and composition of the Convention on the Future of Europe;
- ❖ the recommendations of the Convention and the draft it presented to the IGC;
- ❖ the Treaty Establishing a Constitution for Europe or the Constitutional Treaty 2004;
- ❖ the Lisbon Treaty 2009; and
- ❖ ratification requirements to bring the Constitutional Treaty into law.

Common Pitfalls ✖

Many students give their conclusion in the first paragraph and then do not justify it in the body of their answer. Planning is essential and make sure that you develop your points in support of your overall conclusion.

Answer Structure

This diagram shows the key points to be discussed.

ANSWER

In the 1990s Europe was undergoing many changes as the former Soviet Union was breaking up and many eastern and central European countries were looking to the European Union as a means of protecting their democratic systems of government and raising the standard of living for their citizens. The European Union had 15 Member States at that time, and needed to undertake some reforms in preparation for the enlargement that was imminent. When the **Treaty of Nice** was ratified and came into force in February 2003 it meant that there were eight treaties and many protocols that together built up the primary sources of EU law. The original treaties signed in the 1950s had been amended, extended and revised over the intervening period as the policy areas of the EU had been enlarged and as the institutions had been affected by increased membership. The documentation as far as the treaties were concerned had become very complex. At the IGC in 2000 the European Council agreed that following the Treaty of Nice, with the emphasis on the enlargement of the EU to take place in 2004, priority should be given to reforming the treaties so that there would be one document, one 'constitution', which would simplify the task of identifying the primary source of European law. At the meeting at Laeken in December 2001, the European Council made a declaration establishing the European Convention which was charged with responsibility of agreeing on a 'constitutional treaty' that would be put before the Council for approval. The Declaration identified key issues that the Council wanted to see addressed, including the limitation of competences between the EU and the Member States reflecting the principle of subsidiarity, the status of the Charter of Fundamental Rights and the role of national parliaments in the context of European legislation.

Given that the idea of the Treaty Establishing a Constitution for Europe or Constitutional Treaty was to replace all other treaties apart from EURATOM, it was considered important that the membership of the Convention should be inclusive and transparent. It was important that the European institutions were brought closer to the EU citizen because the decline in voting in European Parliamentary elections was worrying to the Council. The main parties in the debate about the future of Europe were brought together under the chairmanship of Giscard d'Estaing, a former President of France. The Convention included representatives of the existing Member States and those states who were to join the EU in 2004, the European Parliament and the Commission plus representatives of national Parliaments. Other bodies such as the Economic and Social Committee had observer rights. It can be seen that this was quite a large group, too large to discuss the detail of a treaty. Therefore, a number of working groups were established to look at particular issues like subsidiarity and the Charter of Fundamental Rights. These groups produced reports and recommendations which were considered by the Convention as a whole. There was also a Praesidium established which was made up of the chairman, vice-chairmen and nine other members of the Convention. This body was considered to be very powerful in the production of the draft Constitutional Treaty and heavily influenced by its chairman!

The Convention had its first meeting in March 2002 and reported to the IGC in 2004 as requested when it was established. The European Council, now representing the 25 Member States plus the candidate countries of Romania and Bulgaria, signed the Treaty Establishing a Constitution for Europe on 29 October 2004. The Treaty abolishes the three-pillar structure introduced by the Treaty on European Union in 1993, where the dominating pillar was the European Community. The other pillars introduced in 1993, namely the area of Common and Foreign Security Policy and some of the areas of Justice and Home Affairs, remain embedded in the Constitutional Treaty. The Treaty also takes the opportunity of stating what has been reflected in the jurisprudence of the European Court of Justice for many years. The main example of this is the statement that 'the

Constitution shall have primacy over the law of the Member States'. This question of supremacy of Community law was settled in the *Van Gend en Loos* and *Costa v ENEL* cases in the mid–1960s. The Treaty recognises that the EU has received powers from the Member States and any powers or competences not transferred remain with the Member States. There is also a list of competences which are shared between the EU and the Member States and where the EU can only take a co-ordinating or supporting role. This would seem to have met the challenge set for the Convention in the Laeken Declaration.

There are important new developments in the Constitutional Treaty with regard to the EU institutions. Some argue that these changes reflect a shift in power towards the European Council, the main forum for the Member States. Article I-19 of the Constitutional Treaty stated that 'the institutional framework comprises: the European Parliament, the European Council, the Council of Ministers or Council, the European Commission and the Court of Justice of the European Union'. The Court of Auditors is no longer included in this list but is mentioned in the category of 'other institutions and advisory bodies'. Instead of the current six-monthly rotating presidency system of the Council of Ministers, which has been heavily criticised for providing no continuity, there is to be a system of 'Team Presidency'. Under this system the Council was to be chaired by a team of three Member States holding the Presidency for 18 months. This is a little vague at the moment because it merely adds together the traditional six-monthly period for three Member States into one period, but it is intended to provide greater coherence and consistency in the various Council meetings. The system of qualified majority voting or QMV within the Council was also to be changed to reflect the need for a 'dual majority'. This required a qualified majority to reflect not only the voting strength of the Member States but also a minimum percentage of the EU's population. This would allow Member States representing 35% of the EU's population to block any legislative proposal.

Perhaps of greater significance is that there was to be an elected President of the European Council. The President will chair the European Council and 'drive forward' the European agenda. He or she will be elected for two-and-a-half years by the European Council, that is, the Member States, and this term of office will be renewable once. The role of the President of the European Council is to facilitate cohesion and consensus within the Council, which will report to the European Parliament after each of its meetings. It is understandable that the President of the Commission was not enthusiastic about this development, as there could be two individuals with the title of president, and this may confuse the citizens of the EU, who may not appreciate the difference!

As for the European Commission, there are two important developments. The first is that from 2014 the size of the Commission will be reduced and consist of members corresponding to two-thirds of the number of Member States. At present there is one nominated Commissioner for each Member State and it will be interesting to see how the system will work for those who by rotation are not allowed to put forward a candidate for this office. There will also be a Union Minister for Foreign Affairs by merging the present role of the Commissioner for External Relations and the High Representative for the Common Foreign and Security Policy. The European Parliament benefits from an extension to more EU policy areas of the co-decision procedure which gives the Parliament a positive role in legislation. The number of MEPs is capped at 750 so any additional Member States will mean a reduction in the number of existing members. More importantly, the European Council must take into account the outcome of the European Parliamentary elections when nominating a candidate for Presidency of the Commission. This should increase the influence of the European Parliament and encourage greater participation in the election of MEPs.

Much discussion took place in the Convention about how to involve national parliaments more in the EU legislative procedure. One suggestion was to create another chamber in the European Parliament so that representatives drawn from national parliaments could be involved on the basis that all the parliaments of the Member States involved two chambers, so why not at EU level? This was rejected but there is a link between the role of national parliaments and the principle of subsidiarity. National parliaments will have to be informed about draft legislation and given six weeks to respond with their views. Under the **Constitutional Treaty** they were to have the power to send any legislative proposals back for review by the EU institutions if one-third of them agree that it infringes the principle of subsidiarity. There are also to be different terminologies for the laws passed by the European institutions, with the term 'laws' being used in place of regulations and 'framework laws' replacing directives, in order to make such terms easier to understand.

The need for the **Treaty Establishing a Constitution for Europe** was unanimous as the Treaty that emerged from the process of the Convention and the IGC seemed to meet the challenges set by the **Laeken Declaration**, including making the **Charter of Fundamental Rights** part of the Treaty and therefore legally binding. However, the Treaty signed in 2005 will not come into force because it was not ratified by all the existing 25 Member States. Under **Article 48** of the **Treaty on European Union (TEU)**, any Treaty amendments must be ratified by all the Member States in accordance with their respective constitutional requirements. Although those countries whose constitutional system required ratification by their national parliaments, such as Germany, successfully passed the domestic legislation, some Member States requiring ratification by referendum did not fare so well. In Spain, the referendum agreeing to the ratification of the **Constitutional Treaty** was passed by a small majority but the polls held in France and the Netherlands in May and June 2005 gave a 'no' majority. The Treaty should have come into law in November 2006 but following these votes the European Council voted for a period of 'reflection, explanation and discussion'. The outcome of this reflection was the **Reform Treaty**, very similar to the **Constitutional Treaty** in many respects although not seen as a stand-alone treaty but a traditional amending treaty like its predecessors. The Reform Treaty (or the Lisbon Treaty, as that was where it was signed, on 13 December 2007) was rejected in a referendum in Ireland on 12 June 2008. However, it was ratified at a subsequent referendum in Ireland and came into force on 1 December 2009.

QUESTION 50

Critically review the Treaty of Lisbon in the development of the European Union.

How to Answer this Question

This type of essay question is very common for EU courses. It allows you to draw upon your know of the development of the EU and to identify the significant changes that have taken place. The main points to cover are:

- ❖ the historical development leading up to the Treaty of Lisbon;
- ❖ the Laeken Declaration and the preparation for enlargement;
- ❖ the difficulties encountered in specific Member States due to the legal and democratic challenges of enlargement;
- ❖ examples of the institutional and procedural changes included in the Treaty of Lisbon.

Answer Structure

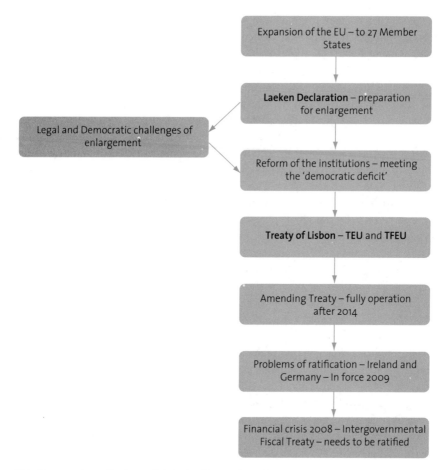

Expansion of the EU – to 27 Member States

Laeken Declaration – preparation for enlargement

Legal and Democratic challenges of enlargement

Reform of the institutions – meeting the 'democratic deficit'

Treaty of Lisbon – TEU and **TFEU**

Amending Treaty – fully operation after 2014

Problems of ratification – Ireland and Germany – In force 2009

Financial crisis 2008 – Intergovernmental Fiscal Treaty – needs to be ratified

This diagram shows the key points to be discussed.

ANSWER

Although representatives of the 27 Member States signed the Treaty of Lisbon in Lisbon on 13 December 2007, it did not come into force until 1 December 2009 due to problems encountered in its ratification. The main delay was associated with the requirement under the Irish Constitution for a referendum in support of the new treaty. The first Irish referendum on 13 June 2008 resulted in a 'no' vote on the Lisbon Treaty. This led to a great deal of debate within the EU leadership. A number of the concerns of the Irish people were set out by the Irish Taoiseach to the European Council who agreed that these concerns would be met provided the Treaty of Lisbon came into force. Perhaps the most important concession to be incorporated into a legally binding protocol to be attached to the next accession treaty was that the Commission will continue to include one national of each Member State. The European Council also agreed that other concerns relating to taxation policy, the right to life, education and the family and Ireland's traditional policy of military neutrality, would be addressed to the mutual satisfaction of Ireland and the other Member States, by way of the necessary legal guarantees. The Irish people voted in favour of ratifying the Treaty of Lisbon on 2 October 2009.

There were other issues raised in Poland and the Czech Republic that had been resolved earlier but a case was brought before the Constitutional Court in Germany. The outcome of this case was recognition that the German Parliament should have a stronger say in EU matters. This was achieved by September 2009, allowing Germany to ratify the Treaty. At the European Council meeting at the end of October 2009 the concerns of the President of the Czech Republic were settled in an agreement for action to be taken at the conclusion of the next Accession Treaty by way of protocols annexed to it. To satisfy the Czech President's concern these protocols will contain the statement that 'competences not conferred upon the Union in the Treaties remain with the Member States' and also add the Czech Republic to Poland and the UK as countries exempt from the Charter of Fundamental Rights. These delays indicate the complex decisions that were being taken to ensure that the Lisbon Treaty came into law, unlike the Constitutional Treaty, which became a historical document. Was the Lisbon Treaty necessary in the development of the EU?

The impetus for a structural change to the EC Treaties was instigated in the 1990s as the European Union contemplated the enlargement of the Community to include many states from Central and Eastern Europe. This has been achieved in the period since 2001, which has seen the Union grow from 15 to 25 in 2004 and then to 27 when Bulgaria and Romania joined on 1 January 2007. At its meeting in Laeken in December 2001, the European Council had made a decision that more work needed to be done in preparation for the enlargement. The Laeken Declaration posed a number of questions on topics such as the division of competences between the Union and the Member States; how could the external action taken by the Union be more coherent and efficient so that the Union could play a larger role in its own right in the world and how could the Union's democratic legitimacy be ensured?

The answers to these questions were initially to be answered by the European Convention on the Future of the European Union, convened by the European Council. The outcome of the deliberations of representations of the heads of government of Member States, the accession states, national parliaments, the European Parliament and the Commission and other Union institutions was a draft Constitution. This was presented to the European Council meeting in Rome on 18 July 2003 and was finally signed by all the Member States at another Council meeting in Rome in November 2004. However, the necessary ratification by each Member States was scuppered when referenda in France and the Netherlands voted against it. A 'period of reflection' was established so that each

Member State could carry out a broad debate. The result was the Treaty of Lisbon, which is an amending treaty rather than a replacement for the previous European Community treaties which was the intention when the Constitutional Treaty was formulated. The result was that from 1 December 2009 there are two Treaties which are of equal importance: a consolidated version of the Treaty on European Union (TEU) and a consolidated version of the Treaty on the Functioning of the European Union (TFEU).

What specific changes has the Lisbon Treaty brought about? Many of the changes reflect the concerns of some Member States to make the Union more democratic so there is a greater role for national parliaments. This may be of benefit, although many commentators consider it to be just 'window dressing'. In the legislative process there is greater involvement of the European Parliament in more areas of Union policy to give it more authority. From 2014 there are to be changes in the qualified majority within the Council so that there will be a 'double majority' to protect the larger Member States like Germany who are net contributors to the EU budget. There is to be a stronger voice for citizens who will be able to call on the Commission to bring forward proposals, but it remains to be seen how realistic this will be given the diversity of 27 Member States. There is to be a clearer distinction between the competences of the Member States and those of the Union, but given the pressure from the European Parliament and the Commission, supported by the ECJ, there is some doubt that this will be consistent. If in the future a Member State thought that it was no longer in its interests to remain a member of the EU, there is now, for the first time, recognition in the Treaty that it can withdraw.

There are also the new posts of President of the Council and High Representative of the Union for Foreign Affairs and Security Policy. Mr Herman Van Rompuy, who was the Prime Minister of Belgium at the time, was unanimously appointed to be the President of the European Council. This is an important new role as the European Council becomes an institution of the Union. As President, Van Rompuy will chair meetings of the European Council and 'drive forward its work'. The European Council also appointed Baroness Catherine Ashton to be the High Representative of the Union for Foreign Affairs and Security Policy. This appointment had to be agreed to by the President of the Commission as the office also makes her a Vice-President of the Commission and, like all European Commissioners, the European Parliament must then agree her appointment. The High Representative conducts the Union's common foreign and security policy. She also has to develop the European External Action Service (EEAS), which is a fundamental change from the previous role of the High Representative. The EEAS is a single service under the authority of the High Representative.

The Treaty of Lisbon was a compromise for the failure of taking the big step towards a 'constitution for Europe', but it has made some important changes towards simplifying the structure and administration of the EU. The term 'community' has gone to be replaced by 'Union'. The three pillars established by the Maastricht Treaty have now been merged to make administration simpler. The compromise reached at the informal European Council meeting in November 2009 reflects the pragmatic approach taken by the Member States and the President of the Commission to resolving political difficulties. This approach illustrates the developments that have led to the Treaty of Lisbon being ratified in all 27 Member States. The latest challenge facing the EU is the response to the financial crisis of 2008, which came ten years after Economic and Monetary Union. After much discussion, and many meetings of the European Council, a Fiscal Treaty was agreed. The full title is the 'Treaty on Stability, Coordination and Governance' which gives a clearer intention of its purpose. It is not an EU treaty because only 25 of the Member States signed it on the 2nd March 2012, with the UK and the Czech Republic refusing to do so. It is an intergovernmental treaty. The Fiscal Treaty is in the process of being ratified by the 25 Member States who are committed to it. Ireland is the only Member State that has to do this by way of a referendum under its constitution and this was achieved at the first time of asking. The Irish voters endorsed the Fiscal Treaty on the 31st May 2012 with a 60% 'yes' vote, although the turnout was only 50%. The focus then turned to Germany where the Constitutional Court was considering whether the Fiscal Treaty violated the German Base Law. At the same time some governments, notably that of Finland, were reconsidering the implications of the Treaty for their economy. The Treaty will come into operation when the Member States providing 90% of the capital have ratified it, so unlike a 'noram' EU treaty it does not have to be unanimous.

> ## Aim Higher ★
> You could select examples of particular issues, such as the Charter of Fundamental Rights or the division of competences, to provide more depth to your answer.

Index